KOSHER COOKERY

Classic & Contemporary

KOSHER COOKERY

Classic & Contemporary

Frances R. AvRutick

jD | **Jonathan David Publishers, Inc.**
Middle Village, New York 11379

KOSHER COOKERY:
Classic & Contemporary
Copyright © 1989
by
Frances R. AvRutick

Jonathan David Publishers, Inc.
68-22 Eliot Avenue
Middle Village, New York 11379

Library of Congress Cataloging-in-Publication Data

AvRutick, Frances R.
    Kosher cookery : classic & contemporary / by Frances R. AvRutick.
    p.   cm.
    Includes index.
    ISBN 0-8246-0341-9
    1.   Cookery, Jewish.   I. Title.
    TX724.A975   1989   89-11806
    641.5'676--dc20   CIP

Layout by Arlene S. Goldberg

Printed in the United States of America

Dedicated to
the cherished and everlasting memory of
my beloved husband,
RABBI ABRAHAM N. AVRUTICK,
and
to my precious children

"And let her that bore thee rejoice."

Proverbs 23:25

Acknowledgments

I owe a debt of gratitude to:

My beloved husband, Rabbi Abraham N. AvRutick, of blessed memory, who convinced me I could do anything I wanted to and taught me to have confidence in what I set out to do.

The deepest debt of gratitude and affection I owe to my immediate family. My daughters—Rena Barth, Judith Berkowitz, and Naomi Simon—who graciously shared with me their prized recipes and culinary knowledge and expertise. Without their advice, encouragement, and help, this book would never have been published.

My beloved son-in-law Rabbi Richard S. Barth, who gave me written assurance that I need not worry about having my manuscript typed. He made good his promise. He uncomplainingly typed and retyped my manuscript on his word processor, assisted by his wife, Rena.

My brother-in-law Louis AvRutick for his devotion and enthusiastic support and practical suggestions at all times during the writing of this book.

A special thanks to my loyal friends who served as a tasting panel. They were always willing to dine at my home even though they knew they might be served the most unbalanced meals. They appraised my culinary adventures. Their comments were constructive and appreciated.

I cannot possibly begin to acknowledge and thank the countless friends who shared their treasured recipes with me, whether original, a family secret, or just plain delicious. There would be no way to stop. I have had their cooperation and encouragement for more years than I can possibly recollect. To all, my appreciation.

Last but not least, I would like to extend a thank you to my publisher, Rabbi Alfred J. Kolatch, who inspired me with enthusiasm to do another book, and to my editor, David Kolatch, for his patience, guidance, and direction.

Contents

Introduction

The enthusiastic response to my first book, *The Complete Passover Cookbook*, encouraged me to yield to the suggestion of many friends, relatives, and readers that I prepare a cookbook for year-round use, one featuring traditional Jewish recipes.

When I began the project, I found that the task would not be easy. I have become very cosmopolitan in my cooking: my repertoire is not limited to the traditional Jewish recipes I learned from my mother and my mother-in-law. Those dishes—borsht from Russia, goulash from Hungary, mamaliga from Rumania—reflect the region from whence the family came and are marvelous in their own right. But over the years friends and relatives have exposed me to a wide variety of cuisines. They shared with me many wonderful recipes from all parts of the world. So today pizza and lasagna are as much at home in my kitchen as are latkes and kreplach.

My changing cooking habits also reflect my health consciousness. I shy away from many nostalgic recipes. I no longer render chicken fat (which I once savored) to use for frying latkes or to spread on rye bread or matzo. I have instead learned to use and enjoy herbs and spices to season food, ingredients that were foreign to my mother and her traditional Jewish cooking.

While I do not profess to be a vegetarian, and while I do not subscribe to the macrobiotic diet, I do adhere to many of their dietary recommendations. Accordingly, I use a wide variety of fruits, vegetables, whole grains, and legumes.

The recent proliferation of kosher food products has made it possible for modern Jewish cooking to make the leap into the "gourmet quality" category. Jewish home cooking today is not the same as the home cooking I recall. There is an evergrowing number of *pareve* ("neutral"—that is, suitable for use with meat or dairy) substitutes for those ingredients that used to pose kashrut problems in many popular recipes—beef stroganoff, for example. Joining pareve margarine, the familiar butter substitute, are pareve coffee lightener (that is, pareve milk), pareve whipping cream, pareve sour cream, and pareve cheese. The availability of a wide variety of processed and prepared pareve foods has made it possible for the kosher cook to please even the most sophisticated gourmet.

Needless to say, all ingredients called for in the recipes herein were available with reliable kosher supervision for year-round and/or Passover use at the time of this writing. However, the buyer must be wary. Never rely on past experience. Check labels for a reliable symbol of kashrut, as manufacturers sometimes do discontinue some items or introduce new ones or change ingredients of existing products.

Be mindful that the fact that a product is kosher does not necessarily make it pareve. For example, not all kosher margarine is pareve, and not all products labeled "nondairy" are pareve. According to United States government regulations, a product may be considered nondairy if it is free of milk or milkfat, even though one of the ingredients may be lactose or sodium caseinate, which are considered dairy according to Jewish dietary laws. Note that some dry cereals contain dairy ingredients.

Remember also that the term "kosher style" is certainly not to be confused with kosher. It simply describes a product that has been made or prepared following a Jewish recipe, but it does not signify that the product is kosher.

In preparing this book, I have sorted through hundreds of Old World recipes. I have selected the best of these traditional Jewish favorites and present them here along with new recipes.

In making my selections, I was cognizant of the emphasis my ancestors and Jews generally put on the home. Placed into focus was and is the important role the home plays in uniting members of the family. It is a bond that helps keep them together, especially when they enjoy home-cooked meals during the Sabbath and holidays.

Jewish traditions are observed and celebrated with family gatherings every Sabbath, from sundown Friday until Saturday evening, and during the holidays throughout the year. Although I have modified some of the traditional Sabbath and holiday recipes, I have done so only in the attempt to create the tastiest possible dishes, not dishes that would be considered "fancy" or "gourmet." My meals have been "taste-tested" numerous times by children, relatives, and friends and have received the stamp of approval.

I recommend that you taste as you cook, for the difference between executing a recipe and creating a delicious dish lies in the tasting. Adjust seasonings to suit your own palate. Make the recipes your own. Centuries ago, the Greeks expressed this thought:

> *For he who rightly cares for his own eating*
> *Will not be a bad cook. And if you keep*
> *Your organs, sense and taste, in proper order*
> *You will not err. But often taste your dishes*
> *While you are boiling them. Do you want salt?*
> *Add some, is any other seasoning needed?*
> *Add it, and taste again, till you've arrived*
> *At harmony and flavor; like a man*
> *Who tunes a lyre till it rightly sounds.* *

It is my hope that this book will meet with enthusiastic acceptance and that you will indeed receive many eating pleasures.

Frances R. AvRutick

---

*From *A Food Lover's Companion*, by Evan Jones.

1

Openings

Hors d'Oeuvres & Appetizers

"In the beginning . . ." (GENESIS 1:1).

Nahit

Serves 8 to 10

Chickpeas, known as *garbanzos* in Spain and Mexico and as *ceci* in Italy, are referred to by Jews as *nahit*. A traditional dish, chickpeas are frequently served at family celebrations. Their nutlike flavor and their crunchy texture makes them a wonderful substitute for nuts—or for popcorn, for that matter. For a savory snack or cocktail appetizer, sprinkle the chickpeas liberally with salt, pepper, and onion and/or garlic powder.

> **1 pound dried chickpeas**
> **2 teaspoons salt**
> **2 to 3 quarts water**
> **Salt and black pepper to taste**

Place the dried chickpeas in a large saucepot and cover with cold water by 3 to 4 inches. Let the beans soak overnight, adding more water if necessary during the soaking period. Drain well. Cover the beans with cold water and bring to a boil. Remove the scum, lower the heat, add the salt and cook uncovered until the beans are almost done, approximately 1 hour. Cover and cook until tender. (Chickpeas are very hard. It is almost impossible to overcook them.) Drain well. Sprinkle with salt and pepper to taste. Serve hot or cold.

Miniature Egg Rolls

Makes 40

Most Chinese restaurants in America serve egg rolls as appetizers, but at many Jewish functions they are served in miniature size as hors d'oeuvres. Ready-to-use kosher wonton wrappers are available, thus simplifying the preparation of these tasty miniatures. The important thing is to fold each wrapper securely over the filling so none seeps out during frying.

> 2 tablespoons oil
> 1 cup thinly sliced celery (white portion only)
> ½ cup finely diced onion
> ¼ cup thinly sliced scallions (green part only)
> 1 cup thinly sliced cabbage
> ⅓ cup sliced fresh mushrooms or 1 can (4 ounces) sliced mushrooms, drained
> Salt and black pepper to taste
> ⅓ cup water chestnuts, chopped
> 40 wonton wrappers
> Oil for frying

In a large skillet, heat the oil until hot but not yet smoking. One at a time, add the vegetables except the water chestnuts. Stir-fry until crisp-tender, then add the salt and pepper and the water chestnuts. Let cool.

To shape the egg rolls, on your work surface place a wonton wrapper with one corner facing you. Place a tablespoon of filling across and just below the center of the wrapper. Fold the bottom point of the wrapper over the filling; tuck the point under the filling. Fold the side corners of the wrapper toward the center, forming an envelope shape. The filling should be completely enclosed in the envelope. Moisten the top corner edges of the wrapper with water. Roll up the wrapper, pressing lightly to seal. Set aside until all are ready to be fried.

To fry, in large skillet heat about 1½ to 2 inches of oil to 375 degrees F. Fry a few egg rolls at a time in the hot fat for 2 to 3 minutes, until golden. Drain on paper towels. Keep warm or let cool and reheat before serving. Serve with sweet-sour sauce or hot mustard.

Filling Variations:

• To the filling, add ½ cup cooked chicken cut into thin slivers.
• To the filling, add 3½ ounces of canned tuna fish. First, drain well, then pour boiling water over the tuna to rinse off all brine. Flake and use.

Note: Egg rolls can be made the standard size and be served as a main dish. Kosher egg roll wrappers are available in the frozen food sections of shops specializing in kosher foods.

Sweet-Sour Sauce:

> **1 cup peach or apricot preserves**
> **½ to 1 teaspoon ground ginger**
> **½ clove minced garlic or ½ teaspoon garlic**
>   **powder (optional)**
> **½ teaspoon dry mustard**
> **3 to 4 tablespoons white vinegar**

Combine all ingredients in a blender jar and process for 15 to 20 seconds, till well blended.

Hot Mustard:

Stir boiling water, a little at a time, into dry mustard until the desired consistency is reached. For ⅓ cup of sauce, use approximately ¼ cup boiling water to ¼ cup dry mustard. Add ⅛ teaspoon salt and 1 teaspoon oil.

Beef-Potato Knishes

Makes about sixty
1-inch knishes

Although knishes are usually associated with Jewish cuisine, they are said to have been created in 1762 for Contades Marshall of France while he was serving in Alsace. There, they were billed as *"pâté de foie gras with a soul."* The name *knish* is Yiddish.

Essentially, knishes are filled pastries. The filling may be made from cheese, potato, liver, beef, kasha, and on and on—whatever you favor. And the dough may be one of many types, ranging from a strudel dough, which has been rolled or stretched thin, to an "Old World" dough made with stale challah.

This recipe features a filling of seasoned ground beef and mashed potatoes encased in an egg-rich yeast dough. Serve them warm as an appetizer, or top with a beef or mushroom gravy and serve as a luncheon or supper dish.

Dough:

   ¾ cup warm water (110 to 115 degrees F.)
   1 envelope active dry yeast
   1 tablespoon sugar
   ¼ cup oil
   ½ teaspoon salt
   2 eggs (graded large)
   3¼ cups unsifted all-purpose flour,
      approximately

Filling:

   1½ pounds ground beef
   1 cup chopped onion
   1 tablespoon oil
   1¼ cups mashed potatoes
   1 teaspoon salt
   ½ teaspoon dried thyme (optional)
   ⅛ teaspoon black pepper
   3 to 4 tablespoons unsalted margarine,
      melted

To prepare the dough, in a large warm bowl combine the water with the yeast and sugar. Stir until dissolved. Add the oil, salt, eggs, and 2 cups of the flour. Beat until smooth. Add enough additional flour to make a soft dough. Turn out onto a lightly floured board and knead until smooth and elastic, about 8 to 10 minutes. Place the ball of dough in an oiled bowl, turning to grease all sides. Cover and let rise in a warm draft-free place until doubled in bulk, about 1 hour.

While the dough is resting, prepare the filling. In a large skillet over medium heat, brown the ground beef and onion in the tablespoon of oil. In a medium-sized mixing bowl, combine the mashed potatoes with the beef mixture. Stir in the salt, thyme, and pepper.

Preheat the oven to 375 degrees F. Grease baking sheets with oil; set aside.

Punch down the risen dough. On a lightly floured board, roll out the dough to a rectangle measuring 15 x 22 inches. Spread the filling over the dough and cut into 3 strips, each about 5 x 22 inches. Starting from the long side, roll up each strip jelly-roll fashion. Seal the edges well. Cut into 1-inch pieces. Place cut pieces on the prepared baking sheets. Cover, place in a warm draft-free place, and let rise again until doubled, about 30 minutes.

Bake for 20 to 25 minutes or until golden brown. Brush with melted margarine. Serve warm.

Note: These knishes may be frozen. To serve, thaw completely and heat in a 400-degree F. oven for about 5 minutes.

Rumaki

Makes 24

A tasty and attractive way to prepare chicken livers. These roll-ups are nice to prepare for a very special occasion.

> 12 chicken livers
> 2 tablespoons prepared mustard
> 12 slices beef fry
> 12 water chestnuts

Preheat the oven to 400 degrees F. Broil the chicken livers and set aside. Cut each beef fry slice and each water chestnut in half. Brush mustard on each liver half, then place a chestnut half next to it and wrap a beef fry strip around both. Secure each roll with a toothpick. Arrange on a cookie sheet and bake until the beef fry is crispy.

Pick-up Chicken Sticks

Serves 6

An ideal choice to serve as a hot hors d'oeuvre. Guests will enjoy nibbling these little "drumsticks."

Grease for the pan
2 pounds chicken wings
1 cup sifted all-purpose flour
1 teaspoon salt (optional)
1 teaspoon onion powder (optional)
½ teaspoon ground ginger
½ teaspoon paprika
⅓ cup sesame seeds
½ cup oil

Grease a 14 x 17-inch baking sheet and set aside. Preheat the oven to 350 degrees F.

Cut off the tips from the wings. Reserve them for future use in making chicken broth. Divide each wing in half by cutting through the joint with a sharp knife. Wash and dry them with paper towels.

Sift the flour, salt, onion powder, ginger, and paprika onto a large dish or pie plate. Stir in the sesame seeds. Pour the oil into a small dish. Roll the chicken pieces, one at a time, in the oil, then roll in the flour mixture to coat generously. Set aside on sheets of wax paper. When all chicken pieces are coated, arrange them, not touching, in a single layer on the prepared baking sheet. Bake for 45 minutes or until tender and richly golden.

Pareve Liver Pâté

Serves 4 as an appetizer,
8 as a spread

This imitation liver pâté is very impressive, if for no other reason than that it tastes and looks so genuine. It is simple to prepare and, probably more often than not, you'll find the ingredients on your kitchen pantry shelf.

1 cup minced onion
3 tablespoons unsalted margarine or oil
2 California sardines in tomato sauce
2 hard-cooked eggs
½ cup walnuts
Salt and black pepper to taste
1 to 2 tablespoons mayonnaise

In a skillet, sauté the onions in the margarine or oil until translucent, about 15 minutes. Scrape off the tomato sauce and skin from the sardines, then debone. Pass the onions, sardines, hard-cooked eggs, and walnuts through a grinder, or chop very fine in a food processor. Season with salt and pepper. Stir in 1 or 2 tablespoons of mayonnaise. Chill well.

The pâté can be served very attractively by molding it in an individual chicken-shaped gel mold. Line the mold with moist cheesecloth, then pack with pâté. Invert the mold onto a lettuce-lined dish. No problem removing the pâté! Now reuse the mold until all the pâté has been used up.

Beef Roll-Ups

Serves 5 or 6

A flavorful make-ahead beef roll-up. So little preparation needed. The roll owes its tart-sweet flavor to the mustard added to the orange marmalade.

1 cup orange marmalade
¼ to ½ teaspoon dry mustard
½ pound roast beef or corned beef, thinly
   sliced
A few tablespoons finely chopped fresh
   parsley

In a small saucepan, heat the marmalade, then pass it through a strainer to remove the orange rind. Add the dry mustard, just enough to give the marmalade a little zing; taste-check to determine the amount needed. With a pastry brush, paint a very thin coating of the dressing on each slice of beef. Roll up each slice lengthwise, then dip each end in the finely chopped parsley. Allow 2 roll-ups per person.

Beef-fry Sticks

Makes 16

These tasty hors d'oeuvres are also simple to prepare. They can be made in advance and refrigerated or frozen.

> **1 loaf (1 pound) of white sandwich-style**
> **bread (16 to 18 slices)**
> **¾ to 1 pound beef fry**

Preheat the oven to 425 degrees F.

Decrust the bread. Roll each slice of bread with a rolling pin to firmly flatten. Roll up each flattened slice lengthwise, jelly-roll fashion, to make a "bread stick." Wrap a slice of beef fry tightly around each stick. Roll the beef fry around the "bread stick" in an overlap fashion, like a barber shop pole. (At this point the fry sticks may be refrigerated or frozen.) Arrange the fry sticks on an ungreased cookie sheet and bake for 10 to 15 minutes, until nice and crispy. Allow 2 to 3 per person.

Variations:

• Wrap a slice of the flattened bread around a frankfurter, then roll the beef fry around the bread. Bake in a 400-degree F. oven for about 15 minutes. The frankfurter could be slit lengthwise and spread with ketchup or mustard or filled with pickle relish before it is wrapped in its "blanket."

• Slices of beef fry may also be wrapped around water chestnuts or pitted dates. Secure each roll with a toothpick. Bake at 400 degrees F. until the beef fry is crispy.

Oriental Chicken Salad

Serves 6 to 8

An unusual way to serve chicken that has been used to prepare chicken broth. The almond slivers and water chestnuts add crunch to the salad, while the soy sauce and ginger give the dish an Oriental flavor.

> 3 cups cut-up cooked chicken
> 2 stalks celery
> ½ cup toasted slivered almonds
> ½ pound mushrooms, sliced
> 1 can (8 ounces) sliced water chestnuts, drained
> ⅔ cup salad dressing or mayonnaise
> 2 to 3 teaspoons soy sauce, to taste
> ½ teaspoon ground ginger

Place the cut-up chicken in a large mixing bowl. Slice the celery on the diagonal. Add to the chicken along with the toasted almonds, mushrooms, and water chestnuts. Toss.

In a 1-cup glass measure, combine the mayonnaise, soy sauce, and ginger. Taste-check for seasoning, adding more soy sauce if desired. Pour the dressing over the chicken and toss well. Cover and refrigerate for 2 or more hours for the flavors to blend. Serve in individual lettuce-lined dishes, garnished with toasted sesame seeds and a light sprinkling of paprika. Or, split popovers in half and spoon about ½ cup chicken mixture into each half.

Chicken Nuggets

Makes 24 to 36 nuggets

A delectable appetizer that requires a minimum amount of cooking. In the variation, the juicy golden chicken pieces team up with a hint of garlic, thyme, and parsley for zip.

> 2 whole broiler or fryer chicken breasts
> ½ stick (¼ cup) unsalted margarine, melted, or oil
> ½ cup cornflake crumbs or seasoned breadcrumbs
> 1 teaspoon salt (optional)
> ¼ teaspoon black pepper (optional)

Preheat the oven to 400 degrees F. Line a baking sheet with aluminum foil; set aside. Bone the chicken breasts. Remove the skin. Cut each breast half into chunks about 1½-inch square. Pour the margarine or oil into a shallow dish. Combine the crumbs with the salt and pepper. (Omit the salt if using seasoned breadcrumbs.) Dip the chicken pieces in the margarine or oil. Roll in the crumbs. Arrange in a single layer on the foil-lined baking sheet. Bake for 10 minutes. Serve hot or cold with cocktail picks.

Variation:

For sautéed chicken chunks, prepare the chicken as above. Measure off ½ teaspoon salt, ¼ teaspoon garlic powder, ¼ teaspoon crushed thyme, and 1 tablespoon chopped parsley. In a large skillet over high heat, melt 6 tablespoons of margarine. Add the chicken and sprinkle with the salt, garlic powder, and thyme. Cook for 5 minutes, stirring constantly. Sprinkle with the parsley. Nice to serve from a chafing dish with cocktail picks.

Note: You can bone the chicken breasts at your convenience. Cut into chunks, wrap in vaporproof, moistureproof wrap, and freeze for later use.

Glazed Sweet-Sour Hot Dogs

Serves 8

Cocktail frankfurters are simmered in a sweet-and-sour sauce.

> 1 jar (10 ounces) currant jelly
> 1 to 2 tablespoons Dijon mustard, to taste
> 1 pound cocktail frankfurters or 1 pound
>   regular-size frankfurters cut crosswise
>   into 4 pieces.

In a 2-quart saucepan over low heat, combine the jelly and mustard. Stir occasionally until blended. Taste to adjust the sweet-sour balance. (If too sweet, add more mustard; if too tart, add more jelly.) Add the cocktail franks to the sauce. Cover and simmer until the hot dogs are heated through thoroughly, about 15 minutes. Serve with frilled toothpicks.

Hot Chicken Salad

Serves 6

A tasty chicken salad variation. Equally good as a hearty hot dish or as a cool, tempting summer salad.

> **2 cups diced cooked chicken**
> **1 cup canned pineapple tidbits, well drained**
> **⅔ cup mayonnaise**
> **½ cup diced celery**
> **½ cup coarsely chopped almonds, divided**
> **¼ cup diced green pepper**
> **¼ cup diced red pepper**

In the top of a double boiler over low heat, heat the chicken and well-drained pineapple for 20 to 25 minutes. Add the mayonnaise and mix lightly. Continue to heat for 5 additional minutes. Remove from the heat and stir in the celery and ⅓ cup of the almonds. Spoon into a serving dish. Sprinkle with the remaining almonds and the diced peppers. Serve at once. Garnish with watercress and spiced crab apples if desired.

Pita Snacks

Pita, which is often referred to as the "pocket sandwich" bread, takes on a new guise when it is split, seasoned, and toasted crisp. You will note its versatility. It can be used as a crunchy snack for munching, as a chip for dipping, or as an unusual soup garnish.

> **Pita**
> **Oil**
> **Paprika**
> **Garlic powder**
> **Sugar**

Preheat the oven to 325 degrees F.

Split each pita in half through the middle. Lightly brush with oil the cut surface of each round. Sprinkle paprika and garlic powder generously on each half. Give each pita half a light sprinkling of sugar, perhaps a scant ⅛ to ¼ teaspoon. Arrange the pita halves on an ungreased cookie sheet. Bake for 10 to 15 minutes, until golden. Check often as they burn easily.

Cool the pita and break into serving-size snacks, about the size of a half-dollar. To use in lieu of crudités for dipping, the size should be larger than for munching. Broken into small-size bits, the pita serve as an unusual soup accessory. Generously seasoned with garlic powder, they are particularly good sprinkled on a *knoble* (garlic) borsht just prior to serving.

Variation:

Using large pitas, lightly spread margarine or oil on each half; then cut into 8 triangles. Sprinkle with sesame or caraway seed. Bake in a preheated 325-degree F. oven for 10 to 15 minutes, until crisp and golden. Four large pitas yield 64 triangles.

French-fried Pasta Dunks

For an unusual accompaniment to your party dips, serve these pasta dunks. They are destined to become a favorite at cocktail parties, for they are more dramatic than potato chips or crackers. Allow about one-half to one cup of Pasta Dunks per person.

>**Various shapes of pasta**
>**Vegetable oil**
>**Salt**
>**Seasonings of your choice: garlic powder,**
>   **onion powder, celery salt, or finely**
>   **grated parmesan cheese**

Prepare several different shapes of pasta according to package directions. Drain well. Blot dry with paper towels. In a deep-fryer, heat oil to 375 degrees F. Fry the pasta in small quantities until golden brown. Drain on paper towels and immediately lightly sprinkle with salt and other seasonings of your choice.

Variation:

For Lasagna Chips, cook lasagna noodles according to package directions. Drain well and blot dry with paper towels. Cut each noodle crosswise into 2-inch pieces. In a skillet, heat 1 inch of oil to 375 degrees F. Fry the lasagna chips until golden. Drain on paper towels. Sprinkle lightly with salt and other seasonings of your choice.

Penguin Eggs

A Penguin Egg consists simply of a hard-cooked egg, three colossal black pitted olives, and five toothpicks. It makes an unusual garnish on an hors d'oeuvre tray and a fun way to serve a whole hard-cooked egg as an appetizer.

For each serving, you will need:

> **1 hard-cooked egg**
> **2 colossal black olives, halved**
> **1 whole colossal black olive**
> **5 toothpicks**

Peel the egg, and chill for firmness. With 2 toothpicks, at the "bottom" (flatter end) of the egg, make legs and affix 2 olive halves as feet. Angle the third toothpick into the back of the egg, forming a tripod so the penguin can stand. Stick a fourth toothpick through the egg; attach the remaining olive halves as flippers. Insert the fifth toothpick into the top (narrow end) of the egg, and spear the whole olive onto it for the head.

Surprise Stuffed Eggs

Makes 12

As a change of pace from the popular deviled eggs, try this eye-catching version. They make for a very attractive garnish on a salad dish on your buffet table.

> 12 hard-cooked eggs
> 4 teaspoons lemon juice
> 1½ teaspoons prepared mustard
> 1 teaspoon prepared horseradish (optional)
> 1 to 2 teaspoons Worcestershire sauce
> ¼ cup mayonnaise
> ¼ to ¾ teaspoon salt, to taste
> ¼ teaspoon white pepper
> Dash of garlic powder
> Surprises: bacos (artificially-flavored
>   vegetable protein chips); nut halves
>   (pecan or walnut); peanuts; cocktail
>   onions; small green olives, etc.
> Finely chopped fresh parsley
> Paprika

Cut the eggs in half lengthwise, and transfer the yolks to a bowl. In order to facilitate assembling the eggs, be sure to keep the matching white halves together. Mash the yolks. Add the remaining ingredients. Blend thoroughly. Fill the white halves with the mixture. Put a surprise in one half and reassemble with the matching half. Cover and chill in the refrigerator. Before serving, roll the flatter end of the egg in the finely chopped parsley and sprinkle the other with paprika.

To prepare eggs a day ahead, wrap each filled egg individually in plastic wrap and refrigerate overnight. Garnish as above before serving.

Variation:

To enhance the appearance of the eggs, insert an artificial (plastic) strawberry leaf in the wider end of the egg (the end that was rolled in the chopped parsley). The leaves are available in party supply or cake decorating shops.

Champignons Farcies
(Stuffed Mushrooms)

Makes 15

Mushrooms are known for their versatility. These mushrooms stand on their own. Their delicate flavor is enhanced by the savory cheese filling.

> 15 large mushrooms
> 1 small onion, finely chopped
> 3 tablespoons unsalted butter or margarine
> ½ cup grated cheese: mozarella, Swiss, or American
> ½ cup to ¾ cup breadcrumbs
> Salt and black pepper to taste
> Grease for the baking sheet

Preheat the oven to 350 degrees F. Clean the mushrooms. Remove the stems and chop finely. In a skillet, sauté the chopped stems with the onions in the butter or margarine. Stir in the cheese and breadcrumbs. Then season with salt and pepper. Stuff the mixture into the mushroom caps, dividing evenly. Arrange on a lightly greased baking sheet and bake for 15 to 20 minutes, until the cheese melts and the mushrooms are golden.

Pareve Stuffed Mushrooms

An ideal canapé or a glamorous garnish.

> Grease for the baking sheet.
> 12 large mushrooms
> 1 small onion, finely minced
> 2 tablespoons unsalted margarine
> 1 tablespoon finely minced fresh parsley or ½ to 1 teaspoon dried parsley flakes
> 1 egg (graded large)
> Salt and black pepper to taste
> 2 to 3 tablespoons breadcrumbs, or more if necessary

Preheat the oven to 400 degrees F. Lightly grease a baking sheet; set aside.

Wipe the mushrooms clean. Separate the stems from the caps. In a food processor or by hand, finely chop the stems. If using a processor, do not run the machine too long; you do not want a pasty purée.

In a saucepan over medium heat, melt the margarine. Combine the chopped mushrooms with the minced onion. Sauté the combination in the melted margarine for about 5 minutes, until some of the liquid evaporates. Stir occasionally. Remove from the heat. Stir in the parsley and egg. Season with salt and pepper. Add breadcrumbs until the mixture is stiff enough to hold together. Stuff each mushroom cap with a spoonful of filling, rounding it slightly but keeping the filling loose.

Place the mushrooms on the prepared baking sheet. Bake in the preheated oven until the stuffing is puffy and crisp, about 15 minutes.

Variations:

• For an aromatic stuffing, add a whole peeled clove of garlic to the food processor when processing the mushroom stems. Or experiment with any herbs you favor.

• Mushroom caps can be filled with sautéed ground meat, chopped liver, or whatever strikes your fancy.

Asparagus Roll-ups

Makes 24 or 36 roll-ups

Crisp-tender asparagus cloaked in a toasted wrap are a superb finger food. These rolls can be frozen. I prefer to toast them before freezing. When ready to use, thaw the rolls then heat them in a 350-degree F. oven for 5 to 10 minutes, or leave them in the oven for 10 to 15 minutes, until the bread is toasted.

> 12 asparagus
> 12 slices sandwich-style white bread
> ⅔ cup mayonnaise
> 1½ teaspoons prepared white horseradish

Break the tough, woody ends from the asparagus. Cut off any large and sandy scales. Wash the stalks very well. Tie the asparagus together and set them upright in a large deep saucepan. Pour in boiling water to a depth of 1½ to 2 inches. Cover the saucepan. (A double boiler may be utilized by setting the asparagus in the lower half and inverting the upper half and using it as a cover.) Steam the asparagus for 10 to 15 minutes, just until crisp-tender. Do not overcook. Remove the asparagus from the pot, place in a shallow dish, and snip off the string. Blot dry with paper towels.

Preheat the oven to 350 degrees F. Decrust the slices of white bread. Flatten each slice evenly with a rolling pin. Combine the mayonnaise with the horseradish, then thinly coat each slice of bread with the dressing. Place an asparagus spear at one end of each slice of bread. Trim the root end of the spear to fit the slice; roll up tightly, jelly-roll fashion. Cut each roll-up in half or thirds. These may be served cold or arranged on a cookie sheet and toasted lightly in a 350-degree F. oven for 10 to 15 minutes.

Pita Pizza

An unconventional Jewish version of an Italian favorite. In Israel the pita is split diagonally. Just one-half of the pita is used. Before topping with the sauce and cheese, the cut side is brushed with salad oil.

For each pizza you will need:

> Oil for the pan
> 1 pita
> ½ cup marinara or spaghetti sauce
> ½ to 1 cup grated mozzarella cheese
> 2 ounces of drained canned sliced
>   mushrooms
> Garlic powder to taste (optional)
> Onion powder to taste (optional)
> Italian seasoning to taste (optional)
> Pizza seasoning to taste (optional)
> 2 to 4 tablespoons grated parmesan cheese

Preheat the oven to 375 degrees F. Generously oil an 8-inch-square baking pan.

Split the pita in half through the middle. Lay one round on the bottom of the greased pan. Spread the round with some of the sauce and about half of the mozarella cheese. Sprinkle with any or all of the optional seasonings. Then lay the other half of the pita on top of it. Spread with the remaining sauce and arrange the rest of the ingredients evenly over the pizza, ending with a sprinkling of the grated parmesan cheese. Bake for about 15 to 20 minutes, until the cheese is melted and golden. Serve very hot.

Variation:

•Ingredients can be varied according to what you have on hand. For a meat meal, the cheese can be replaced with grated salami, ground meat, or thin rounds of frankfurters.

•Pizza Bits: Toasted melba garlic rounds double for pita in these cocktail pizzas. Spoon pizza filling (tomato sauce, grated cheddar cheese, oregano, and garlic powder) on melba garlic rounds and heat.

Bagel Pizzas

Makes 8

The shiny crusted bagel, once considered a Jewish specialty, is now popular throughout the United States. Although most of us immediately associate the bagel with cream cheese and lox, it also can be used to make a wonderful pizza treat. An appetizer delight for kids.

> 4 bagels, cut in half
> 1 can (10½ ounces) tomato sauce with
>   mushrooms (1¼ cups)
> Garlic powder to taste
> Onion powder to taste
> ½ teaspoon Italian seasoning
> 1 cup shredded mozzarella cheese

Preheat the oven to 350 degrees F. Arrange the bagel halves cut side up on a cookie sheet. Spread each half with sauce. Sprinkle each with garlic powder, onion powder, and Italian seasoning. Top with shredded mozzarella cheese. Bake just until the cheese melts, about 8 to 10 minutes. Or broil until the cheese melts, about 4 minutes.

Note: To freshen bagels that are more than one-day old, split the bagels crosswise, and sprinkle the cut surfaces lightly with warm water. Wrap in foil and bake at 325 degrees F. for 15 to 20 minutes, until heated through. Serve warm.

Alternate method: Put the bagels in a brown paper bag and sprinkle the bag with water. Place in a 325-degree F. oven for about 15 minutes, until the paper bag is thoroughly dry.

2

From the Kettle

Soups & Garnishes

"Take thou also . . . wheat and barley and beans and lentils and millet and spelt and put them in one vessel" (Ezekiel 4:9).

Corn Chowder

Serves 6

This soup evokes happy childhood memories, for I learned to make it in cooking class when I was in the sixth grade.

> 1 small onion, finely chopped
> 2 tablespoons unsalted butter or margarine
> 2 cups boiling water
> 2 cups potato cubes
> 1 carrot, diced
> 1 celery stalk, diced
> 1 can (16½ ounces) cream-style corn
> Salt and black pepper to taste
> ½ to 1 cup milk
> Chopped fresh parsley

In a 2-quart saucepan, sauté the onion in the butter or margarine. Add the boiling water, potato cubes, carrot, and celery. Cook until the potatoes are soft. Add the corn and seasoning and bring to a boil. Reduce the heat; add the milk. Heat through and serve. Garnish with parsley.

Vegetable Soup
With Split Pea Base

Serves 6 to 8

"Pease porritch 'ot, pease porritch cold" is an old nursery rhyme. In England pease porritch was a dried pea soup. Here is a dried pea soup that is high in protein and enriched with fresh and frozen vegetables.

> 1 pound split peas, green or yellow
> 2 stalks celery, diced
> 1 large carrot, cut up
> 1 medium-sized parsnip, cut up
> 1 large onion, diced
> A few celery leaves, chopped
> A few parsley sprigs (optional)
> 3 quarts cold water
> Salt and black pepper to taste
> 1 package (20 ounces) frozen mixed
>   vegetables

Wash the peas in cold water. Drain well. In a large pot, combine the peas, celery, carrot, parsnip, onion, celery leaves, and parsley sprigs. Cover with 3 quarts of cold water. Bring to a boil. Lower the heat. Simmer covered for 1½ to 2 hours, until the peas are tender. Stir occasionally.

Purée the soup in a blender until the vegetables are smooth, or rub the vegetables through a sieve. Season with salt and pepper. Return the soup to the pot and add the package of frozen mixed vegetables. Cook until the vegetables are tender. If the soup is too thick, add boiling water. Dot not overcook the frozen vegetables. Taste and add additional salt and pepper if necessary. Serve with croutons.

Vegetarian Cholent Soup

Serves 8 to 10 generously

This is a very thick and hearty stick-to-the-ribs vegetable soup made with a variety of legumes. If cooked long enough, the soup becomes an excellent stand-in for a side dish of cholent. Ideal to serve in the *sukkah* on a cool evening.

> ½ cup dried yellow split peas
> ½ cup dried green split peas
> ⅓ cup dried lentils
> ⅓ cup barley
> ½ cup kidney beans or pinto beans
> ¼ cup baby lima beans
> ¼ cup Great Northern beans
> 2 quarts cold water
> 1 large onion, diced
> 2 large carrots, cut into ½-inch slices
> 1 to 2 stalks celery, finely sliced
> 2 large potatoes, cubed
> 1 parsnip, cut into ½-inch slices
> 3 ounces tomato paste
> Salt and black pepper to taste
> Garlic powder or 1 small garlic clove,
>   minced (optional)

Sort and wash all the dry legumes in cold water. Combine them in a 4-quart soup pot. Cover with the 2 quarts of cold water and soak overnight. The next day prepare and add the fresh vegetables and the tomato paste. Season to taste. Bring to a boil, then lower the heat, cover, and simmer gently for 1 to 1½ hours, until the beans are tender. Taste to correct seasoning. If the soup is too thick, thin with boiling water to the desired consistency. However, to serve as an accompaniment, simmer until the consistency is like cholent, thicker than stew.

Variation:

For a more robust nonvegetarian soup, add 1 to 2 pounds of meat or meat bones to the pot before adding the fresh vegetables. Bring to a boil, remove the scum, then proceed as above. Additional water (½ quart) may be needed.

Pareve Lentil Soup

Serves 6 to 8

Lentil soup may have its origin in the Bible, for we read in Genesis 25:34, "Jacob gave Esau bread and potage of lentils." Lentils are extremely nutritious, and they make a hearty and flavorful soup.

> 1 onion, diced
> 2 tablespoons oil or unsalted margarine
> 2 cups lentils, washed and drained
> 2 carrots, diced or sliced
> 3 stalks celery, diced
> 1 teaspoon salt
> ¼ teaspoon black pepper
> 1 teaspoon sugar (optional)
> 2 quarts hot water
> Minced fresh parsley

In a 3-quart soup pot, brown the onions in the oil or margarine. Add the lentils, carrots, celery, seasonings, and 2 quarts of hot water. Bring to a boil, lower the heat, cover, and simmer for 2½ to 3 hours, until the lentils are tender. Taste and correct the seasoning.

If you prefer a thick, smooth soup, purée in a blender or pass it through a sieve. Bring to a boil and serve hot. Garnish with parsley.

Variations:

• For a shorter cooking time, the lentils may be soaked overnight in cold water to cover. Drain before proceeding as above.

• Add ½ cup barley with the lentils.

• For a meat meal, enrich the soup by adding soup bones and 1½ to 2 pounds of soup meat. Serve the soup in individual bowls garnished with parsley, and serve the meat as a main dish.

• Slice 2 frankfurters into ½-inch rounds. Add them to the soup during the last 10 minutes of cooking. The frankfurter "pennies" floating on top of the lentil soup adds a contrast of color as well as additional flavor.

Chilled Cucumber Soup

Serves 4

A welcome change from borsht. You can serve the soup as an appetizer, or enjoy it with crackers and salad for a light lunch.

> 1 cup plain yogurt
> ¾ cup creamed cottage cheese
> 2 cucumbers, peeled, seeded, and coarsley
>   chopped
> 2 tablespoons snipped fresh dill
> Salt and black pepper
> 4 small sprigs of dill

Place the yogurt, cottage cheese, and chopped cucumber into the container of an electric blender. Process until smooth. Pour into a bowl or saucepan. Add the chopped dill. Season well with salt and pepper. Mix and chill for at least 1 hour. Before serving, stir the soup. Garnish each serving with a small sprig of dill.

Serving Variations:

• A small dollop of sour cream sprinkled with additional snipped fresh dill makes an attractive garnish.

• Float 1 to 3 thin cucumber slices on each serving, and top each slice with a dab of sour cream or yogurt sprinkled with dill.

Israeli Zucchini Soup

Serves 6

Make the meal a memorable one by starting with this smooth chilled soup. The flavor of dill is quite pronounced.

My daughter Naomi, who shared this recipe with me, uses an entire bunch of dill weighing approximately one-quarter pound. I personally use less, about three-fourths that amount.

> 2 tablespoons unsalted margarine
> 1 large onion, sliced
> 3 cloves garlic, sliced
> 6 medium-sized zucchinis, peeled and
>   thinly sliced

6 cups water
1 bunch dill
Salt and black pepper

In a saucepan, melt the margarine. Add the onion and sliced garlic cloves. Sauté over low heat until the onions are translucent. Add the thinly sliced zucchini and the water. Bring to a boil, reduce the heat, cover, and simmer until the zucchini are very tender, about 20 minutes.

Remove the soup from the heat. Add the dill to the hot soup. Stir. Pour the soup through a strainer, reserving the liquid. Transfer the solids to a blender jar or food processor. Add 2 cups of the cooking liquid and process until smooth.

Return the puréed soup to the pot and add boiling water if necessary to achieve a vichyssoise-like (rich cream soup) consistency. Season to taste with salt and black pepper. Simmer briefly. Bring the soup to room temperature, then chill. The soup may also be served warm.

Variation:

For a creamy soup, substitute 1 cup of pareve milk for 1 cup of the liquid added before puréeing. Heat but do not bring to a boil.

Vichyssoise

Serves 4 to 6

Add this classic cream of potato and leek soup to your repertoire of cold soups. A nice alternative to schav (sorrel soup).

2 tablespoons unsalted butter or margarine
1½ cups finely sliced leeks
1 cup diced celery
1 sliced onion
4 large potatoes, peeled and thinly sliced
3 cups boiling water
2 vegetable bouillon cubes
1 cup light cream or pareve milk
Salt and black pepper
Minced chives and paprika for garnish

Melt the butter or margarine in a 2-quart saucepot. Add the leeks, celery, and onion. Sauté until tender. Add the potatoes and boiling water. Cook until the vegetables are very soft. Dissolve the bouillon cubes in the soup. Taste and correct the seasoning. Purée the soup in a blender. Chill thoroughly before stirring in the cream. Serve very cold, garnished with minced chives and a sprinkling of paprika.

Cream of Mushroom Soup

Serves 4

An easy, made-from-scratch soup. If you're concerned about keeping your figure, try using skim milk.

> ½ pound fresh mushrooms
> 4 tablespoons (½ stick) unsalted margarine
>   or butter, divided
> 2 tablespoons flour
> 1 teaspoon salt
> ⅛ teaspoon black pepper
> 2 cups milk
> 1 onion, thinly sliced
> 1 tablespoon lemon juice (optional)

Wash, dry, and chop the mushrooms. In a heavy skillet, melt 2 tablespoons of the margarine or butter. Sauté the mushrooms for about 5 minutes. In the top part of a double boiler, melt the remaining 2 tablespoons of margarine or butter. Stir in the flour, salt, and pepper. Gradually add the milk and stir until smooth. Add the sliced onion and cook until thickened. Add the sautéed mushrooms and heat thoroughly. Stir in the lemon juice. Serve piping hot.

Turkey Frame Broth

Makes about 2 quarts

Waste not, want not! The party is over and you have a large turkey carcass left with slivers of meat here and there. Prepare this tasty soup. A chicken carcass may be used to make a chicken broth using the same procedures as for this turkey broth.

However, decrease the amount of vegetables and water used to compensate for the smaller size of the carcass.

> Carcass of a 12- to 14-pound turkey
> 2 stalks celery with leaves, cut in half
> 2 carrots, peeled and quartered
> 1 medium-sized whole onion, pierced
>   several times with a fork
> 1 parsnip, peeled and cut in half
> 1 parsley root, peeled and cut in half
> A few sprigs of fresh parsley
> A few sprigs of fresh dill
> Salt and white pepper to taste
> 2½ quarts cold water

In a large soup pot, combine the turkey carcass with the prepared vegetables. Season with the salt and pepper. Pour cold water over all; bring to a boil. Lower the heat to simmer; remove any scum that may have risen to the surface. Cook uncovered for 2 to 2½ hours. Remove the bones from the broth.

When the bones are cool enough to handle, remove any meat still adhering to them. Use the meat in recipes, or cut the meat into slivers and return to the broth. Chill the broth in the refrigerator to facilitate removing the fat. The vegetables may be used to prepare soup green pancakes, or they may be puréed in a blender and returned to the broth. Before chilling, taste and adjust the seasoning.

"Cream" of Chicken Soup

Serves 4 to 6

A quick-to-prepare nondairy cream of chicken soup.

> 2 cups chicken broth
> Salt and black pepper to taste
> ¼ cup cream of rice (cereal)
> 1 cup nondairy creamer
> 1 cup water
> Yellow food coloring (optional)
> ½ cup diced cooked chicken

Combine the chicken broth with the seasoning in a 2-quart pot. Scald. Sprinkle in the cream of rice and cook for 1 minute, stirring constantly. Remove from the heat. Cover and let set for 5 minutes. Dilute the pareve cream with the water and add to the chicken broth. Turn the mixture into a blender jar and whirl until smooth, or beat with a hand or electric mixer. (Blending or beating the mixture may be omitted, but then the soup will not be as smooth and creamy.) Return to the pot. Add the diced chicken and 1 drop of yellow food coloring. Heat thoroughly, but do not boil.

Variation:

For Chicken Bisque, add the cooked chicken to the soup before whirling in the blender.

Kaparah Chicken Soup

Makes 2½ to 3 quarts

Many religious Jews of Eastern European origin practice a religious ritual known as *shlugen kaporos* on the morning preceding the Day of Atonement. A fowl (or, in its place, money) is used as a *kaparah* (an expiatory ransom offering). Prayers petitioning God for a year of life are recited. The value of the fowl (or the money used) is given to charity, and the owner utilizes the fowl by making chicken soup for the forthcoming holiday.

> 1 chicken (4 to 5 pounds), quartered
> 4 quarts cold water
> Chicken giblets (except liver), cleaned
> 1 large onion
> 1 parsnip, peeled
> 1 parsley root, peeled
> 1 small celery knob, peeled
> 3 carrots, scraped
> 2 to 3 celery stalks, including leaves
> Salt and white pepper to taste
> A few sprigs of fresh parsley (optional)
> A few sprigs of fresh dill (optional)

Scald the chicken and clean it very well. Place the quartered chicken into a large soup pot with the cold water. Add the cleaned giblets. Bring the water to the boiling point, reduce the heat, and simmer uncovered. Skim off the scum from the top as it rises. When no more scum seems to appear, cover the pot and simmer for 1 hour. Add all of the prepared vegetables along with the salt, pepper, and optional herbs. Simmer covered for an additional 1½ hours or until the chicken is fork-tender.

With a slotted spoon remove the chicken and vegetables. Set aside. Strain the soup and chill to degrease. To serve, return the chicken and vegetables to the broth and bring it slowly back to simmer.

Variation:

For a gilded-lily kind of chicken soup, discard the greens and purée the vegetables in a blender. Return to the soup, which will now take on a creamy consistency.

Note: *Goldena yoich* came to be used as an appellation for chicken soup because of the golden globules of fat often seen floating on top of the broth. If you degrease your soup, you can still enjoy a *goldena yoich* by adding a few drops of pure yellow food coloring to the cooked broth.

Chicken Consommé With Julienne Vegetables

Serves 8 or more

Traditional chicken noodle soup is brightened by a crunch of raw vegetables and further enhanced by speckled chicken *quenelles*.

> 1 chicken (4 to 5 pounds) and giblets
> (except liver)
> 4 quarts cold water
> 1 teaspoon salt
> 1 onion
> 1 parsnip, peeled
> 1 parsley root, peeled
> 1 small celery knob, peeled
> 2 to 3 carrots, scraped

⟶

> **2 to 3 stalks of celery, including leaves**
> **4 sprigs of parsley or cilantro**
> **4 sprigs dill**
> **Salt**
> **White pepper**
> **1 chicken bouillon cube (½ ounce)**
> **16 to 20 chicken quenelles (see below)**
> **½ green bell pepper**
> **½ red bell pepper**
> **½ small zucchini**
> **1 cup cooked fine noodles**
> **Finely chopped parsley**

Clean the chicken very well. Disjoint the chicken and put the pieces in a 6-quart soup kettle. (It is optional to remove the skin from the chicken.) Add the giblets, cold water, and 1 teaspoon of salt. Cover the kettle and bring to a boil. Remove the cover, reduce the heat, and simmer for 10 to 15 minutes. Skim the surface carefully to remove the scum as it rises. When there is no more foam, add the onion, parsnip, parsley root, celery knob, and carrots. Tie together the celery, parsley, and dill to make a *bouquet garni*. Add to the pot. Cover and simmer for 2½ hours or until the chicken tests tender when pierced with a fork. With a slotted spoon remove the chicken and vegetables. Set aside. Strain the soup and chill.

While the soup is cooling in the refrigerator, prepare the chicken *quenelles*. When the soup is chilled, remove the grease from the surface, then return the soup to the kettle and bring to a boil again. Season with the chicken bouillon cube, additional salt if necessary, and pepper to taste. Simmer for about 10 minutes.

Quenelles (knaidlach):

> **2 eggs (graded large), lightly beaten**
> **2 tablespoons oil**
> **½ cup finely ground chicken**
> **½ teaspoon snipped fresh dill**
> **½ cup matzo meal**
> **1 teaspoon salt (optional)**
> **2 tablespoons water or chicken stock**

Lightly beat the eggs with the oil. Add the ground chicken, dill, matzo meal, and salt. When well blended, add the stock or water. Cover and refrigerate for at least 20 minutes. In a 2-quart pot, bring 4 cups of water to a brisk boil. Reduce the heat a bit. With a teaspoon, form approximately 30 small balls of dumpling mixture. Drop into the bubbling water. Cover the pot and cook for 30 to 40 minutes.

Cut the green pepper, red pepper, and zucchini into very thin julienne strips about 1½ to 2 inches long. Set aside. With a slotted spoon, transfer the chicken *quenelles* to the pot of chicken soup. Allow to simmer for about 5 minutes. To serve, put a portion of the julienne vegetables and cooked noodles in each dish. Ladle in some broth with 2 or 3 of the chicken quenelles. Garnish with a light sprinkling of chopped parsley.

Oriental Egg Drop Soup

Serves 8 or more

Water chestnuts add a new dimension to a traditional Chinese soup.

> 2 quarts chicken soup
> ¾ cup minced cooked chicken
> 3 to 4 water chestnuts, coarsely chopped
> 1 tablespoon cornstarch
> 3 tablespoons water
> 3 eggs (graded large)

In a 3-quart saucepan over medium-high heat, bring the chicken soup, chicken, and water chestnuts to a boil. In a cup, mix the cornstarch with the water. Pour the mixture into the soup, stirring constantly. Cook until clear. Beat the eggs and pour in a stream into the boiling soup. Cook until the eggs are set. Taste to correct seasoning.

Gazpacho

Serves 6 to 8

Gazpacho, a cold Spanish soup, can be thought of as a liquefied vegetable salad. There are countless versions. Some are made spicy hot by adding cayenne or hot pepper sauce. Some are thickened and some are sharpened with wine or wine vinegar. Adding slices of bread to the mixture serves as a thickener.

> 3 tomatoes, peeled and quartered
> 1 large cucumber, peeled, seeded, and cut
>   into chunks
> 1 small onion, peeled and quartered
> 1 sweet green pepper, seeded and chopped
> 1 sweet red pepper, seeded and chopped
> 1 or 2 cloves fresh garlic, peeled and
>   chopped
> 3 cups tomato juice
> ¼ cup oil
> 1 to 2 teaspoons lemon juice
> Salt and pepper to taste

Garnishes:

> Finely snipped parsley
> 1 cup garlic-seasoned or plain croutons
> 1 cup thinly sliced or diced cucumber
> ¾ cup diced green pepper
> ½ cup chopped scallions
> ½ cup chopped celery

Combine the tomatoes, cucumber, onion, peppers, and garlic in the container of an electric blender and whirl until smooth. Transfer to a large mixing bowl. Add the tomato juice, oil, lemon juice, and salt and pepper to taste. Stir to mix. Chill thoroughly.

Serve in chilled bowls with some snipped parsley drifted over each serving. Pass the various garnitures in individual dishes so each diner can add to his soup any combination of garnishes desired.

Variations:

• For a different texture, finely chop, but do not purée, all the vegetables. If using a processor, use the steel blade.

• Add 2 slices of trimmed white bread to the blender when whirling the vegetables.

• Serve with toasted pita triangles or garlic bread.

• For those who like their soup spicy hot, have hot pepper sauce or cayenne pepper available.

Garlic Soup

Serves 3 or 4

One of the past presidents of our congregation happens to be a physician, and his wife, Jean Chameides, once told me of a very unusual soup she had been served: garlic soup. It intrigued me! I did some research and learned that in France garlic soup was believed to be a cure-all. I have Americanized the delicate French classic by adding vegetables and thickening the soup with cream of rice rather than egg yolks. The flavor of the soup is pleasingly rich yet subdued. (See the Forty-clove Garlic Chicken on page 78.)

> 1 bulb of garlic (12 or more cloves)
> 6 sprigs of fresh parsley
> 1 bay leaf
> ⅛ teaspoon dried sage
> ⅛ teaspoon dried basil
> ⅛ teaspoon dried oregano
> 1 whole clove
> 1 tablespoon olive oil
> 5 cups hot water
> 2 vegetable bouillon cubes or 1 chicken
>   bouillon cube (for a meat meal)
> ⅛ teaspoon black pepper
> 4 tablespoons cream of rice
> Salt and black pepper to taste

Peel the garlic cloves. In a medium-sized (2-quart) soup pot, combine the cloves of garlic with the parsley, bay leaf, sage, basil, oregano, clove, and olive oil. Add the hot water. Crumble the bouillon cubes into the pot. Stir to dissolve. Bring the contents to a boil. Cover the pot, turn down the heat, and simmer for 1 hour. Remove the bay leaf. Slowly add the cream of rice. Cook for 30 seconds. Cover the pot and let set for 3 more minutes. Cool enough to be able to purée in the blender. Taste to correct seasoning. Return to the pot and reheat, stirring occasionally. If the puréed soup is thicker than you like, merely thin it with boiling water, adding a little at a time until you arrive at the desired consistency.

Note: Prepared with the vegetable cubes, I have served this soup cold. A nice change from borsht or schav.

Beet Borsht

Serves 8

Borsht originated in the Ukraine, and the very name *borsht* has its origin in the old Slavic word for beets. Borsht takes on several forms—hot with meat, hot without meat, cold without meat.

This meatless borsht can be served hot in the winter or cold in the summer, either as a soup or a refreshing cold beverage.

> 2 bunches (approximately 2¼ to 2½ pounds,
>   8 medium-sized) beets, scraped and sliced
> 1 onion, peeled and sliced
> 2 quarts cold water
> 2 teaspoons salt
> 3 tablespoons sugar
> 2 tablespoons cider vinegar
> Juice of 1 lemon

Place the beets and onion in a 4-quart soup kettle. Add the water, salt, sugar, vinegar, and lemon juice. Bring to a boil, turn down the heat, cover, and simmer until the beets are tender. Strain. Put the beets, onion, and 2 cups of the borsht liquid into a blender jar or food processor bowl. Process until the solids are chopped very fine or puréed. Return the processed solids to the soup. Taste to correct the seasoning, adding more sugar or lemon juice if necessary to arrive at the perfect balance of sweet and sour.

To serve cold, chill thoroughly. Serve in a glass as a beverage or in a bowl with a dollop of sour cream afloat. To serve hot, serve in a bowl with or without a hot boiled potato. For a dairy meal, top with a dollop of sour cream. Or, you may serve the soup ungarnished and pass condiment bowls of sliced hard-cooked eggs, thinly sliced cucumbers, finely cut scallions, fresh chopped dill, and boiled potatoes.

Variations:

• For a thick borsht, with a wire whisk beat 2 eggs in a bowl. While whisking, very gradually add a ladle or two of the hot soup. Then slowly add the beaten egg mixture to the soup, whisking all the while. Simmer until hot. Do not boil or the eggs will curdle.

• For a bright pink creamy borsht, fortify the borsht with sour cream. Blend the cream into the borsht in a blender.

• For a clear borsht, purée, correct the seasoning, then strain.

Russian Cabbage Borsht

Serves 6

Borsht is traditionally a beetroot soup, but some versions of this Russian classic contain no beets at all. Rather, they feature cabbage as the predominant vegetable.

This cabbage borsht with meat makes a robust meal. Serve the soup with *sucherkis* (page 348), and then serve the meat as the main dish.

> 2 to 3 pounds of flanken or brisket
> A few beef bones
> 2½ cups peeled, seeded, and chopped fresh
>   tomatoes or 1 can (1 pound 4 ounces)
>   tomatoes
> 2 onions, chopped
> 2½ quarts cold water
> 1 medium-sized head of cabbage, shredded
> 2 teaspoons salt
> ¼ cup sugar
> Juice of 1 lemon

In a large 4-quart soup kettle, combine the meat, bones, tomatoes, and onions. Cover with the cold water and bring to a boil. Remove the scum. Cover, reduce the heat, and simmer for 1 hour. Add the cabbage, salt, sugar, and lemon juice. Simmer for an additional 1½ hours or until the meat is fork-tender. Taste and correct seasoning, adding more salt, sugar, or lemon juice until you achieve that perfect balance between sweet and sour.

Semolina (Farina) Squares

Makes 64 squares

Farina is not only good in the morning as a breakfast cereal, but prepared as squares it serves as an attractive soup garnish.

> **1 cup semolina (farina)**
> **3 cups boiling water**
> **½ teaspoon salt**
> **1 tablespoon finely minced fresh parsley**

Slowly pour the cup of farina into the 3 cups of boiling water seasoned with the salt. Cook until done. Stir in the chopped parsley. Spread out the cooked farina in an 8-inch-square pan. Chill completely. Cut into 1-inch squares before adding to soup.

Variation:

For special occasions, cut the cooked semolina into fancy shapes using small cookie cutters or aspic cutters.

Egg Rivels

*Makes enough for
2 quarts of soup*

An easy soup garnish, similar to the Lithuanian soup dumpling known as *rivvels*, although the Lituanian version has a dash of nutmeg added.

1 cup sifted all-purpose flour
¼ teaspoon salt
1 egg (graded large)
Black pepper (optional)

Sift the flour and salt into a bowl. Make a hollow in the center and break in the whole unbeaten egg. Sprinkle with a few grains of pepper. With your fingers or a fork, work the egg into the flour until the mixture resembles cornmeal. Rub the mixture between the palms of your hands to drop small shreds into boiling hot soup; or, with a spoon, sprinkle the mixture into boiling hot soup. Cover tightly and cook gently for 10 to 15 minutes, until the rivels are tender.

Soup Lotus

Makes about 24

Add a touch of elegance to chicken soup by setting a "lotus" flower adrift with a sprig of fresh parsley resting in its center. Truly a dramatic soup garnish. A few strands of fine noodles, the classic accompaniment to chicken soup, will not detract from the effect.

2 eggs (graded large)
Pinch of salt
½ teaspoon sugar (optional)
1¼ cups sifted all-purpose flour
Oil for frying

In a medium-sized bowl, beat the eggs with the salt and sugar. Add the flour to make a soft dough. Knead for several minutes, until elastic. On a lightly floured surface, roll out the dough to ⅛-inch thickness. With a 2¼-inch daisy cookie cutter, cut out dough daisies. Wet the center of 1 daisy cutout with a little cold water, then place another daisy on top. With a finger, press the center so the 2 cutouts will adhere to each other. Let stand for about 10 minutes.

In a deep fryer or a skillet at least 2½ inches deep, heat a minimum of 1 inch of oil to 375 degrees F. Drop a few daisies at a time into the oil and fry until delicate brown, turning if necessary. They must be watched, as they fry quickly. Drain on absorbent paper.

Variation:

In the absence of a daisy cutter, substitute a round cookie cutter and proceed as above. To make little roses, cut into circles of three varying sizes. Place the circles one on top of the other, with the smallest on top. Press in the center, as above.

Einlauf
(Egg Drop)

Makes enough for
6 to 8 cups of soup

A simple Jewish and German garnish for a clear soup.

> 2 eggs (graded large), well beaten
> ½ teaspoon salt
> Dash of black pepper
> ½ cup water
> ½ cup less 2 tablespoons all-purpose flour
> 1 tablespoon finely minced parsley
>   (optional)

In a small mixing bowl, stir all the ingredients together until smooth. Pour in a steady thin stream directly from the mixing bowl into boiling soup. Stir once, cover, and simmer for 5 to 10 minutes.

Egg Fluff

Serves 8 to 10

A low-cholesterol soup garnish.

> 3 egg whites
> 2 quarts boiling clear chicken soup
> Chopped fresh parsley, chopped fresh dill,
>   or a dash of paprika (optional)

In a large soup tureen or large bowl, beat the egg whites until stiff. Pour the boiling chicken soup over the beaten egg whites. Serve the soup with a portion of the fluff on top. Garnish with chopped parsley or dill or a dash of paprika.

Egg-Parsley "Noodles"

Makes twelve
3-inch noodles

A soup garnish that will lend flavor and color to a bowl of clear chicken soup.

2 eggs (graded large), well beaten
3 tablespoons all-purpose flour
Dash of salt and black pepper
2 tablespoons minced parsley, divided
2 to 3 tablespoons unsalted margarine

Combine the eggs, flour, salt and pepper, and half of the parsley. For each "noodle" drop the batter from a tablespoon into hot melted margarine in a medium-sized skillet. Cook just till golden, turning once. Drain on paper towels. Cool and cut each noodle into wedges, or roll each noodle jelly-roll fashion and cut into strips. Serve 2 of the egg-parsley wedges or a few noodles in each bowl of boiling chicken broth. Sprinkle each serving with some of the remaining parsley.

Puffed Crackers

A new and exciting way to serve square soda crackers. Serve as a soup or salad accompaniment.

Square soda crackers
Unsalted butter or margarine

Soak the crackers upside down in a shallow pan of ice water for 5 minutes. With a spatula, remove one cracker at a time and place it right side up on a greased baking sheet. Dot with butter or margarine. Bake in a preheated 450-degree F. oven for 8 to 10 minutes without opening the oven door. If not nice and brown, continue baking for a few more minutes. Cool slightly and serve. Prepare 3 or more crackers per serving.

Variation:

For seasoned crackers, brush the tops of any crisp crackers with melted butter or margarine. Flavor with a sprinkling of any of the following: onion powder, garlic powder, or paprika; caraway, celery, poppy, sesame, or dill seed. Arrange the crackers on a greased baking sheet. Bake in a preheated 350-degree F. oven for approximately 5 minutes, until crisp.

3

Colorful Compositions

Salads & Relishes

"[I give] all the green plants for food" (Genesis 1:30).

Tabbouleh

(Bulghur Salad)

Serves 6 to 8

Tabbouleh, frequently served in pita bread, makes a wonderful party salad or side dish. Flavored with a traditional Middle Eastern dressing of olive oil and lemon juice, and seasoned with parsley and mint, tabbouleh has a lovely aroma. Other herbs, such as oregano or dill, may be added.

A dramatic way to serve tabbouleh is on a mound of shredded lettuce surrounded by cherry tomatoes, ribbons of green pepper, black olives, and sprigs of parsley. For a Middle Eastern touch, serve with three-inch lengths of lettuce to be used as "scoops" with which to eat the salad.

> **1 cup dry bulghur (cracked wheat)**
> **½ to 1 cup chopped scallions, to taste**
> **1½ cups boiling water**
> **1 cup chopped parsley**
> **½ teaspoon crushed dried mint**
> **1 teaspoon minced garlic**
> **¼ cup olive oil or salad oil**
> **¼ cup lemon juice**
> **1 to 2 tablespoons sugar, to taste**
> **Salt and black pepper to taste**
> **2 tomatoes (1½ cups coarsely cut)**

Place the dry bulghur into a medium-sized bowl. Stir in the chopped scallions. Cover with the boiling water. Set aside to soak for at least 1 hour. Drain off excess water. Combine the chopped parsley, dried mint, and minced garlic with the bulghur. In a small bowl, prepare a dressing with the remaining ingredients. Pour over the salad. Toss well. Taste to correct the seasoning. Best if refrigerated covered for 2 to 4 hours so that the flavors can blend. Just before serving, cut the tomatoes into small pieces and mix into the salad.

Variations:

Additions to the salad may include one or more of the following: ½ cup cooked chickpeas, ½ cup grated carrots or squash, ½ cup sliced radishes or diced green pepper, 1 cup green peas.

Baba Ghanouj
(Eggplant Salad)

Makes 2½ to 3 cups

Add a Middle Eastern accent to your salad bar. Serve Baba Ghanouj either as a dip or as a salad.

Two of Israel's favorites—the staple eggplant, baked and peeled, and tahina (sesame seed paste) dressed with lemon juice and crushed garlic—team up in a delicious dip or salad. When I was in Israel, I was intrigued by the color of the eggplant salad. My suspicion that mayonnaise gave the eggplant its unusual color was wrong: it's tahina!

> 1 large eggplant (approximately 1½ pounds)
> 1 medium-sized onion, finely minced or
>   grated
> ¼ cup finely minced pasley
> ½ cup tahina
> 2 to 4 tablespoons lemon juice, to taste
> 2 to 3 cloves garlic, finely chopped, to taste
> 1 to 2 teaspoons water (optional)
> Salt to taste
> Dash of freshly ground black pepper

With a fork, puncture the eggplant in a 4 or 5 places. Place on a foil-lined baking pan and bake in a 450-degree F. oven, turning occasionally until the eggplant feels soft to the touch, about 30 minutes. Remove from the oven. Cool. Cut the eggplant in half. Scoop out the pulp.

In a chopping bowl, chop the eggplant with the onion and parsley. In a large measuring cup, blend the tahina with the lemon juice and garlic. If the tahina is too thick, stir in a teaspoon or more of water. Stir the dressing into the chopped eggplant. Season with salt and pepper.

The excellence of the dish will depend largely on the balance of the ingredients. Taste and add more lemon juice, garlic, or seasonings to please your palate.

Vegetable Salad

Serves 10 or more

In lieu of crudités and a dip, my daughter Judith will frequently prepare this tasty salad, which includes ingredients usually not found in a combination salad.

> **Florets from 1 head of broccoli**
> **4 large carrots, cut julienne**
> **½ pound snow pea pods**
> **1 pound fresh mushrooms, sliced**
> **1 small can (8 ounces) sliced water**
> ** chestnuts**
> **1 jar (7 ounces) miniature corn**

In individual pots, steam the broccoli florets and the carrots for no more than 5 minutes. Drain and, in order to retard cooking, immediately run under cold water. Steam the snow peas for 3 minutes. Combine the broccoli, carrots, and peas in a large salad bowl. Add the sliced mushrooms, water chestnuts, and miniature corn. Toss together, but do not dress until serving time.

Dressing:
> **1 cup vegetable oil**
> **¼ cup white vinegar**

Juice of 2 lemons
2 teaspoons prepared mustard
2 teaspoons salt
1 teaspoon black pepper
¼ cup soy sauce

In a blender container or a screw-top jar with a tight- fitting lid, combine all the ingredients. Chill and toss with the salad to serve.

Colombian Tossed Salad

Serves 6

Our Latin friends are generous in their use of fiery hot chilies in their cooking. But they also use many spices that are flavorful but not hot. One favorite is *comino*, Spanish for cumin.

This subtly exotic recipe calls for ground cumin seed. The salad is crowned with sliced tomatoes, julienne beets, and hard-cooked eggs.

½ head lettuce
1 cup shredded cabbage
½ cup thinly sliced carrots
½ cup sliced Spanish onion
½ cup sliced celery
¼ cup olive oil or salad oil
1 tablespoon fresh lemon juice
1 tablespoon cider vinegar
½ to 1 teaspoon salt, to taste
½ to 1 teaspoon sugar, to taste
⅛ teaspoon black pepper
⅛ teaspoon garlic powder
½ teaspoon ground cumin seed
2 medium-sized tomatoes, sliced
½ cup cooked beets, sliced julienne
2 hard-cooked eggs, sliced

Tear the lettuce into bite-sized pieces. Place in a salad bowl. Add the cabbage, carrots, onion, and celery. In a 1-cup glass measure, prepare the salad dressing by combining the oil, lemon juice, vinegar, and seasonings. Stir to blend. Pour the dressing over the salad. Toss lightly. Arrange the sliced tomatoes and beets on top of the salad. Garnish with the sliced hard-cooked eggs.

Ensaladas de Palmitas
(Hearts of Palm Salad)

Serves 8

Hearts of palm, a tropical vegetable with a delicate flavor, are the tender young buds of the palm tree. This salad, with its flavor in some ways reminiscent of the Mexican ceviche, is an elegant party appetizer. For a variation, substitute artichoke hearts for the hearts of palm—or use a combination.

> 2 cans (14 ounces each) whole hearts of
>   palm, drained and sliced
> 1 large onion, finely diced
> 6 tomatoes, cubed
> 1 avocado, cut into small squares
> 3 ounces pimento-stuffed small olives
> Fresh lemon juice, enough to cover the
>   vegetables
> 5 tablespoons olive oil
> 7 ounces (⅞ cup) ketchup
> Salt and black pepper

In a large deep dish or bowl, combine all the cut-up vegetables. Cover with lemon juice. Add the oil and ketchup. Season to taste with salt and pepper. Toss the salad to mix well. Cover and refrigerate for at least 2 hours to blend the flavors. This salad is good-natured and will not object to being refrigerated overnight. Drain off some of the marinade before serving.

Mock "Crabmeat" Salad

Serves 4 to 5

You can fool your friends into thinking you are serving fish when in reality the "seafood" in this salad is all vegetables.

2 cups shredded raw parsnips
1 cup finely chopped celery
1 tablespoon chopped pimento
⅓ cup chopped black olives
½ cup mayonnaise
1 tablespoon lemon juice
½ teaspoon salt
Shredded salad greens
2 teaspoons finely sliced scallion
Parsley sprigs

Into a medium-sized bowl, place the shredded raw parsnips. Add the celery, pimento, and chopped olives. In a measuring cup, blend together the mayonnaise, lemon juice, and salt. Combine this mixture with the parsnip mixture in the bowl. Toss well. Serve over salad greens, garnished with onion slices and a few sprigs of fresh parsley.

Israeli Carrot Salad

Serves 4 to 6

Israeli carrot salad is popularly dressed with orange and lemon juice. This savory version, which was introduced to me by Dr. and Mrs. Joseph Korn, friends who spent a sabbatical year in Israel, does not contain the traditional orange or lemon juice. It is laced with garlic. An excellent condiment to serve with meat.

½ pound (4 medium-large) carrots
1 to 2 cloves garlic
3 tablespoons mayonnaise or salad dressing
Dash of black pepper (optional)

Peel the carrots and, on the medium openings of a grater, grate them into a medium-sized bowl. Finely mince the garlic or put it through a garlic press directly into the grated carrots. Stir in enough mayonnaise or salad dressing to bind the carrots. Add pepper to taste. Refrigerate for at least an hour for the flavors to blend.

Variations:

- Two tablespoons of finely minced parsley will add color.
- Ground ginger (⅛ teaspoon) will give the salad a little zip.
- Salt and perhaps ½ teaspoon of sugar may also be added.
- Israelis, on occasion, substitute beets for the carrots and proceed as above.

Fresh Broccoli Salad

Serves 8 or more

A salad that is ready when you are. Prepare it the day before you plan to serve it. Refrigerate overnight so the flavors can blend. The secret to this salad is the use of pimento-stuffed olives. The green of the olives blends in with the broccoli, while the pimentos add a dash of color. The salad will keep well in the refrigerator three to four days.

> ¼ cup dehydrated onions
> 1 cup cold water
> 1 head of broccoli (approximately 1½
>   pounds)
> ⅓ cup of pimento-stuffed green olives
> 2 hard-cooked eggs, chopped
> ¼ cup slivered almonds
> Garlic powder to taste
> Salt and black pepper to taste
> 1 heaping tablespoon mayonnaise

Reconstitute the dehydrated onions in the cup of cold water while preparing the broccoli. Trim off the large leaves from the broccoli. Remove the tough ends from the bottom of the stalks. Wash the broccoli thoroughly. Remove the flowerets from the stalks and separate them into bite-sized pieces. Turn them into a large bowl. Peel the stalks and chop them coarsely. Add to the flowerets.

Thoroughly drain the onions. Rinse the olives to remove the brine. Dice them into the bowl with the broccoli. Add the onions, chopped eggs, and almonds. Season with the garlic powder, salt, and pepper. Add the mayonnaise and toss gently. Refrigerate overnight.

Variations:

• Chopped or sliced green onions can be substituted for the dehydrated onions.

• A medium-sized carrot, finely grated, makes a colorful addition.

• For additional seasoning, grated parmesan cheese can be sprinkled on the salad before serving.

Mock Lobster Salad

Serves 6

For devotees of fish, here is a blend of fish and seasonings that will surprise and delight. Be careful not to overcook the fish. Fish cooks quickly, and extended cooking will make it flavorless.

> 2 pounds halibut or haddock fillets
> 1 medium-sized onion, sliced
> 1 stalk celery
> 2 sprigs parsley
> ⅛ teaspoon black pepper
> 1 teaspoon salt
> 1½ cups boiling water
> ½ teaspoon paprika
> ¼ cup French Dressing (page 258)
> Mayonnaise
> 3 hard-cooked eggs

Place the fillets in a saucepan lined with the onion, celery, parsley, pepper, and salt. Add the boiling water and simmer until the fish is just tender, about 5 to 8 minutes. Drain. Remove the fish and vegetables. Flake the fish. Sprinkle with paprika. Moisten with French Dressing and chill thoroughly. Serve on lettuce with mayonnaise. Garnish with hard-cooked eggs.

Smoked Salmon Salad

Serves 4

You will score points when you serve this easily prepared and extraordinarily different and good-tasting salmon salad.

1 can (7¾ ounces) salmon
¼ teaspoon liquid smoke
Black pepper
Lemon juice

Open the can of salmon. Add the liquid smoke. Cover the top of the can with plastic wrap. Refrigerate overnight. When ready to serve, drain off the liquid. Flake the salmon and pile the large colorful flakes onto a bed of chiffonade of lettuce (lettuce that has been finely shredded). Sprinkle with a little freshly ground pepper from the mill. Add a squeeze of lemon juice. Dark pumpernickel bread makes an ideal accompaniment to the salad.

Garden Salmon Salad

Serves 12 as an appetizer,
6 as a luncheon main course

One of the best ingredients to combine in a salad is canned salmon. It blends perfectly with any other salad ingredients. In this particular dish, color plays an important role. The orange of the salmon is offset by bright-colored vegetables and rice.

1 cup peas, cooked
1 cup diced carrots, cooked
1 cup diced string beans, cooked
1 cup chopped radishes
1 cup chopped celery
1 cup chopped scallions
1 can (7¾ ounces) salmon, drained and
   flaked
3 cups cooked rice
5 to 6 tablespoons French Dressing
   (page 258)
6 hard-cooked eggs
8 ounces cream cheese, at room
   temperature
½ cup mayonnaise
Salt and black pepper to taste
Watercress

In a large salad bowl, combine the vegetables, salmon, rice, and

French Dressing. Stir to blend the ingredients. Cut the eggs in half crosswise. Remove the yolks and mash with the cheese and mayonnaise. Season with salt and pepper. Fill the egg whites with the yolk mixture and arrange around the edge of the salad. Garnish with watercress. Refrigerate until ready to serve.

Note: For a celebration, place the salad in a fish mold. Before doing so, line the mold with a damp piece of cheesecloth and you will have no difficulty in unmolding the salad onto a serving platter. Garnish the mold by adding fish features, such as a pimento-stuffed olive or a small slice of carrot for the eye, layers of thinly sliced cucumber for scales, and so on. Surround the mold with greens.

Herring Salad

Serves 6 to 8

Looking for a different herring salad? Consider this one. The combination of wine sauce, sour cream, and mayonnaise provides a refreshingly different flavor. The beet tidbits add dramatic color.

> 1 jar (12 ounces) herring fillets in wine
>   sauce
> 1 can (16 ounces) beet tidbits
> 1 apple, cored but unpeeled
> 1 large sour or half-sour pickle
> 2 hard-cooked eggs
> 1 potato, boiled and peeled
> ½ cup sour cream
> ½ cup mayonnaise

Drain the herring and reserve the wine sauce in a small bowl. Cut the herring into bite-sized pieces. Place the herring and the onions in a large bowl. Add the can of undrained beet tidbits. Cut the apple, sour pickle, and cooked eggs into bite-sized pieces; add to the herring-beet mixture. Combine the sour cream and mayonnaise with the reserved wine sauce. Pour the dressing over the herring mixture. Toss the salad with the dressing. Cover and let marinate overnight. Keeps very well in the refrigerator.

Three-Bean Salad

Serves 8 to 10

When thoughts of a bean salad turn you on, try this one, which is both colorful and stimulating to the appetite. Note that canned vegetables are not used in this dish, which can be frozen successfully.

> ½ cup dried red kidney beans
> ½ cup dried chickpeas
> 1 tablespoon sugar
> 1 box (10 ounces) frozen baby lima beans
> 1 box (10 ounces) frozen whole-kernel corn
> 1 box (9 ounces) frozen cut green beans
> 1 red onion, thinly sliced
> ½ to ¾ cup sugar
> ½ cup wine vinegar or cider vinegar
> 2 tablespoons water

Place the kidney beans and the chickpeas in 2 separate bowls. Add cold water to cover and soak overnight. The next day, drain the beans and cook them individually in small covered saucepans, each containing 2 cups of water. The kidney beans can be seasoned with 1 tablespoon sugar or the equivalent in sugar substitute. Cook the frozen vegetables in individual pans according to package directions. Do not overcook. When done, thoroughly drain the cooked vegetables and cooked beans.

Combine them all in a large bowl. Add the sliced onion.

In a medium-sized bowl, prepare the dressing by combining the sugar, vinegar, and water. There are no strict rules. Add more or less sugar to taste. Pour the dressing over the salad. Toss to mix. Refrigerate for a few hours, or chill overnight so the beans have time to marinate and the flavor of the dish to develop.

Variations:

• Add one or more of the following vegetables: a green pepper, cut into strips or cubes; a medium-sized cucumber or zucchini squash, cubed; ⅓ cup coarsely chopped celery; ⅓ cup shredded carrot.

• If you are inclined to use herbs, try ½ teaspoon of tarragon, ½ teaspoon basil leaves, or 2 tablespoons fresh parsley.

Quick Three-Bean Salad

Serves 10 or more

If you want a head start on tomorrow's meal, prepare this marinated bean salad. It is very easy on the cook and is full of flavor. Keeps well in the refrigerator for a few days.

1 can (17 ounces) whole-kern corn
1 can (16 ounces) cut green beans
1 can (16 ounces) cut wax beans
1 can (16 ounces) red kidney beans
½ cup diced green pepper
½ cup thinly sliced onion
½ cup salad oil
½ cup wine vinegar
½ cup sugar
1 teaspoon salt
½ teaspoon black pepper
Dash of lemon juice

Drain all the vegetables and combine them in a large mixing bowl. In a 4-cup glass measure, combine the dressing ingredients. Mix well and pour over the combined vegetables. Refrigerate for a few hours. Use a slotted spoon to serve.

Variation:

You may add any of the following to the above: canned baby lima beans, garbanzo beans (chickpeas), black-eyed peas. The amount of the dressing may have to be increased to compensate for the addition of more vegetables.

Curried Walnut and Rice Salad

Serves 6 to 8

For a refreshingly different dish, brown rice is combined with curry and a tangy lemon dressing.

5 cups cooked brown rice
1 cup chopped scallions
1 large carrot, grated
½ cup chopped fresh parsley

————————➤

> 1½ cups coarsely chopped walnuts
> Salt and black pepper to taste
> 1 large apple, peeled

Lemon Dressing:

> ½ cup oil
> ⅓ cup lemon juice
> 2 tablespoons honey
> 1 tablespoon mayonnaise
> 1 to 3 teaspoons curry powder, to taste
> 2 cloves garlic
> Salt and black pepper to taste

Combine the rice, scallions, carrot, chopped parsley, and chopped nuts. Add the salt and pepper to taste. Toss to blend the ingredients. Set aside the apple.

In a blender jar, combine the Lemon Dressing ingredients. Blend until smooth. Dice the peeled apple into the dressing. Pour the dressing over the rice mixture. Mix well and serve.

Party Pasta Salad

Serves 8 or more

My daughter Judith, though not a vegetarian, is noted for her salads. She gets a head start by preparing them in advance. Here is a very colorful pasta salad that is enhanced by the dressing added just prior to serving. You may substitute vegetables of your choice for the cauliflower and zucchini.

Salad:

> 1 package (12 ounces) rainbow corkscrew
>   pasta
> ½ head cauliflower
> 2 small zucchini
> 1 sweet red pepper, diced

Cook the pasta according to package directions. Trim the cauliflower and cut into bite-sized flowerets. Slice the zucchini; cut the red pepper into squares. Carefully toss the vegetables into the cooked pasta. Other cup-up vegetables of your choice are a welcome addition. Set aside in the refrigerator till serving time. Before serving, spoon the dressing over the salad and toss.

Dressing:

> ¼ cup olive oil
> 2 cloves garlic, minced
> 1 tablespoon sugar
> 3 tablespoons dry white wine
> 2 tablespoons lemon juice
> 1 teaspoon dried basil
> 1 teaspoon salt
> 1 teaspoon black pepper
> 4 dashes Tabasco sauce
> 1 tablespoon dried parsley

In a screw-top jar, combine all the ingredients. Shake well to blend. Makes a generous ½ cup.

Bella's Potato Salad

Serves 6 to 8

My friend Bella Weisfogel shared this marvelous potato salad recipe with me. She said her son likes it so much that he can eat it as a dessert.

> 10 to 12 medium-sized potatoes (2 to 2¼
>   pounds)
> 1 onion, finely chopped (⅜ cup), or 2
>   tablespoons dehydrated onion, reconstituted
> Salt and black pepper to taste
> 2 hard-cooked eggs
> 2 tablespoons vinegar
> 1 tablespoon sugar
> 2 tablespoons water
> ¾ to 1 cup mayonnaise or salad dressing

Cook the potatoes in their jackets until tender; do not overcook. Cool and peel. Slice the potatoes very thin into a large mixing bowl. Add the finely chopped onion. Season well with salt and pepper. Separate the whites and yellows of the hard-cooked eggs. Chop the whites and add to the potato mixture.

In a small mixing bowl, prepare the dressing as follows: Mash the yolks well. Add the vinegar, sugar, and water. Mix well. Pour the dressing over the potatoes. Add the mayonnaise or salad dressing. Toss to mix well.

Mashed Potato Salad

Serves 4

Here, with an assist from packaged dried potato granules, an old-fashioned mashed potato salad is prepared in an easy new way. The dill pickle adds zip.

A different way of serving this salad at a meat meal: Heat thick slices of bologna in a little hot fat just until the meat "cups." Fill with potato salad.

> **Potato granules to make 4 cups mashed**
> **potatoes**
> **½ cup salad dressing**
> **1 to 2 teaspoons salt, to taste**
> **2 teaspoons dry mustard**
> **1 cup diced celery**
> **1 to 2 chopped dill pickles**
> **4 hard-cooked eggs, chopped**

Prepare the mashed potatoes, substituting ½ cup salad dressing for 1 cup of the liquid. Season with salt and mustard. Fold in the celery, chopped pickle, and chopped hard-cooked eggs. Refrigerate overnight for flavors to blend. Next day, scoop out onto tomato slices.

Variation:

Chopped scallions and/or chopped green pepper may be added to the basic potato salad. Colorful cooked vegetables such as diced beets, carrots, or tiny green peas are welcome additions.

Homemade Sauerkraut

Makes 1 pint

Sauerkraut, a German word meaning "sour cabbage," is an Old World German specialty. How well I remember my mother stashing away a barrel of sauerkraut in the basement, next to the barrels of sour pickles and sour tomatoes. She would layer finely shredded cabbage with salt and allow it to ferment in the brine made of its own juice. She was meticulous in seeing that the cabbage was properly weighted down and submerged in the juices. Occasionally she would add caraway seeds. Fresh sauer-kraut has a milder, less acidic flavor than the canned.

> 1 small firm green cabbage (approximately
>   1 pound)
> 2 teaspoons salt

Remove soiled or bruised leaves from the cabbage. Wash and shred finely into a large bowl. Add the salt and mix thoroughly. Let stand for 5 to 10 minutes, until the cabbage starts to become limp and some liquid is released. Press all the cabbage tightly into a 1-pint canning jar; add the cabbage liquid. Press the cabbage down, then top it with some crumpled wax paper to hold the cabbage under the liquid. Cover the jar with the lid, but do not close too tightly. Place the jar in a glass bowl and let it stand at room temperature for 8 to 10 days or until fermentation stops (bubbles will no longer rise to the surface). Some liquid may seep up and out of the jar. Always keep the cabbage submerged under liquid. Add another wad of wax paper if necessary to weight it down.

Note: For larger amounts, use 2 teaspoons of salt per pound of cabbage and allow more time for fermentation to stop (that is, for 2 pounds of cabbage, allow about 15 days fermentation).

Hungarian Fruit Salad

Serves 6 to 8

Bella Weisfogel, who introduced me to this fruit salad, always referred to it as a Hungarian fruit salad, for it was the favorite of many of her Hungarian relatives. The salad may be served on a bed of thinly sliced lettuce or as a dessert in a coupe dish.

> 1 can (15½ ounces) crushed pineapple
> 1 can (11 ounces) mandarin orange sections
> 1 banana
> 2 apples, peeled
> ½ tablespoon lemon juice
> ¼ cup chopped walnuts
> 1 package (12 ounces) frozen red
>   raspberries, defrosted

In a medium-sized mixing bowl, combined the crushed pine-apple and mandarin orange sections. Slice in the banana and coarsely grate in the apples. Add the lemon juice. Fold in the chopped walnuts and package of thawed raspberries. Let rest for 30 minutes to 1 hour for flavors to blend.

Fruit Strata Salad

Serves 6 to 8

The uniqueness of this salad is the spiked orange-apricot dressing. You can adapt this fruit cup to all seasons by adding segments, slices, or cubes of a variety of the seasonal fruits available. An oversized brandy snifter makes a dramatic serving dish.

> 1½ cups honeydew balls
> 1½ cup cantaloupe balls
> 2 cups whole strawberries
> 1½ cups pineapple cubes
> 1 cup blueberries
> 3 kiwi fruits, peeled and sliced

Orange-Apricot Dressing:

> ½ cup apricot preserves
> ⅓ cup hot water
> ¼ cup Sabra or other orange liqueur
> ⅓ cup frozen orange juice concentrate

In a large bowl, layer the fruit, arranging the sliced kiwi on top. In a small mixing bowl, blend the apricot preserves with the hot water, liqueur, and orange juice concentrate until well blended. Pour the dressing over the salad. Cover and chill for a few hours for fruit to macerate in the dressing. Toss before serving. This dressing may be put to many good uses. Drizzle it over cut grapefruit, cantaloupe, or honeydew melon.

Note: Be sure the kiwi is well chilled before peeling. Rub off the fuzzy part of the skin, then peel. Cut into slices.

Spicy Cranberry Relish

Makes 2½ cups

A perfect relish for cold chicken or turkey.

> **1 can (1 pound) whole cranberry sauce**
> **½ cup canned drained crushed pineapple**
> **¼ teaspoon cinnamon**
> **¼ teaspoon nutmeg**
> **¼ teaspoon dry mustard**

In a medium-sized mixing bowl, combine all the ingredients. Chill for at least 1 hour to allow the flavors to blend.

Cranberry Salad

Serves 6 or more

An easy-to-make salad—a blend of cranberries, crushed pineapple, and citrus fruits. A perfect complement for poultry and game.

> **1 can (16 ounces) whole cranberries**
> **1 can (8¼ ounces) crushed pineapple**
> **1 can (16 ounces) grapefruit and orange**
> **sections**

In a medium-sized mixing bowl, mash the cranberries. Drain the juice from the pineapple and grapefruit and orange sections. Add to the crushed cranberries. Cover and refrigerate for a few hours to allow the flavors to blend.

Cranberry-Pineapple Taffies

Serves 6

Jellied cranberry is incredible. Because of its high pectin content, you can broil it and it will remain in plump firm slices. Make this very colorful dish to serve with your roast chicken or turkey.

½ cup firmly packed brown sugar
1 tablespoon unsalted margarine
6 canned pineapple rings
1 can (1 pound) jellied cranberry sauce

Crumble the brown sugar together with the margarine. Arrange the pineapple slices on a foil-lined broiler pan. Cut the jellied cranberry sauce into 6 slices. Arrange a slice on top of each slice of pineapple. Carefully sprinkle the sugar-margarine mixture over the top. Place the pan in the broiler so that the cranberry-pineapple taffies are about 3 inches from the flame. The taffies are done when the brown sugar topping is bubbling.

Variations:

• Omit the pineapple slices and proceed as above.
• To add pizazz, use cookie cutters to cut the cranberry slices into fancy shapes (chickens, turkeys, etc.) before placing them on the pineapple.

Cranberry Relish

Serves 4 to 6

A crispy vegetable medley that is appropriate to serve throughout the year.

1 can (1 pound) whole cranberry sauce
2 carrots, grated
½ cup diced celery
¼ teaspoon nutmeg
1 teaspoon lemon juice

Drain the cranberry sauce. Combine with the remaining ingredients. Stir well. Refrigerate for several hours so that the flavors can blend.

Cranberry Citrus Relish

Makes 3 cups

Curry powder adds a delightful change to citrus-seasoned cranberry sauce. It is an excellent accompaniment to poultry or meat, but you may serve it as a side dish with other foods as well.

> 1 orange, whole
> ½ lemon, unpeeled
> 1 can (1 pound) whole or jellied cranberry
>   sauce, crushed
> 1 cup crushed pineapple, drained
> 1 teaspoon curry powder

Pass the orange and ½ lemon through the food chopper or food processor. In a medium-sized mixing bowl, combine the orange-lemon mixture with the cranberry sauce. Fold in the crushed pineapple. Stir in the teaspoon of curry powder. Blend well. Chill thoroughly before serving.

Bombay Fruit

Serves 12 or more
as an accompaniment

Curry lifts these canned fruits from the ordinary to the exotic. An excellent recipe to prepare for a large dinner party. Ease the last-minute rush and prepare this in advance. Warm before serving.

> 1 can (29 ounces) sliced cling peaches
> 1 can (29 ounces) sliced pears
> 1 can (16 ounces) apricot halves
> 1 can (16 ounces) pineapple chunks
> ¼ cup dark raisins
> Scant ¼ pound unsalted margarine
> ⅓ cup firmly packed dark brown sugar
> 3 to 4 teaspoons curry powder, to taste
> ¼ cup toasted sliced almonds
> A few maraschino cherries for decoration

Preheat the oven to 325 degrees F. Drain all the canned fruits; reserve the juices for some other recipe if desired. In a 9 x 13-inch baking pan, arrange the canned fruits and the raisins.

In a small saucepan over medium heat, melt the margarine and the brown sugar. Stir frequently. Stir in the curry, reduce the heat to low, and simmer for one minute to blend the flavors. Drizzle the syrup over the fruit, sprinkle the almonds on top, and bake for 45 minutes, adding the maraschino cherries after half the cooking time. Serve warm.

Crunchy Peach Halves

Serves 6

Peaches with a snappy crunch are filled with mint jelly, making them a sensational accompaniment to veal.

> 6 canned large cling peach halves
> 2 tablespoons unsalted margarine, melted,
>   or 2 tablespoons oil
> ¾ cup cornflake crumbs
> ½ teaspoon curry powder
> 6 teaspoons mint jelly

Preheat the oven to 350 degrees F. Drain the peaches well. Blot dry. Dip the peach halves into the melted margarine or oil, then into the cornflake crumbs mixed with curry powder. Press down so that the crumbs adhere to the peaches. Arrange the peach halves rounded side up in a shallow baking pan, 7½ x 11½ x ⅞ inches. Bake for 15 minutes or until hot and invitingly browned. Turn over each peach half and spoon mint jelly into each pit cavity. Serve as an accompaniment to veal.

4

Poultry in Many Guises

Chicken, Duck & Turkey

"The Lord God formed every beast of the field and every fowl of the air" (Genesis 2:19).

Forty-clove Garlic Chicken

Serves 4

Most folk remedies do not stand up to scientific scrutiny, but garlic may be an exception. Dr. Gerhard Schrauzer, professor of chemistry at the University of California at San Diego, claims that "garlic is a simple nonprescription drug that helps detoxify the body and prevent disease." Dr. Paavo Aerola, a well-known nutritionist, agrees: "Garlic is definitely a miracle food and a miracle medicine."

If, as I do, you accept the word of the good doctors, you will not hesitate to try this chicken recipe. Some years ago James Beard introduced a recipe with forty cloves of garlic. Here is my version. You will need a heavy 6-quart casserole with a tight-fitting lid.

> 4 stalks celery, sliced crosswise into ¼-inch
>   pieces
> 1 onion, sliced
> 2 carrots, sliced julienne
> ⅓ cup oil
> 1 onion, finely diced
> 6 sprigs parsley, finely minced

1 teaspoon dried basil
½ teaspoon dried tarragon
¼ teaspoon nutmeg
1 large broiler chicken, quartered
   (3 to 3½ pounds)
Paprika
1 teaspoon salt
¼ teaspoon black pepper
1 cup dry red wine (or sweet wine if you
   prefer)
40 cloves garlic, peeled

Preheat the oven to 375 degrees F. Line the bottom of a heavy 6-quart casserole with the sliced celery, sliced onion, and julienne-sliced carrots.

Pour the oil into a shallow dish or pan. Add the finely diced onion, minced parsley, basil, tarragon, and nutmeg. Blend together well. Dip the chicken pieces into the oil; turn them to coat all sides evenly with the oil mixture. Arrange the chicken pieces on the sliced vegetables. Lightly sprinkle with paprika, salt, and pepper. Distribute the remaining dressing over the chicken pieces. Tuck the garlic cloves around and between the chicken pieces. Pour in the wine. Cover the top of the casserole with the lid. If the lid is not tight-fitting, cover the casserole tightly with aluminum foil and place the lid over the foil to prevent steam from escaping. Bake for 1½ hours. Serve the chicken with the pan juices and whole garlic cloves. Offer thin slices of warmed French bread on the side.

Note: The softened cooked garlic is surprisingly mild, tender, and buttery. Its flavor is subdued and it lends itself to be spread easily on bread. The quantities of chicken and vegetables may be adjusted to serve any number of guests. Just don't forget the 40 garlic cloves.

Interesting note: There is a prestigious restaurant on the West Coast that bakes whole heads of garlic in oil and serves each guest an entire head of garlic accompanied by lightly toasted bread. Each clove is pulled off the garlic bulb and is squeezed at its root end to release the garlic paste onto the toasted bread. The garlic is very mellow and spreads like butter.

Queen Victoria Chicken Breasts

Serves 8

A regal chicken dish: chicken rolls crowned with cherries. Sure to receive rave reviews. The flavorful combination of veal and chicken, the texture of the baked puffed pastry robe, and the color of the Cherry Jubilee Sauce turns this dish into a glamorous meal.

Filling:

> 1½ pounds ground veal
> ¼ pound mushrooms, sautéed
> 2 eggs (graded large), beaten
> ½ teaspoon onion powder
> 1 to 2 tablespoons seasoned breadcrumbs
> 8 chicken cutlets
> 1 package puff pastry dough squares

To prepare the filling, combine the ground veal with the sautéed mushrooms. Add the beaten eggs and season with the onion powder. Stir in the breadcrumbs. Mix well.

Preheat the oven to 400 degrees F. Lightly grease a 10 x 15 x 1-inch baking pan; set aside. Pound each chicken cutlet to flatten slightly. Spoon an eighth of the filling across the center of each cutlet. Roll up. Roll out each puff pastry square to accommodate the chicken roll. Place the chicken roll seam side down on the pastry. Roll the pastry around the chicken.

Fold up the pastry edges and seal. Arrange the rolls seam side down on the prepared baking pan. Place in the preheated oven and bake for 10 minutes. Lower the heat to 325 degrees F. and continue baking for an additional 45 to 50 minutes, until golden brown. Serve with Cherry Jubilee Sauce.

Cherry Jubilee Sauce:

Makes about 2 cups

> 1 can (17 ounces) dark sweet pitted cherries
> 1 tablespoon cornstarch
> 1 tablespoon cold water
> 1 to 2 tablespoons sugar
> 1 to 2 tablespoons brandy or rum (optional)

Into a 1-cup measure, drain the syrup from the cherries. Add water, if necessary, to make 1 cup of liquid.

In a small saucepan, dissolve the cornstarch in the tablespoon of water. Add the sugar and blend in the syrup. Stir until smooth. Cook over low heat, stirring constantly until the mixture thickens and bubbles, about 1 minute. Stir in the cherries and optional liquor.

Chicken Breasts in Tarragon Sauce

Serves 6

This recipe can be prepared in advance. To reheat, merely cover and warm in a low oven. This is as attractive to serve as it is delicious.

> **6 chicken cutlets**
> **Salt and white pepper to taste**
> **3 tablespoons unsalted margarine**
> **3 tablespoons flour**
> **¾ cup pareve milk**
> **¾ cup dry white wine**
> **2 teaspoons dried tarragon**

Preheat the oven to 400 degrees F. Lightly grease a large roasting pan, or coat it with vegetable-spray. Lay the chicken cutlets flat in the pan. Sprinkle with salt and pepper.

In a small saucepan over low heat, melt the margarine. Blend in the flour. Stir in the pareve milk and wine and cook until thickened, stirring occasionally. Add the tarragon and additional salt and pepper if desired. Pour the sauce over the breasts. Bake uncovered for 20 to 30 minutes, until the cutlets are fork-tender.

Crispy Baked Chicken

Serves 8

This oven-baked chicken is quick to prepare and a treat to eat. Minimal attention is required while the chicken bakes.

> **4 chicken breasts, boned and cut in half**
>   **(8 pieces)**
> **1 cup mayonnaise**
> **1 teaspoon dried oregano**
> **½ teaspoon lemon juice**
> **1 to 1½ cups cornflake crumbs**

Preheat the oven to 350 degrees F. Rinse the chicken breasts and dry with paper towels. In a bowl, combine the mayonnaise, oregano, and lemon juice. Brush the chicken on all sides with the mayonnaise mixture. Dredge the chicken in the crumbs.

Arrange the chicken on a baking sheet. Cover with aluminum foil. Bake for 1 hour or until fork-tender. Remove the foil and bake for an additional 10 minutes, until crispy.

Variations:

•Omit the oregano and add ½ to 1 envelope of onion soup mix. Stir the onion soup mix into the cornflake crumbs. This gives the crumb coating a zesty flavor.

•Add ¼ cup sesame seeds to the cornflake crumbs. Omit the oregano.

•Remove the skin from the chicken breasts before brushing with the mayonnaise.

Moroccan Chicken I

Serves 6 to 8

This is a nice recipe to add to your repertoire because you can prepare chicken soup when you cook the chicken, then serve the cooked chicken in a "foreign" dress.

Here, bite-sized pieces of chicken are baked in prune juice or chicken broth and are flavored with a variety of spices. The marvelous mingling of flavors results in a dish that is irresistible.

Moroccans use an enormous range of spices. I recommend that the first time you make this dish you use the lesser amount of spices. Then, after tasting the dish, adjust the quantities to please your taste.

3 tablespoons unsalted margarine
1 pound (5 or 6) onions, diced
1 chicken (3½ pounds), cooked
1 to 3 teaspoons cinnamon
1 to 3 teaspoons cumin
1 to 3 teaspoons turmeric
1 to 3 teaspoons ginger
1 to 3 teaspoons nutmeg
Salt and black pepper to taste
6 ounces pitted prunes
4 ounces slivered almonds (a scant cup)
1 cup prune juice or chicken broth

Preheat the oven to 325 degrees F. In a medium-sized skillet, melt the margarine. Add the diced onions and sauté until translucent. Transfer them to a teflon or vegetable-sprayed 9 x 13-inch baking pan. Cut the chicken into bite-sized pieces, discarding the skin and bones. Season the cut chicken generously with the spices and salt and pepper. Arrange the prunes over the chicken. Sprinkle with the almonds. Add the prune juice or chicken broth. Bake covered for 45 minutes. Rice or couscous is a great go-along.

Variation:

Add ½ cup raisins at the same time you add the prunes.

Moroccan Chicken II

Serves 6

This recipe is not as dramatic as the previous one. It contains no fruit or nuts, but the parsley adds a dash of color. The chicken costars with the subtly spiced seasoned onions, which enrich the sauce.

1 chicken (3 to 3½ pounds)
1 pound (5 or 6) onions, thinly sliced
2 tablespoons turmeric, divided
2 tablespoons cinnamon, divided
1 tablespoon dried parsley

Preheat the oven to 350 degrees F. Cut the chicken into eighths and place in a teflon or vegetable-sprayed roasting pan. Bake for 1 hour. Simultaneously, place the sliced onions in a saucepan with water to barely cover. Cook at a slow boil until the onions are tender and the liquid is very much reduced.

With a slotted spoon, transfer the onions from the saucepan to a very large skillet. Add some of the onion liquid, but the liquid should not cover the onions. Sprinkle a tablespoon each of turmeric and cinnamon over the onions. Arrange the chicken on top of the onions. Season the chicken with the remaining turmeric and cinnamon. Cover the skillet and cook for 1 to 1½ hours, until the chicken is fork-tender. Spoon a portion of the onions over each serving.

Chicken Marbella

Serves 8 to 10

This is a Mexican dish that my daughter Naomi's friend, Adina Singer, shared with me. It was served to me warm but is also very tasty at room temperature.

The list of ingredients in Chicken Marbella looks formidable, but everything is easily obtained. The combination of wine and vinegar sweetened with prunes and brown sugar gives the sauce a distinctive sweet-sour flavor unlike a typical sweet-and-sour sauce.

> **2 medium-sized chickens (about 3 pounds each), quartered**
> **½ head of garlic, peeled and puréed**
> **2 tablespoons dried oregano**
> **Coarse salt and freshly ground black pepper to taste**
> **¼ cup red wine vinegar**
> **¼ cup olive oil**
> **½ cup pitted prunes**
> **¼ cup pitted green olives**
> **¼ cup capers**
> **1 to 2 teaspoons of juice from the capers**
> **3 bay leaves**

½ cup chopped Italian parsley or fresh
   coriander
½ cup firmly packed brown sugar
½ cup white wine (optional)

Arrange the chicken quarters skin side down in a large roasting
pan. In a mixing bowl, combine the remaining ingredients except for the sugar and white wine. Pour the marinade over the
chicken. Cover and refrigerate overnight. Before roasting, add
the sugar to the wine. Combine with the marinade in the pan.

Roast covered in a 350-degree F. oven for 15 minutes. Uncover
and turn over the chicken. Continue roasting uncovered for an
additional 45 minutes, until the chicken is fork-tender.

Polynesian Glazed Chicken

Serves 4

Chicken is very versatile. It blends well with a variety of ingredients and seasonings. Here, the emphasis is on a savory
glaze.

1 broiler-fryer chicken (2½ to 3 pounds),
   disjointed
½ cup flour
¼ teaspoon salt
⅛ teaspoon black pepper
¼ teaspoon garlic powder
½ cup oil
1 jar (10 ounces) apricot preserves or
   apricot and pineapple preserves
½ cup bottled barbecue sauce
1 to 2 tablespoons soy sauce (to taste)
1 small onion, chopped
¼ cup white raisins (optional)

Preheat the oven to 350 degrees F. Cut up the chicken. In a pie
plate or large dish, combine the flour, salt, pepper, and garlic
powder. Coat the chicken. In a large frying pan, heat the oil over
medium heat. Add the chicken and brown on all sides.

In a large measuring cup, mix together the preserves, barbecue sauce, soy sauce, onion, and raisins until well blended. Place the chicken in a single layer, skin side up, in a 9 x 13-inch pan. Pour the sauce over the chicken. Cover with aluminum foil and bake for about 1 hour, until fork-tender.

Orange-Apricot Chicken

Serves 6 or more

Toby Stein, a college classmate whose friendship I cherish, has shared recipes with me for over four score years. One Passover she introduced to me this roast chicken that encases a most unusual and succulent dressing. It is party fare destined for special occasions.

Stuffing:

4 cups matzo farfel
1 cup orange juice
¼ cup unsalted margarine
⅓ cup chopped onion
⅓ cup chopped celery
⅓ cup chopped red pepper
1 egg (graded large), lightly beaten
½ cup golden raisins or chopped dried apricots
½ teaspoon salt
½ teaspoon grated orange rind
Salt and black pepper (optional)
1 roasting chicken (6 to 8 pounds)

Glaze:

¾ cup apricot preserves
6 tablespoons orange juice
2 tablespoons brandy

In a large bowl, soak the farfel in the orange juice. In a skillet, melt the margarine. Sauté the onion, celery, and red pepper until soft. Add the sautéed vegetables to the farfel. Stir in the egg, raisins or apricots, ½ teaspoon salt, and orange rind. Mix well.

Preheat the oven to 350 degrees F. Wash the chicken inside and out. It is optional to sprinkle the neck and body cavity with salt and pepper. Spoon the stuffing loosely into the neck and body cavities. Secure the stuffing with poultry pins. Place the chicken on a rack in a shallow roasting pan, breast side up. Sprinkle with additional salt and pepper if desired.

Combine the glaze ingredients until well blended. Brush the chicken with the glaze. Place the chicken in the oven and roast for about 2 hours, basting the glaze every half-hour. Combine the pan drippings with the remaining glaze. Skim the fat off the surface. Serve the sauce in a gravy boat along with the chicken.

Chicken Florentine

Serves 8

Veal cutlets or fish fillets can be substituted for the chicken, and the result is equally delicious. If using the latter, substitute fish or vegetable broth for the chicken stock. The topping tastes like cream, but it is a pareve cream sauce and you'd never know it.

> 2 packages (10 ounces each) frozen chopped
>   spinach
> 2 tablespoons flour
> ⅓ cup pareve cream
> 1 tablespoon unsalted margarine, melted
> 2 cloves garlic, mashed
> 2 pounds chicken cutlets

Topping:

> 3 tablespoons unsalted margarine
> 3 tablespoons flour
> ¾ cup pareve cream
> ¾ cup chicken stock
> Salt and black pepper

Preheat the oven to 400 degrees F. Cook the spinach according to package directions. Drain very well. In a small bowl, blend the flour with the pareve cream. Add the margarine and mashed garlic. Add the mixture to the drained spinach. Spread the spinach mixture in a 9 x 13 x 2-inch baking pan. Arrange the cutlets on the spinach.

In a small saucepan over low heat, melt the 3 tablespoons of margarine. Blend in the flour and stir until thick. Remove from the heat. Stir in the pareve cream and chicken stock. Add salt and pepper to taste. Whisk until well blended. Pour the mixture over the chicken cutlets. Bake for 20 to 25 minutes, until the topping has thickened and the cutlets are tender.

Florentine Chicken Roll

Serves 8 generously

This elegant chicken dish takes a little time to prepare, but it is well worth the effort. Serve it on special occasions.

> 1 large onion, minced
> 2 stalks celery, chopped
> 2 medium-sized carrots, finely diced
> 2 tablespoons oil
> ½ to 1 teaspoon dried sage, to taste
> ¼ to ½ teaspoon dried thyme, to taste
> ¼ teaspoon onion powder
> ¾ cup boiling water
> 4 cups ground (medium fine) cooked
>   chicken
> 1½ cups breadcrumbs
> ½ teaspoon salt (optional)
> ½ teaspoon black pepper
> 3 eggs (graded large)
> ¼ cup chopped walnuts, reserved (optional)

Spinach Filling:

> 2 packages (10 ounces each) frozen chopped
>   spinach
> ¼ teaspoon black pepper
> ½ teaspoon salt (optional)
> ⅛ teaspoon nutmeg
> 1 egg (graded small)

In a medium-sized saucepan, combine the onion, celery, carrots, and oil. Sauté over medium heat for 6 to 7 minutes, stirring occasionally. Blend in the sage, thyme, onion powder, and boiling water. Lower the heat, cover, and simmer slowly for 3 to 4 minutes so that the flavors will blend.

In a large mixing bowl, thoroughly combine the chicken with the sautéed vegetables. Stir in the breadcrumbs, salt, pepper, and eggs. Mix well. Set aside.

To prepare the filling, cook the spinach according to package directions. Drain thoroughly, extracting as much liquid as possible. Transfer to a bowl. Add the pepper, salt, nutmeg, and egg. Blend together.

Preheat the oven to 350 degrees F. Brush an 11 x 17-inch sheet of aluminum foil with oil. Form the chicken mixture into a rectangle 10 inches x 15 inches, keeping all edges as straight as possible. Sprinkle the chopped walnuts over the chicken. Spread the spinach filling evenly over the chicken layer, leaving a ½-inch border on all sides. Using the foil to assist you, roll up meat and filling lengthwise. Brush another piece of foil with oil. Using 2 spatulas, carefully transfer the roll to the prepared foil. Bring the exposed lengths of foil together over the top of the roll. Pull the foil in close to the roll. Fold together. Fold in the end pieces of foil. Transfer the foil-wrapped loaf to a 12 x 18-inch baking pan. Bake for 30 minutes. Open the foil and continue to bake for an additional 25 minutes. You may serve this with a mushroom gravy, but it truly stands on its own laurels. Freezes well.

Note: For a more robust chicken filling, substitute chicken broth for the water.

Chicken à la King

Serves 4

A nifty way to disguise leftover boiled chicken and use up a small amount of chicken broth.

> 1 tablespoon unsalted margarine
> ¼ cup chopped green pepper
> 1 tablespoon grated onion
> ¼ cup diced celery
> ½ cup chicken broth

———————▶

1 cup pareve milk
2 tablespoons flour
¾ teaspoon seasoned salt
1 tablespoon chopped pimento
1 cup diced cooked chicken
Salt and black pepper to taste

In a medium-sized saucepan over medium heat, melt the margarine. Sauté the green pepper, onion, and celery in the margarine. Set aside.

In a blender cup, combine the chicken broth and pareve milk. Add the flour and salt. Cover and blend at high speed until foamy. Transfer the mixture to a medium-sized heavy saucepan. Cook, stirring constantly to make a smooth sauce. Add the sautéed vegetables, pimento, and chicken. Heat thoroughly together. Add salt and pepper to taste. Serve hot over rice or toast if desired. Or, to add pizazz, serve in a patty case covered with the lid.

Chicken Divan

Serves 5

More and more people are eating less and less red meat. One excellent alternative is poultry, which is so versatile. Its delicate flavor marries well with assertive sauces or subtle ones, such as the pareve Béchamel Sauce called for here.

This preparation is actually chicken and broccoli in a one-dish dinner. The chicken stays undercover, which keeps it moist and tender.

Grease for the pan
5 skinless and boneless chicken breasts or
cutlets
1 bunch of broccoli, blanched
2 cups Béchamel Sauce (see below)
¼ cup dry sherry

Preheat the oven to 350 degrees F. Generously grease a 9 x 13-inch baking pan. Arrange the chicken breasts in the pan. Slice the broccoli into serving-size pieces and place on top of the chicken. Cover the broccoli with the Bechamel Sauce. Pour the sherry into the corners of the baking pan. Bake in the preheated oven for 20 to 25 minutes, until the chicken is fork-tender.

Béchamel Sauce:

This is a basic white sauce.

> 1 cup water
> 1 cup pareve milk
> 2 tablespoons unsalted margarine
> ¼ cup all-purpose flour

In a 2-cup glass measure, combine the water and the pareve milk. In a medium-sized saucepan over low heat, melt the margarine. Stir in the flour and whisk together for several minutes. Do not brown. Stir in ½ cup of the liquid, then the remainder. Cook until thickened.

Chicken-Vegetable Custard Pie

Serves 4

A different way of dealing with leftover cooked chicken. The appearance of the pie is reminiscent of the popular quiche.

> 1 tablespoon unsalted margarine
> ½ cup finely chopped onion
> ¼ cup chopped red pepper
> 1 tablespoon boiling water
> 1½ cups chopped cooked chicken
> ½ cup chopped water chestnuts
> 1 cup frozen chopped broccoli, cooked and
>   drained
> 3 eggs (graded large), slightly beaten
> 1½ cups pareve milk
> 2 teaspoons Dijon mustard
> ½ teaspoon salt
> ⅛ teaspoon black pepper
> 1 deep 10-inch pie shell, prebaked for 5
>   minutes

Preheat the oven to 350 degrees F. In a small saucepan over low heat, melt the margarine. Add the chopped onion and red pepper. Sauté until the onions are golden. Add the tablespoon of boiling water and simmer for an additional 2 minutes.

In a medium-sized bowl, combine the cooked vegetables with the chicken, water chestnuts, and drained broccoli. Blend in the beaten eggs. Season the pareve milk with the mustard, salt, and black pepper. Pour the mixture over the chicken and vegetables. Stir the mixture to blend thoroughly. Pour into the prebaked pie shell. Bake for 30 to 40 minutes, until the custard is set and the top is nicely browned.

Savory Chicken Sandwich

Serves 8

A savory chicken mixture is held together by a tender yeast dough. This hearty knife-and-fork sandwich could be enhanced by cloaking it with a hot mushroom sauce.

> **1 envelope active dry yeast**
> **1 tablespoon sugar**
> **¾ cup warm water (110 to 115 degrees F.)**
> **1 egg (graded large)**
> **1 teaspoon salt**
> **2½ cups sifted all-purpose flour**
> **¼ cup unsalted margarine**
> **½ cup chopped celery**
> **½ cup chopped onion**
> **¼ cup chopped green pepper**
> **¼ cup chopped red pepper**
> **½ cup chopped mushrooms**
> **½ teaspoon salt**
> **¼ teaspoon poultry seasoning**
> **⅛ teaspoon black pepper**
> **3 cups diced cooked chicken**

In a medium-sized bowl, dissolve the yeast and sugar in the warm water. Let stand for 5 minutes, then stir in the egg. Sift the salt with the flour. Gradually add the flour to the yeast to form a soft dough. Let rise in a warm draft-free place until doubled in bulk, about 1 to 1½ hours. Meanwhile, prepare the chicken.

Preheat the oven to 425 degrees F. In a small saucepan over low heat, melt the margarine. Add the vegetables and sauté until the onions are golden. Remove from the heat and add the seasonings. Stir the vegetables and chicken into the dough. Mix very well so that the vegetables are distributed evenly throughout. Turn the dough into a well greased 9-inch-square pan. Cover and let rise until doubled in bulk, about 45 minutes to 1 hour. Bake for 20 to 25 minutes, until golden brown.

Duckling in Bing Cherry Sauce

Serves 4

When it comes to poultry, duck is one of the easiest birds to roast, for after pricking the skin, it is self-basting. In this recipe, however, the skin and fat are removed from the duck before cooking.

> **1 duckling (5 pounds)**
> **½ small onion**
> **3 tablespoons unsalted margarine or oil**
> **1 can (1 pound 4 ounces) bing cherries**
> **½ cup water**
> **¼ teaspoon salt**
> **¼ teaspoon black pepper**
> **1 bay leaf**
> **¼ teaspoon dried savory (optional)**
> **1½ teaspoons cornstarch**
> **2 tablespoons water**

Cut the duckling into quarters. With a sharp knife, pull off the skin and the fat adhering to the duck meat. Finely slice the onion. Melt the margarine in a large skillet. Add the onion and cook until transparent but not browned. Add the duck pieces and brown well on all sides. Drain the cherries. Set aside 1 cup of the juice. Combine the remaining cherry juice, water, salt, pepper, bay leaf, and savory. Pour this over the duck in the skillet. Cover and cook gently for 45 to 55 minutes, until tender. Remove the duck pieces to a dish.

In a measuring cup, mix the cornstarch with the 2 tablespoons water to form a smooth paste. Combine with the reserved cherry juice. Pour into the skillet and cook over medium heat, stirring constantly until thickened. Discard the bay leaf. Return the duck pieces and drained cherries to the juice. Cook for 10 minutes.

Turkey-Nut Puffs

Makes 12 large puffs

A fantastic way to use leftover turkey (or leftover chicken, which works equally well). These taste like cream puffs with a filling baked into them. To serve as hot hors d'oeuvres, make the puffs miniature-sized.

> **Grease for the baking sheet**
> **¾ to 1 cup finely chopped turkey**
> **⅓ cup chopped toasted almonds**
> **1 cup chicken broth**
> **½ cup oil**
> **1 teaspoon salt**
> **Pinch of cayenne pepper**
> **½ teaspoon celery seed (optional)**
> **1 tablespoon parsley flakes**
> **1 cup sifted all-purpose flour**
> **4 eggs (graded large)**

Preheat the oven to 400 degrees F. Grease a baking sheet and set aside. In a small bowl, mix the turkey with the nuts; set aside.

In a 2-quart saucepan, combine the chicken broth, oil, salt, cayenne, celery seed, and parsley flakes. Bring the mixture to a boil. Remove the saucepan from the heat and immediately pour in all of the flour. Stir briskly at once. When the mixture is smoothly blended, return the saucepan to low heat. Cook and beat vigorously until the mixture forms a ball that leaves the sides of the saucepan. Remove from the heat. Add the eggs, one at a time, beating well after each addition, until the egg is well absorbed. Mix until the dough is smooth and glossy (a portable electric mixer will serve you well). Add the turkey mixture and mix well.

Drop the mixture by the heaping tablespoonful onto the greased baking sheet. Bake in the preheated oven without opening the door for 15 minutes, then reduce the heat to 375 degrees F. and bake for an additional 25 minutes or until browned. Serve hot.

Variations:

Substitute a 6-ounce can of tuna or an 8-ounce can of salmon for the turkey. Instead of the chicken broth, add water to the liquid drained from the tuna or salmon to make 1 cup.

5

The Mainstay

Meat Entrées

> "These are the living things which ye may eat among
> all the beasts that are on the earth: whatsoever parteth
> the hoof, and is wholly cloven-footed, and cheweth the
> cud" (Leviticus 11:2-3).

Oven-smoked Brisket

Serves 8 or more

No need to have a smokehouse or smoker to prepare smoked brisket. The robust smoky flavor of the roast is due to the liquid smoke.

> **1 brisket (4 to 5 pounds)**
> **Salt, pepper, garlic powder, onion powder,**
>   **and paprika**
> **Dash (salt-free) seasoning, to taste**
> **Liquid smoke**

Line a roasting pan with a piece of heavy-duty aluminum foil large enough to bring up over the meat and completely enclose it. Massage the brisket with the various seasonings to taste. Brush the brisket generously with liquid smoke. Place the meat, fat side down, in the pan. Seal with the foil and refrigerate overnight.

Next day, roast for 1 hour at 300 degrees F. Uncover and turn the brisket so the fat side is up. Lower the heat to 275 degrees F., cover, and continue roasting for an additional 2 to 2½ hours, until tender. Cool and slice thin.

Variation:

After the first hour of roasting, make a paste of 2 tablespoons firmly packed brown sugar, a tablespoon of mustard, and 2 teaspoons of vinegar. Spread over the top of the roast. Cover and continue roasting.

Stuffed Breast of Veal

Serves 6 or more

There is an infinite variety of savory fillings with which a breast of veal can be stuffed. The stuffing serves several purposes: it adds to the appeal of the dish; it increases the number of servings; and it adds substance to a breast of veal that may not be too meaty.

> 2 small onions, finely minced
> 2 cloves garlic, finely minced
> 2 to 3 tablespoons oil
> 2 packages (10 ounces) frozen chopped
>   spinach
> 1 egg (graded large)
> 2 teaspoons dried tarragon, divided
> ¼ cup chopped fresh parsley
> 1 cup breadcrumbs, seasoned or plain
>   or a combination
> 1 pound ground veal
> Salt and pepper to taste
> 1 breast of veal (4½ to 5 pounds) with a
>   pocket for stuffing
> 1 tablespoon oil
> ½ teaspoon paprika

In a small skillet, sauté the onions and garlic in the oil until the onions are translucent. Cook the spinach according to package directions; drain well. Transfer the spinach to a mixing bowl. Beat in the egg. Add a teaspoon of tarragon, the chopped parsley, the sautéed onions and garlic, and the breadcrumbs. Mix together. Lastly, add the ground veal and mix to blend thoroughly. Add salt and pepper if desired.

Preheat the oven to 350 degrees F. Stuff the veal pocket with the meat mixture; reserve any extra filling. Set the stuffed breast on a greased rack in a roasting pan. Massage the top of the veal breast with the tablespoon of oil, remaining tarragon, and the paprika. Form any extra filling into a little loaf and roast it alongside the breast. Cover the roast with aluminum foil. Roast for 2½ hours.

Pot Roast

Serves 6

> 2 tablespoons oil
> 3 pounds lean boneless beef chuck
> 6 small onions, peeled
> 4 carrots, peeled and cut into thirds
> 1 stalk celery, cut up
> 1 bay leaf
> 1½ teaspoons salt
> Generous dash of freshly ground black
>   pepper
> 1 cup red wine or apple juice
> 1 cup water
> 6 small potatoes, peeled
> 3 large sweet potatoes, peeled and halved
> Chopped fresh parsley
> 1 tablespoon cornstarch or potato starch
> 2 tablespoons cold water

In a large Dutch oven, heat the oil over medium heat. Add the beef; brown well on all sides. Add the onions, carrots, celery, bay leaf, salt, pepper, wine or apple juice, and the water. Cover and simmer over low heat for 1 hour, or place in a 300-degree F. oven for 1 hour.

Remove the pot from the oven. Add the potatoes and sweet potatoes. Cover and return to the oven for 1 more hour, or continue to simmer until the potatoes are fork-tender.

Remove the meat to a serving platter. Slice and arrange the vegetables around the meat. Garnish with parsley. Dissolve the cornstarch or potato starch in the cold water. Add to the gravy and cook until thickened. Pour some of the gravy over the meat and vegetables. Serve the remaining gravy on the side.

Cholent

Serves 8 or more

"Ye shall kindle no fire throughout your habitations upon the Sabbath Day" (Exodus 35-3).

Cholent is traditionally prepared for the Sabbath because it is a convenient way to have a hot meal for Saturday lunch while still conforming to the law of Sabbath. The preparation is assembled on Friday before sunset and left to cook or bake all night, ready to be served after *shul* on Saturday. The aroma that permeates the house all night is indescribable. It is a delectable meal which owes its distinctive flavor to the very long, slow cooking. The method used to prepare Boston Baked Beans would be comparable.

Basically, cholent consists of meat and potatoes and, more often than not, a combination of different types of beans. The ingredients called for below can be varied by choosing different beans, omitting the meat, adding a dumpling or derma, or altering the seasonings.

> 1 cup dried pea beans
> 1 cup dried lima beans
> ½ cup coarse barley
> 2 medium-sized onions, sliced
> 10 small peeled potatoes
> 3 pounds beef brisket, short ribs, flanken,
>   or chuck
> Salt and pepper to taste
> Water

Thoroughly wash the pea beans, lima beans, and barley. Alternatively, the beans may be soaked overnight in cold water. Drain well.

Line a heavy 6- to 8-quart pot with the sliced onions. Add the soaked beans and washed barley. Sink the meat in the center.

Put the peeled potatoes, cut in half, on top. Season with salt and pepper. Add enough water so that everything is covered. Be sure there is at least 1 inch of headroom in the pot after the water has been added.

Bring the cholent to a boil over high heat. Skim off any foam from the top of the liquid. Turn down the heat. Cover the pot and cook for 2 hours. Remove the cover and check the water level. The water should cover all ingredients. Cover tightly and place the pot in a 200-degree F. oven. Cook slowly in the oven overnight. Remember, no peeking.

If you'd like, the cholent may be cooked on top of the stove on a *blech* (a tin placed over the fire) over low heat. It should simmer gently overnight.

When served, the cholent should be very thick. If all the liquid has not been absorbed, use a slotted spoon to remove the cholent from the pot.

Variations:

Any of the beans called for may be eliminated, substituted, or the quantity used increased or decreased. Possible bean substitutions include kidney beans, pinto beans, navy beans, or chickpeas. Brown rice may be substituted for the barley. Seasonings can be altered by adding 1 or 2 whole cloves of garlic, a hearty dash of paprika, or a bay leaf.

Sweet-and-Sour Shortribs

Serves 4

A welcome change from barbecued shortribs.

> 2½ pounds shortribs
> ½ stick (¼ cup) unsalted margarine
> ½ cup chopped green pepper
> ½ cup chopped onion
> 2 large cloves garlic, finely minced
> 1 tablespoon cornstarch
> ¼ cup cider vinegar
> 1 cup pineapple juice
> 3 tablespoons sugar
> ⅛ teaspoon black pepper

Preheat the oven to 350 degrees F. Arrange the shortribs in a shallow baking pan and roast uncovered for 1 hour. Pour off accumulated grease. Do not turn off the oven.

In a small saucepan over low heat, melt the margarine. Add the green pepper, onion, and garlic. Sauté until tender. Remove from the heat. Dissolve the cornstarch in the vinegar. Combine it with the pineapple juice. Add this mixture to the sautéed vegetables. Return the saucepan to low heat. Cook, stirring constantly, until the mixture thickens and comes to a boil. Remove from the heat. Stir in the sugar and pepper. Pour the sauce over the shortribs. Return the roasting pan to the oven; continue roasting, basting occasionally until tender, about 30 to 40 minutes.

Beef Stroganoff

Serves 6

Beef Stroganoff is reportedly named after Count Paul Stroganoff, a nineteenth-century Russian diplomat. This dish, particularly popular in the Baltic countries, consists of beef cut into strips, seared, then cooked. It is served topped with a cream-enriched sauce. Pareve milk makes an admirable substitute for the sour cream.

> 1½ pounds shoulder steak
> ½ teaspoon salt
> ⅛ teaspoon paprika
> ⅛ teaspoon black pepper
> ¼ cup unsalted margarine
> 1 small onion, chopped
> ⅓ cup sliced mushrooms
> 1 cup bouillon made with a cube
> 8 ounces egg noodles
> 1 cup pareve milk

Cut the steak into 2-inch squares or transversely into ½-inch strips. Season with the salt, paprika, and pepper. In a large heavy skillet, melt the margarine. Add the meat along with the onion and cook until browned. Add the mushrooms and cook them for a few minutes. Pour in the bouillon. Simmer for 15 minutes.

Cook the noodles according to package directions. Drain and transfer to a serving dish. With a slotted spoon, arrange the meat over the cooked noodles. Add the pareve milk to the sauce in the pan. Scrape the cooked-on juices from the bottom and sides of the pan. Heat the sauce, stirring constantly. Pour over the meat and serve immediately.

Beef Sukiyaki

Serves 4

The ingredients used in this tasty Japanese dish are familiar ones. Meat and vegetables are cooked in a savory sauce satisfying to the heartiest of appetites. In Japan, sukiyaki is prepared at the table over a hibachi (charcoal brazier). A chafing dish would serve as an adequate alternative for table preparation.

> 1 pound shoulder or tenderloin steak
> 3 stalks of celery, thinly sliced
> 2 large onions, thinly sliced
> ½ pound mushrooms, thinly sliced
> 1 bunch scallions, cut into 1½-inch lengths
> 1 can (8 ounces) bamboo shoots, drained
>   then cut into bite-sized pieces
> 3 tablespoons water
> ⅓ cup soy sauce
> ⅛ cup sugar
> 1 chicken bouillon cube dissolved in ½ cup
>   hot water
> ½ pound fresh spinach leaves, cut into
>   1-inch strips
> 3 cups cooked rice

Cut the steak into thin strips 2½ inches long. In a large nonstick skillet, brown the meat. Add the celery and onions. Cook for 3 to 5 minutes, stirring occasionally. Add the mushrooms, scallions, bamboo shoots, water, soy sauce, sugar, and chicken bouillon. Simmer until the vegetables are tender, about 10 minutes. Add the spinach strips and cook for an additional 5 minutes. Serve over a bed of rice.

Chinese Pepper Steak

Serves 4

The secret of this dish lies in its quick cooking. The meat should be tender but firm and the vegetables crisp.

> 1 pound flank or chuck steak
> ¼ cup oil
> 1 clove garlic
> ½ cup coarsely chopped onion
> 2 cups bite-sized pieces of green pepper
> ½ teaspoon salt
> Freshly ground black pepper to taste
> ⅛ teaspoon ginger
> 1 tablespoon cornstarch
> 1 cup bouillon made with a beef cube
> 1 to 3 teaspoons soy sauce, to taste

Cut the steak diagonally across the grain into thin slices, then cut into strips about 2 inches long. In a large skillet or wok, over medium heat, heat the oil. Cut the clove of garlic in half; place in the hot oil for about 3 minutes, long enough to infuse the oil with the flavor, then remove. Add the meat to the skillet and cook over medium heat, turning as needed until browned.

Mix in the onion, green pepper, and seasonings. Cook over medium heat, stirring constantly until tender. In a small bowl, blend the cornstarch with the bouillon and soy sauce until smooth.

Gradually stir this mixture into the contents of the skillet. Bring to a boil and cook, stirring constantly, until the liquid is thickened. Taste-check the seasoning. Serve hot over cooked rice.

Variations:

• For Chinese Mushroom Steak, substitute a pound of sliced mushrooms for the green pepper.

• For Chinese Onion Steak, substitute 3 or 4 medium-sized onions, cut into rings, for the green pepper.

• For Chinese Bean Steak, substitute a pound of green beans, cut diagonally into one-inch pieces, for the green pepper. Cook until the beans are crisp-tender.

Layered Beef-Vegetable Casserole

Serves 4 to 5

A colorful one-dish meal starring corn and green peas.

> **1 pound ground beef**
> **½ teaspoon salt (optional)**
> **2 cans (16 ounces each) whole-kernel corn,**
> **drained**
> **1 medium-sized green pepper, sliced**
> **1 medium-sized onion, sliced**
> **¼ teaspoon black pepper**
> **Salt (optional)**
> **1 can (20 ounces) tomato sauce or 2½ cups**
> **homemade tomato sauce**
> **1 package (10 ounces) frozen peas, slightly**
> **thawed**

In a 10-inch skillet over medium-high heat, cook the ground beef seasoned with the salt until the meat is lightly browned, about 10 minutes. Stir frequently. Spoon off and discard excess fat.

Preheat the oven to 400 degrees F. In a 2-quart casserole, spread 1 can of drained corn. Top with half of the meat, then with all the green pepper slices and onion slices. Sprinkle with the pepper and salt if desired. Next, top with half of the tomato sauce. Then add the remaining corn, meat, and tomato sauce, in that order. Top all with the peas. Cover the casserole and bake for 1 hour.

Tongue in Apricot Sauce

Tongue is one of the variety meats that does not enjoy universal appeal. Prepared in apricot sauce, the prejudice may very well change. Tongue gives life to any menu because it introduces an interesting flavor and texture.

> **1 pickled tongue, size of your choice (see**
> **below)**
> **Cold water**

> **4 cups apricot nectar**
> **1 tablespoon firmly packed brown sugar**
> **1 cup dried apricots**
> **½ cup raisins**

Soak the tongue in cold water for 3 hours before cooking; drain. In a large pot, place the tongue. Cover with cold water. Bring to a boil. Reduce heat and cook over low heat for 30 minutes per pound, until tender.

Plunge the hot tongue into cold water. This will help loosen the skin. Cut away the roots, small bones and gristle at the butt end, then remove the outer skin. Slice the tongue into thin slices; set aside while preparing the sauce.

In a medium-sized saucepan, combine the apricot nectar, brown sugar, dried apricots, and raisins. Bring to a boil, cover, and simmer for 20 minutes. Correct the seasoning. Add the sliced tongue (including the odd-shaped pieces) and heat for about 5 minutes. Serve.

Yield: If sliced ⅛-inch thick, a 2½-pound tongue will yield 26 to 28 slices; a 3½-pound tongue will yield 28 to 30 slices; and a 4½-pound tongue will yield 32 to 34 slices and will serve 10 or more. Thicker slices will yield a lesser amount.

Variations:

Once the tongue has been cooked and prepared as above, it can be served with various sauces. Try this one in place of the apricot sauce.

> **1 quart ginger ale**
> **1 bottle (12 ounces) ketchup**
> **1 can (6 ounces) frozen lemonade**
> **½ to 1 cup raisins**

In a medium-sized saucepan, combine the ginger ale, ketchup, lemonade, and raisins. Bring to a boil. Add the sliced tongue. Reduce the heat and simmer until heated through. One-quarter cup slivered blanched almonds makes an unusual garnish.

Meat Rolled in Cabbage

Serves 12,
3 rolls per serving

Ground meat plus cubed apples, bound together with rice, cook together lazily inside green cabbage leaves in a sweet-and-sour tomato sauce. This is a large recipe that freezes very well.

1 large head of cabbage (about 6 pounds)
2 pounds chopped meat
1 cup cooked rice
2 large apples, peeled, cored, and cubed
½ cup raisins
1 teaspoon cinnamon
1 teaspoon salt (optional)
1 large onion
A few meat bones
1 can (6 ounces) lemonade, defrosted
1 can (6 ounces) tomato paste
½ cup firmly packed brown sugar
1 bottle (16 ounces) ketchup
2 cups water
Cinnamon to taste
Sugar to taste
Salt to taste

Place the head of cabbage in the freezer for 24 hours. Remove from the freezer; let thaw. The cabbage leaves will now be easy to peel off. (Alternatively, you may core the cabbage, then boil it for 10 minutes in order to be able to separate the leaves.)

In a large bowl, mix together the chopped meat, rice, apples, raisins, cinnamon, and salt. Lay a cabbage leaf flat on a dish. In the middle of the leaf, place 2 to 3 tablespoons of the meat mixture. Fold the thick end up over the filling, then fold both sides toward the middle. Roll up tightly, jelly-roll fashion. Set aside on a large baking sheet. Continue this method of filling each leaf until all cabbage leaves have been filled and rolled up. Shred or chop any cabbage that remains after peeling off the large leaves. Set aside.

To prepare the sauce, slice the onion into a large saucepot. Rest the bones on the onions and stew over low heat until the fat on the bones is rendered and the onions are limp. Stir occasionally. Simultaneously, in a medium-sized saucepan, combine the defrosted lemonade with the tomato paste, brown sugar, and ketchup. Rinse the cans and bottle with the 2 cups of water; pour the liquid into the saucepan. Stir well. Cook over low heat until the sauce has a smooth, thick consistency.

Arrange a layer of the prepared cabbage rolls over the bones in the bottom of the large saucepot. Add a portion of the reserved chopped or shredded cabbage, and top with a portion of the sauce. Continue in this manner until all the cabbage and sauce has been used up. Sprinkle lightly with cinnamon. Pour 2 additional cups of water into the pan in which the sauce has been cooked. Swirl around and pour into the cabbage pot. Cover and cook over very low heat for 3 hours. Taste to adjust seasonings, adding white sugar and salt if necessary.

Variations:

•Substitute 1 can (15 ounces) of tomato sauce for the ketchup.

•Substitute the juice of 2 lemons for the lemonade, and use ¼ cup brown sugar with ¼ cup white sugar.

•Line the bottom of the pot by arranging the chopped cabbage over the bones.

Surprise Cabbage Roll

Serves 6

This variation on the traditional meat rolled in cabbage looks like a masterpiece, but it's easy to make. A meat loaf mixture is packed into a cabbage-lined ring mold and topped with a tomato sauce containing a surprise ingredient: cranberry sauce. The meat is served in slices rather than in individual cabbage rolls.

> 1 egg (graded large)
> ½ teaspoon nutmeg
> 1 tablespoon chopped fresh parsley
> 1 tablespoon sugar
> 1 small onion, finely minced

———————➤

1¼ pounds ground veal
1 cup cooked rice
Salt and pepper to taste
1 head of cabbage (2 pounds)
Grease for the mold
1 can (16 ounces) jellied cranberry sauce
1 can (8 ounces) tomato sauce

In a large mixing bowl, beat the egg well with the nutmeg, chopped parsley, and sugar. Add the onion, ground veal, and cooked rice. Add salt and pepper to taste. Mix to blend well.

Parboil several large cabbage leaves in hot water for a few minutes until flexible, or put the head of cabbage in the feezer overnight.

Preheat the oven to 350 degrees F. Grease a 2-quart ring mold. Line the mold with a double layer of cabbage leaves. Pack the prepared meat solidly in the cavity of the cabbage-lined mold. In a saucepan, cook the cranberry sauce and tomato sauce over medium heat until smooth, stirring frequently. Spoon over the meat in the mold, reserving any extra sauce to serve later. Cover the top of the mold with foil. Place the mold on a baking sheet. Bake for 1 to 1¼ hours. Invert on a platter to serve. Garnish by placing small round Israeli carrots in the center. Slice to serve, using reserved dressing to spoon over or alongside each portion.

Note: The jellied cranberry sauce and tomato sauce combination makes an interesting dip for chicken hors d'oeuvres.

Meat-filled French Loaf

Serves 6 or more

Ground meat, onion, and carrot are encased in a loaf of French bread and baked. One-half pound of meat will serve six or more. A perfect dish to serve at a patio party.

1 large onion, diced
2 tablespoons pareve margarine or oil
½ pound ground veal or ground beef

3 tablespoons chopped fresh parsley
1 large carrot, grated
1 teaspoon salt
¼ teaspoon black pepper
½ teaspoon poultry seasoning
1 loaf French bread
1 onion, grated
1 large clove garlic, minced (optional)
½ cup tomato juice or water

Preheat the oven to 350 degrees F.

In a medium-sized saucepan, sauté the onion in the fat until golden brown. Add the meat and cook until browned. Add the parsley, carrot, and seasonings and cook for an additional 5 minutes. Cut off one end of the bread and set aside. With a long fork, pull out the soft center of the loaf. (If the loaf is too long to be able to scoop out all the bread from one end, cut off the other end as well. Proceed to fill, then reattach both cut-off ends.)

Mix the bread with the meat mixture. Add the grated onion, minced garlic, and tomato juice or water. Blend well. Stuff the filling into the loaf. With a skewer, reattach the cut-off end of the loaf. Put the filled loaf on a baking sheet and bake for 25 minutes.

Variations:

• Double the recipe and use 6 grinder or ranch rolls. Cut off one end of each roll and, with a long fork, pull out the soft center. Stuff with the filling and bake as above. Can be served with or without a mushroom gravy. Freezes very well.

• For salmon rolls, substitute a 15½-ounce can of red salmon for the meat. Substitute onion powder for the poultry seasoning. Add to the sautéed vegetables and proceed as above. May be served with or without a mushroom or mushroom-vegetable gravy.

To prepare a mushroom-vegetable gravy, cook a 10-ounce package of frozen mixed vegetables or peas and carrots according to package directions. With a slotted spoon, spoon a portion of vegetables over the salmon roll, then dress with Mushroom Sauce (page 261).

Lasagna

Makes 9 generous portions

Here is a new kosher version of an Italian favorite. Pareve cheese is substituted for the traditional parmesan or mozzarella cheese.

1 large onion, finely chopped
1 tablespoon oil
1½ pounds ground meat
3½ cups tomato sauce
1 can (6 ounces) tomato paste
¾ cup water
2 cloves garlic, minced
¼ teaspoon dried basil
1 tablespoon sugar
1 pound lasagna noodles
10 ounces Parvcheezy, divided
2 eggs (graded large), lightly beaten
1 tablespoon dried parsley flakes
Dash of black pepper
Oil for the pan

In a deep saucepan, sauté the onion in the oil until translucent. Add the ground meat and sauté until it loses its red color. Stir in the tomato sauce, tomato paste, water, minced garlic, basil, and sugar. Simmer for about 20 minutes, stirring occasionally.

Preheat the oven to 350 degrees F. Grease a 9 x 13 x 2-inch pan; set aside.

Cook the lasagna noodles as directed on the package; set aside.

Grate half of the Parvcheezy into a small bowl. Combine with the eggs, parsley, and pepper. Blend well.

Into the prepared pan, spoon a thin layer of the meat sauce. Arrange a layer of lasagna noodles. Spread with a thin layer of the Parvcheezy-egg mixture. Now spoon a layer of the meat sauce over this and top with thin slices of the Parvcheezy. Repeat until all the ingredients have been used up. Save enough of the sauce and Parvcheezy-egg mixture to use over the top layer of noodles. Finish by grating the remaining Parvcheezy over all.

Bake for 30 minutes or until bubbly. Let set 10 minutes before serving.

Note: This lends itself to buffet service. Needs only a crisp green salad for accompaniment.

Easy Meat Lasagna

Serves 6 to 8

This impressive baked casserole consists of giant noodles, ground meat, tomato sauce, and tofu. The latter gives the illusion that the dish contains cheese. Excellent for buffet service. Only a crisp salad is needed as an accompaniment.

> 1 generous tablespoon oil
> 1 to 2 large cloves garlic, cut into halves
> 1 large onion, finely diced
> 1½ pounds ground beef or veal
> Optional seasonings: minced garlic or garlic
>   powder, crushed dried oregano, chopped
>   fresh parsley
> 12 lasagna noodles
> 1 tablespoon oil
> 1 pound firm tofu
> 4 cups Italian-style tomato sauce
> Oil for the baking pan

In a large skillet over medium-high heat, heat the oil. Add the cut garlic and sauté until lightly browned to infuse the oil with the flavor. Remove the garlic; add the diced onion. Sauté until translucent. Add the ground meat. Add the optional seasonings. Stir until the meat is browned.

In a large pot, bring 4 quarts of water to a boil, adding the tablespoon of oil. Add the lasagna noodles and cook until tender but not soft. Drain and rinse thoroughly with cold water. Chop the tofu in a food processor or blender, or mash very well with a fork. Reserve about ¼ cup to sprinkle on top of the lasagna.

Preheat the oven to 350 degrees F.

Lightly coat with oil the bottom and sides of a deep 9 x 13-inch pan. Coat the bottom of the pan with a small portion of the tomato sauce. Arrange a layer of noodles on the sauce, followed by a layer of ground meat (about a third of it). Sprinkle with a portion of the tofu and cover with another third of the tomato sauce. Repeat layering until all the ingredients are used up. The top layer of noodles should be completely covered with the sauce. Sprinkle the top with the reserved tofu. Bake for 25 to 30 minutes, until bubbly hot.

Moussaka

Serves 4 to 6

Moussaka is popular not only in Greece but throughout the Balkans, Turkey, and the Middle East. Although there are many variations on the basic recipe, the dish consists basically of eggplant layered with a savory mixture of ground lamb or ground beef.

1 medium-sized eggplant (approximately
   1¼ pounds)
Oil
2 tablespoons oil
1 cup chopped onion
Salt and pepper to taste
1 pound ground beef or lamb
1 cup tomato sauce
1 can (6 ounces) tomato paste
2 tablespoons chopped parsley
1 garlic clove, minced, or ½ teaspoon garlic
   powder
1 teaspoon cinnamon
3 tablespoons dry red wine
Grease for the pan
Sliced tomatoes to cover the top of the
   meat (each slice ⅜-inch thick)
3 eggs (graded large)

Preheat the oven to 375 degrees F. Peel and slice the eggplant, but not too thin. Brush each slice with oil and arrange on a baking sheet. Bake for 10 minutes; set aside.

In a large skillet, heat the 2 tablespoons of oil. Add the chopped onion and seasonings. Sauté until the onion is translucent, stirring occasionally. Add the ground meat, and cook until the meat is browned. Drain excess grease from the pan.

In a small bowl, combine the tomato sauce, tomato paste, parsley, garlic, cinnamon, and dry wine. Stir to mix. Pour into a skillet and cook over low heat until the ingredients are thoroughly blended.

In a lightly greased 1½-quart baking casserole, layer the eggplant, meat, and sauce. Arrange the sliced tomatoes on top. Beat the eggs and pour over all. Bake for 35 minutes. Serve piping hot.

Moussaka Puff

Serves 6

Here, the traditional moussaka is treated in a novel way.

> **1 large eggplant (1½ pounds)**
> **Boiling water**
> **½ pound ground veal or ground beef**
> **1 small onion, grated**
> **1½ cups soft breadcrumbs, divided**
> **½ teaspoon salt**
> **½ teaspoon dried basil**
> **⅛ teaspoon nutmeg**
> **½ cup tomato sauce**
> **4 eggs (graded large), separated**

Pare the eggplant and dice the pulp. In a medium-sized saucepan, place the eggplant in a small amount of boiling salted water. Cover and cook until soft. Drain well. Measure off 1½ cups of cooked pulp.

In a medium-sized teflon-coated skillet (if using a regular skillet, coat with a vegetable spray), brown the ground veal. Cook for about 5 minutes. Stir in the drained eggplant, onion, and 1 cup of the breadcrumbs. Add the seasonings and tomato sauce. Remove from the heat. Let cool.

Preheat the oven to 350 degrees F.

In a large bowl, beat the egg yolks until creamy thick. Blend in the cooled eggplant-meat mixture. In a separate bowl, beat the egg whites until they form soft peaks. Gently fold the whites into the yolk mixture, just until no whites show. Pour the mixture into an ungreased 6-cup soufflé or straight-sided baking dish. Sprinkle the remaining ½ cup of breadcrumbs on top and bake for 45 minutes or until puffy firm and golden. Best if served at once.

Cherry Tomato Meatballs

Serves 3 to 4

Newport, Rhode Island, is not only the home of the first synagogue in the United States, it is also the home of the Corne House, which bears a marker with the legend HOME OF THE ARTIST MICHELE FELICE CORNE, WHO INTRODUCED THE TOMATO INTO THIS COUNTRY. We shall be ever grateful, for the tomato enhances countless dishes. This recipe uses cherry tomatoes as a surprise relish filling for meatballs.

Grease for the pan
1 pound ground beef
1 egg (graded large), beaten
¼ cup water or tomato juice
¼ cup finely minced onion
⅓ cup matzo meal
Salt and freshly ground black pepper
Garlic powder (optional)
12 small cherry tomatoes

Preheat the oven to 375 degrees F. Lightly grease a 9 x 13 x 2-inch baking pan.

In a medium-sized bowl, thoroughly mix all ingredients except the cherry tomatoes. Shape about ¼ cup of the meat mixture around each cherry tomato to form a round meatball. Place the meatballs in the prepared pan and bake for 25 to 30 minutes, until the meat is nicely browned.

Savory Stuffed Hamburger Patties

Serves 6

There are many more ways to serve chopped beef than merely as a hamburger in a roll. The ground meat can appear wrapped in a cloak of cabbage or encased in a variety of vegetables. Try these oversized stuffed burgers prepared with your favorite meat or chicken stuffing. Serve them plain or garnished with a little warmed tomato sauce or ketchup. Serve with a green salad.

> **2 eggs (graded large), beaten**
> **¼ cup tomato juice or water**
> **Crumbs from 1 slice of bread**
> **2 tablespoons snipped fresh parsley**
> **¼ teaspoon salt**
> **Dash of freshly ground black pepper**
> **2 pounds ground beef**
> **1 recipe Rice Stuffing, Potato Stuffing, or**
> **the stuffing of your choice**
> **1 tablespoon oil**

In a small bowl, mix together the eggs and tomato juice or water. Add the breadcrumbs, parsley, salt, pepper, and beef. Blend lightly but thoroughly. Divide the mixture into 12 equal portions. Shape each into a 4-inch patty. Place 6 patties on a piece of wax paper. Center a portion of stuffing atop each patty. Place the remaining patties atop the stuffing, and press the edges together to seal the patties.

To pan-broil, heat the oil on a griddle (or use a teflon griddle or skillet and omit the oil). Using a broad pancake turner, transfer the stuffed hamburgers to the griddle. Lower the heat to medium-low. Brown the patties lightly on each side, turning carefully. Or, you may bake them in the oven at 350 degrees F., turning once.

Rice Stuffing:

Makes 1¼ cups

> **⅛ cup chopped onion**
> **1 tablespoon unsalted margarine or oil** ⟶

    1 cup cooked rice
    Salt and pepper to taste
    2 tablespoons chopped almonds (optional)

In a small saucepan over medium heat, cook the onion in the margarine or oil until translucent, not brown. Stir in the rice and seasonings. Add the almonds; mix lightly. Divide into 6 portions.

Potato Stuffing:

Makes 1½ cups

    1¼ cups peeled and shredded raw potato,
       drained well
    ½ cup chopped onion
    ¼ cup shredded carrot
    3 tablespoons unsalted margarine or oil
    ½ cup matzo meal or breadcrumbs
    1 egg (graded large), beaten
    ¼ teaspoon salt
    ⅛ teaspoon black pepper

In a medium-sized skillet, sauté the vegetables in the margarine or oil until tender. Add the remaining ingredients to the vegetables. Mix well. Divide into 6 portions.

Corned Beef Hash

Serves 4 to 5

From Cornwall England comes the ditty of the Sunday roast: "Hot on Sunday ... cold on Monday ... hashed on Tuesday ..." and so on for the rest of the week. Here, you disguise yesterday's (or Sunday's) leftover corned beef as ... corned beef hash! Prepared with chopped beets, this dish is known as red flannel hash.

    Grease for the pan
    1 pound leftover corned beef
    3 medium-sized potatoes, cooked
    1 small onion

½ large green pepper
1 small stalk of celery
¼ cup chopped fresh parsley (optional)
Stock from corned beef

Preheat the oven to 425 degrees F. Grease a shallow 9-inch pan.

Into a medium-sized mixing bowl, mince all the ingredients. Mix well, adding enough stock to moisten. Turn the mixture into the prepared pan and bake for about 20 minutes, until a brown crust forms. Fold over as you would an omelette and serve with tomato sauce.

Alternatively, you may prepare the hash in a large greased skillet. Heat the skillet over high heat until hot. Spread the meat mixture in it. Reduce the heat and cook covered until well browned on the bottom. Fold over as you would an omelette and serve.

Variations:

•Substitute leftover beef for the corned beef. Moisten with leftover gravy.
•Substitute 2 cooked carrots for the green pepper and celery.
•Omit the green pepper and celery and add 1 cup chopped beets. Moisten with ¼ cup of water.

Hot Bologna Rolls

Serves 8

The ever-popular bologna is served with a new twist: it is ground and enhanced with relish and mayonnaise before being encased in a hot dog roll to be baked in the oven.

These rolls may be prepared in advance and refrigerated. Remove from refrigerator about two hours before baking.

¾ pound bologna or salami
⅓ cup mustard relish spread
¼ cup mayonnaise
8 frankfurter rolls

Preheat the oven to 300 degrees F. Grind the bologna. Add the mustard relish spread and mayonnaise. Mix until well blended. Split rolls partway lengthwise. Fill with bologna mix. Arrange in a large casserole, cut side up. Bake covered for 30 minutes.

Salami Quiche

Serves 6

This is a classic quiche with an unclassic filling (salami combined with chopped scallions, mushrooms, and zucchini). A colorful and tasty dish.

> 1 deep 9-inch pie shell
> 4 eggs (graded large)
> ⅔ cup nondairy creamer
> 1 teaspoon salt (optional)
> ⅛ teaspoon black pepper
> 1 cup thinly sliced salami
> 2 scallions, chopped
> 2 large mushrooms, thinly sliced
> ½ cup thinly sliced zucchini

Prick the pie shell all over with a fork and prebake in a 350-degree F. oven for 10 minutes. Set aside while preparing the filling.

Beat the eggs with the nondairy creamer, optional salt, and pepper. Layer the salami, chopped scallions, mushrooms and zucchini in the pie crust. Pour the egg mixture into the crust. Bake for 50 minutes or until the top of the quiche has set and is lightly browned. Allow to rest for 5 minutes before serving.

6

From the Waters

Fish Delicacies

"*These may ye eat that are in the waters, whatsoever hath fins and scales . . .*" (Leviticus 11:9).

Baked Fish Fillets

Serves 3

"Fish," Grandma used to say, "is brain food." Whether or not that's true, we do know that fish is highly delicious and protein-rich.

Here, fish bakes under a lemony, buttery crumb topping, and garlic powder and parsley add a little zing. This party-perfect dish was served at one of our congregational donor dinners. Ceil Finman, head of the kitchen detail, graciously shared the recipe with me.

> **Grease for the pan**
> **1 pound lemon sole fillets**
> **1 wedge of lemon**
> **½ cup unsalted cracker crumbs and ½ cup**
>   **flavored breadcrumbs**
> **2 tablespoons unsalted butter or margarine**
> **1 to 2 teaspoons freshly squeezed lemon**
>   **juice**
> **¼ teaspoon garlic powder**
> **2 tablespoons chopped fresh parsley**
> **Paprika**

Preheat the oven to 350 degrees F. Lightly grease 9 x 13-inch baking pan. Arrange the fish in the pan. Squeeze the lemon over the fish. Combine the cracker crumbs with the bread-crumbs. In a saucepan over low heat, melt the butter or mar-garine. Add the lemon juice and garlic powder. Stir in the pars-ley and crumbs and toss together until well mixed. Spoon the mixture over the fish to cover. Sprinkle with paprika. Bake for 20 minutes, or longer if the fish is thick, until the fish flakes easily when poked with a fork.

Rolled Fish Fillets With Vegetable Stuffing

Serves 4

Fillets of fish lend themselves to a variety of methods of preparation: poaching, broiling, frying, baking. Here is an ap-pealing recipe: fillets of flounder are rolled up to encase a color-ful and succulent filling. The lemon juice adds flavor to the fish as it bakes.

> **Grease for the pan**
> **1 cup shredded raw vegetables of your**
> **choice (celery, cabbage, carrot, and green**
> **pepper are a good combination)**
> **1 onion, minced**
> **2 tablespoons prepared French dressing**
> **4 thin flounder fillets**
> **½ teaspoon salt**
> **⅛ teaspoon white pepper**
> **Juice of 1 lemon**

Lightly grease a baking pan and set aside. Preheat the oven to 325 degrees F.

Prepare a filling for the fish by tossing together the cup's worth of shredded vegetables in a small mixing bowl. Add the minced onion, then stir in the French dressing. Spread one-fourth of the mixture over each of the fillets, then roll up each fillet jelly-roll fashion. If necessary, skewer with toothpicks. Place the fish rolls seam side down in the prepared baking pan. Sprinkle with the salt, pepper, and lemon juice. Cover the pan with foil and bake for 25 minutes, until the fish flakes easily when poked with a fork.

Layered Fish

Serves 8 to 10

Cheese and sour cream go into this tempting fish dish. The fish is breaded, fried, then baked in the sour cream dressing.

Grease for the pan
2 eggs (graded large)
1 tablespoon water
½ cup all-purpose flour
1 cup breadcrumbs or matzo meal
Salt and pepper to taste
12 small flounder fillets
Fat for frying
1 pint sour cream
1 cup grated Cheddar or Muenster cheese
Onion powder to taste
Garlic powder to taste

Lightly grease a 9 x 13-inch baking pan and set aside. Preheat the oven to 275 degrees F. In a shallow bowl, beat the eggs with the water. Place the flour in a flat dish and the crumbs or matzo meal and salt and pepper in another. Dip each fish fillet into the flour to coat, then into the egg, and finally into the crumbs or matzo meal. In a large skillet over medium-high heat, heat the fat. Fry the fish lightly until golden on each side. Layer the fillets in the prepared pan.

Combine the sour cream and grated cheese with enough onion powder and garlic powder to give it a "tang." Pour the mixture over the fish fillets. Cover the pan and bake for 30 minutes. Uncover and continue baking for an additional 15 minutes.

Pickled Herring

How ironic! To some, herring is considered a lowly fish, while an English proverb proclaims, "Of all the fish in the sea, herring is the king." In Jewish cuisine, herring has long been a favorite. There are many types of herring available—shmaltz, matjes, and bismarck are some—and each can be prepared in a variety of ways. This recipe makes wonderful pickled herring.

> Shmaltz herrings
> Vinegar
> Water
> Sugar
> White pepper
> Onions
> Pickling spice (whole pepercorns, bay
>   leaves, allspice, etc. Do not use red
>   peppers or cloves.)

Clean thoroughly as many herrings as you wish to pickle. Peel, then wash them well. Slice each herring into about 8 slices. Place the herring slices in cold water and let soak in the refrigerator overnight. Drain.

Make a marinade of vinegar and water using 1 part vinegar to 2 parts water. Add sugar to taste (it is difficult to specify the exact quantity, as it depends on the strength of the vinegar and personal preference). Add a dash of pepper. Cut the onions into rings (1 medium-sized onion for each herring).

Arrange the herring and onions in layers in a glass jar, sprinkling each layer with a few pickling spices. Pour the vinegar marinade over all. Cover the jar and refrigerate for 3 days before using.

Note: After cleaning the herrings, fillet them—that is, cut each in half lengthwise, remove the bones, then cut into 2-inch slices. Proceed as above.

Marinierte Fish

(Pickled Fish)

Serves 5 or 6

In lieu of pickled herring, many serve pickled (marinated) fish to break the fast on Yom Kippur night. Vinegar, onion, and lemon flavor this zesty pickled fish. The recipe works well with all kinds of fish.

> 2 pounds sliced fish of your choice (carp,
>   salmon, white, pike), sliced about ¾-inch
>   thick   ⟶

> ¾ cup white vinegar
> ½ cup water
> ½ cup sugar
> 1 tablespoon salt
> 1 tablespoon mixed pickling spice
> 2 to 3 onions
> 1 lemon

Arrange the sliced fish in the bottom of a glass container. In a large measuring cup, combine the vinegar, water, sugar, and salt. Stir to dissolve the sugar and salt. Sprinkle the pickling spice over the fish, then pour on the marinade. Cover and marinate in the refrigerator overnight. The next day, slice the onions into a 2-quart saucepan, arrange the fish on the bed of onions, then pour in marinade. Bring to a boil, then cover and simmer for 30 minutes over medium heat. To serve, transfer the fish to a deep platter and top each piece with a slice of lemon. Pour the marinade over the fish. Refrigerate for at least 24 hours before serving. Keeps very well in the refrigerator.

Ceviche

Serves 6 or 7 as an appetizer

Sashimi, artfully carved raw fish, has been standard fare in Japan for thousands of years. Ceviche, another raw fish dish, said to have been created by the Indians of South and Central America, found its way north with the Spaniards. My daughter Naomi's Mexican friend, Adina Singer, introduced the preparation to us.

Ceviche is remarkable in that the fish is cooked not by placing it over or under a heat source but by marinating it in lemon or lime juice. The fish develops a very interesting texture—and no one will suspect that the fish was not literally cooked!

> 1 pound firm-fleshed white-meated fish
>   (haddock, cod, sole, etc.)
> Juice of 3 or 4 lemons or limes, enough to
>   cover the fish completely
> 1 medium-sized onion, finely chopped

1 large or 2 medium-sized tomatoes, cubed
A few coriander leaves, cut into small
   pieces
¼ cup pimento-stuffed small olives
   (optional)
¼ cup olive oil
⅞ cup ketchup
1 medium-sized avocado, cut into small
   squares (optional)
Salt to taste

Wash the fish and cut it into uniformly small squares. Place them in a deep dish and cover with lemon or lime juice. Refrigerate and let marinate overnight. When "cooked," the fish will appear to be a deeper white. Strain off about two-thirds of the lemon or lime juice. Add the remaining ingredients. Gently toss to mix well. Cover and refrigerate for at least 1 hour to blend the flavors.

To serve, with a slotted spoon remove the fish and vegetables from the marinade. Place atop lettuce leaves or into individual coupe dishes. If you'd like, spoon some of the marinade over each serving. A delicious fish course.

A standing slice of lime atop each coupe serving of ceviche makes a lovely garnish. To prepare, slice a lime thinly. Cut through the rind and through the center of the slice three-fourths the way to the other side. Then twist the slice so it will stand up.

Pickled Fillet of Sole

Serves 4

This is a modern version of ceviche. You will note that this recipe differs from the classic recipe in that the fish is "cooked" in a combination of three citrus fruits and is flavored with pickling spice.

Once the fish is "cooked" in the prepared marinade, it is ready to be served. Nice main dish for a dairy meal. It keeps well in the refrigerator for a few days.

> 1 pound fresh fillets of sole or 1 pound
>   frozen fillets of sole
> 1 cup orange juice
> Juice of 1 lemon
> Juice of 1 lime
> ¼ cup white vinegar
> 1 teaspoon salt
> ¼ teapoons black pepper
> 1 to 2 tablespoons sugar
> 1 to 2 tablespoons mixed pickling spice
> 1 medium-sized onion

Cut the sole into strips. In a mixing bowl, combine the juices with the vinegar, salt, and pepper. Add sugar to taste. Arrange the fish in a glass bowl. Slice the onion into rings and distribute over the fish. Sprinkle with the pickling spice. Pour the liquid over the raw fish. Cover and refrigerate for at least 24 hours. The fish will then be beautifully "cooked and pickled."

Salmon Pasta

Serves 6

If you are tired of serving the usual spaghetti with tomato sauce or meat sauce, try these large shells stuffed with a fish filling and baked on a green sauce. The white shells framed by the green sauce makes an eye-appealing dish.

> 3 quarts boiling water
> 1 tablespoon salt (optional)
> 12 large pasta shells
> 1 can (7¾ ounces) salmon
> 1 pound ricotta cheese
> 3 tablespoons unsalted butter
> 3 tablespoons flour
> ½ teaspoon salt
> Dash of pepper
> Dash of nutmeg
> 1 cup milk
> 1 cup chopped spinach, cooked and drained

Grease for the pan
¼ to ½ cup grated parmesan cheese
Parsley sprigs

Cook the pasta shells in the boiling salted water for 45 minutes or until tender. Drain. Rinse with cold water to remove excess starch and stop the cooking. Set aside.

Generously grease an 8-inch-square baking dish; set aside. Preheat the oven to 350 degrees F. Drain and flake the salmon. Add the ricotta cheese. Mix well.

In a saucepan over medium heat, melt the butter or margarine. Blend in the flour and seasonings. Add the milk gradually and cook until thick and smooth, stirring constantly. Stir in the chopped spinach. Blend thoroughly. Pour the green sauce into the prepared baking dish. Fill the pasta shells with the salmon mixture and arrange over the sauce. Sprinkle with parmesan cheese. Bake for 30 minutes. Garnish each stuffed shell with a sprig of parsley. To serve, do not cloak the pasta shells with the sauce. Rather, let the sauce serve as a background for the shells.

Salmon Quiche

Serves 6 to 8

They say, "Men don't eat quiche." I defy any man not to like this one. Salmon-lovers will give this a five-star rating.

1 deep 9-inch pie shell
3 large onions
2 tablespoons unsalted margarine
1 can (7¾ ounces) salmon
3 eggs (graded large)
1½ cups pareve milk
Salt and pepper to taste
1 tablespoon chopped fresh dill

Preheat the oven to 350 degrees F. and bake the pie crust for about 6 minutes; remove from the oven and set aside. Do not turn off the oven.

In a medium-sized skillet over medium heat, sauté the onions in the margarine until translucent. Transfer the onions to the pie shell, distributing them evenly. Crumble the drained salmon and sprinkle over the onions. Beat the eggs in a small bowl; blend in the pareve milk. Season with salt and pepper, and pour the mixture over the salmon. Sprinkle the fresh dill over all. Bake for about 1 hour, until the custard is set and the top is golden.

Salmon-filled Potato Pancakes

Makes 8 pancakes

To convert an ordinary potato pancake into an epicurean pancake, tuck a salmon patty into each pancake before frying or baking.

> 1 can (7¾ ounces) salmon
> 2 tablespoons finely chopped onion
> 1 teaspoon onion powder
> 2 eggs (graded large)
> 1 tablespoon plain or seasoned breadcrumbs
> ½ teaspoon salt
> ⅛ teaspoon pepper
> ⅛ teaspoon onion powder
> 1 medium-sized onion, grated
> 2 generous cups grated raw potato
> 2 tablespoons flour
> ¼ cup oil

Skin and bone the canned salmon. Chop very well. Combine the chopped onion, onion powder, and 1 of the eggs. Blend together very well. Stir in the breadcrumbs. Shape into 8 small salmon patties. Set aside.

Beat together the remaining egg and seasonings. Blend in the grated onion and potatoes. Last, stir in the flour. Mix well. This recipe is enough for 8 filled pancakes.

In a large skillet, heat half of the oil to 375 degrees F. Drop the potato mixture by large spoonfuls to make 4 pancakes, or as many as the pan will comfortably accommodate without the pancakes touching. Place a salmon patty on each pancake and cover completely with another spoonful of potato mixture. Cook slowly until brown, then turn and brown the other side. Add the remaining 2 tablespoons of oil, and proceed to cook the next 4 pancakes. Drain on paper towels.

Alternatively, the potato mixture may be shaped to form pancakes in the palm of the hand. Place a salmon patty on each pancake and cover with potato mixture. Carefully arrange on a greased cookie sheet and bake in a 400-degree F. oven, turning once to brown both sides.

Variation:

Prepare hamburger patties with ½ pound ground meat and prepare meat-filled pancakes as above.

Smoked Salmon Rolls

Serves 4

Enjoy a facsimile of smoked salmon. This smoked salmon is more economical than the real thing. Start the recipe the night before you plan to serve it.

> 1 can (7¾ ounces) salmon
> ¼ teaspoon liquid smoke
> 9-inch pastry circle
> Freshly ground black pepper
> 1 tablespoon finely chopped scallions or
>   chives
> 1 egg (graded large)
> 1 teaspoon cold water

Preheat the oven to 425 degrees F. Open the can of salmon. Add the liquid smoke to the liquid in the can. Cover the top of the can with plastic wrap and refrigerate overnight.

Drain the liquid from the salmon, flake it, and sprinkle the flakes over the pastry circle. Sprinkle with a little freshly ground black pepper and the finely chopped scallions or chives. Cut the pastry circle with its garnish into 8 wedge-shaped pieces. Roll each wedge tightly from the outside wide edge to the center. Arrange the rolls on a baking sheet. Beat the egg with the cold water till well blended. Brush the rolls with the egg wash, then bake for 15 minutes, until golden. Serve hot.

Variation:

Substitute the mock smoked salmon in your favorite recipe for salmon patties or salmon croquettes.

Epicurean Salmon and Spinach

Serves 8

"Delicious" best describes this seafood dish with its spinach soufflé topping. The creamy salmon baked topped with a spinach soufflé will earn you a "terrific cook" reputation.

The Filling:

> 1 pound fresh salmon, cooked and flaked,
>   or 1 can (1 pound) salmon, flaked
> 1½ tablespoons unsalted butter or
>   margarine
> 2½ tablespoons flour
> 1¼ cups dairy or pareve milk
> ¼ teaspoon salt (optional)
> A few grains of pepper

Place large flakes of salmon on the bottom of eight 10-ounce individual baking dishes. In a medium-sized saucepan, melt the butter or margarine over low heat. Add the flour and mix well. Gradually add the milk and cook, stirring constantly until thickened. Add the seasoning. Spoon portions over the salmon. Set aside and prepare the soufflé topping.

The Topping:

> 3 tablespoons unsalted butter or margarine
> 4 tablespoons flour
> 1 cup dairy or pareve milk
> Salt and pepper to taste
> 3 eggs (graded large), separated
> 1½ cups finely chopped fresh spinach or 1
>   box (10 ounces) chopped spinach, thawed
>   and drained

Preheat the oven to 325 degrees F.

In a saucepan, melt the margarine over low heat. Add the flour and mix well. Gradually add the milk, stirring constantly until thickened. Add ¼ to ½ teaspoon salt and a few grains of pepper.

Gradually stir a small amount of the hot mixture into the egg yolks to warm them. Then stir the warmed egg yolk mixture into the remaining hot mixture. (This is done to prevent the yolks from curdling.) Cool slightly, then add the uncooked spinach. While the cream sauce is cooling, beat the egg whites in a clean bowl until they are stiff but not dry. Fold in the stiffly beaten egg whites. Cover the prepared salmon with this spinach soufflé. Place the baking dishes in a hot water bath and bake for 30 to 40 minutes, until the center is set and the top is golden.

Sweet-and-Sour Canned Salmon

Serves 8 as an appetizer,
4 as a main dish

Sweet-and-Sour Salmon is an excellent choice for a casual luncheon. The beauty of the recipe is that it can be prepared days in advance. The creamy topping looks and tastes scrumptious, and the salmon itself is savory.

> 1 can (1 pound) red salmon
> 3 medium-sized onions
> 2 tablespoons flour
> 6 tablespoons sugar, or to taste
> ½ teaspoon salt
> ½ cup vinegar
> ¼ cup golden raisins
> 2 egg yolks

Drain the salmon. Remove the skin and bones. Break the salmon into large pieces and arrange in a deep 8-inch pie dish. Slice the onions into a small saucepan. Add sufficient cold water to cover. Simmer uncovered over medium heat until tender, about 20 minutes. Drain the onions, reserving 1 cup of the liquid. Arrange the sliced onions over the salmon. In a small saucepan, mix together the flour, sugar, and salt. Add the onion liquid, vinegar, and raisins. Stirring all the while, heat to the boiling point, then simmer for 5 minutes.

Beat the egg yolks in a large measuring cup or deep dish. Ladle out a few tablespoons of the hot liquid and gradually but rapidly whisk them into the beaten egg yolks to prevent curdling. Return the mixture to the saucepan, continually stirring. (By whisking the hot liquid into the beaten egg yolks and returning the mixture to the saucepan, the eggs do not curdle.) Simmer gently, stirring all the while until smooth and thickened, about 5 minutes. Taste the sauce to correct the seasoning, adding more sugar if desired. Spoon the dressing over the salmon and onions. You may serve this dish warm, but it is truly best served cold. As a main dish, hot or cold, serve with hot parslied potatoes.

Tuna Quiche

Serves 6 to 8

Tuna and Swiss cheese bake smooth and velvety in a rich custard. This recipe was prepared for a sisterhood card party. By popular demand, the recipe was subsequently printed in the Sisterhood's bulletin.

> 1 deep 9-inch pie shell
> 3 eggs (graded large)
> 1 cup sour cream
> 1 cup grated Swiss cheese
> 1 can (7 ounces) tuna in water

Preheat the oven to 350 degrees F., and bake the pie shell for 10 minutes. Remove the prebaked shell and set aside, but do not turn off the oven.

In a medium-sized bowl, beat the eggs just to mix. Add the sour cream and beat together. Blend in the grated Swiss cheese and the tuna fish, including the liquid. Pour the mixture into the pie shell. Bake for 40 minutes, until lightly golden.

Amazing Tuna Pie

Serves 6 to 8

An amazing pie because there is no fussing, no preparing of a rolled pie crust. The filling (be it tuna, meat, poultry, cheese, or vegetables) is prepared and spread in a pie plate. A blender mixture is poured over it. The pancake mix separates and forms a crust, while the eggs and milk bind together the pie's filling.

> **Butter or margarine for pie plate (not oil)**
> **1 can (6½ ounces) tuna, drained**
> **1 cup shredded American cheese**
> **1 package (3 ounces) cream cheese, diced**
> **¼ cup sliced scallions**
> **¼ cup chopped pimento, drained**
> **2 cups dairy or pareve milk**
> **1 cup Hungry Jack pancake mix**
> **4 eggs (graded large)**
> **¾ teaspoon salt**
> **Pinch of nutmeg**

Preheat the oven to 400 degrees F.

Lightly grease a 10 x 1½-inch pie plate. Mix together the tuna, cheeses, scallions, and pimento and transfer to the pie plate. Pour the milk, pancake mix, eggs, salt, and nutmeg into a blender cup. Blend until smooth, about 15 seconds on high speed, or beat with a rotary beater for 1 minute. Pour the mixture into the pie plate. Bake for 35 to 40 minutes, until a knife inserted in the center comes out clean. Let cool for 5 minutes. Serve in wedges garnished with sliced tomatoes.

Kosher Scallops

Serves 6 to 8

Easy but elegant seafare. These "scallops" team together well with tartar sauce. Let everyone spear his own scallops, then dunk into tartar sauce.

2 thick slices codfish, haddock, or halibut—
   approximately 1-inch thick
½ cup all-purpose flour
1 egg (graded large)
1 tablespoon water
½ teaspoon salt
A few grains black pepper
¼ teaspoon paprika
1 cup matzo meal
Oil for frying

Cube the fish. Put the flour in a flat dish. In a shallow bowl, beat the egg with the water. In another shallow bowl, combine the salt, pepper, and paprika with the matzo meal. Coat the cut fish by dipping it first in the flour, then in the beaten egg, then in the matzo meal. Toss to cover thoroughly. Transfer to a piece of wax paper. Let the coated fish set for ½ hour.

In a large skillet, heat 1½ inches of oil to 375 degrees F. Transfer some of the fish to the pan, but be sure not to overcrowd the skillet. Stir and turn so the cubes brown evenly on all sides. With a slotted spoon remove the "scallops" from the pan and transfer to paper toweling to drain. Repeat until all the fish is cooked.

Variation:

Place the coated fish cubes on a well-oiled baking sheet and bake in a 450-degree F. oven, turning once or twice until all sides are browned.

Mock Oysters

Makes about 20

Eggplant can be prepared in numerous ways. Ratatouille is a delicious stew, and baba ghanouj is a marvelous relish or dip. Here, eggplant parades as "mock oysters." Purists serve them plain. You may wish to serve them with a cocktail sauce made by mixing equal parts of prepared horseradish and ketchup, stirring in lemon juice to taste.

Oil for the baking sheet
2 pounds eggplant (2 cups cooked and
    mashed—see method)
¾ cup breadcrumbs
Salt to taste
Dash of paprika
1 egg (graded large)
½ to 1 cup additional breadcrumbs

Preheat the oven to 400 degrees F. Oil a baking sheet and set aside.

Peel the eggplant and cut into cubes. Cook over medium-high heat, in boiling water to cover, until tender. Drain well. Mash. Measure off 2 cups of the eggplant and place it in a medium-sized mixing bowl. Stir in the breadcrumbs, salt, and dash of paprika. In a small bowl, beat the egg well. Place the breadcrumbs in a shallow dish.

With 2 forks, shape the eggplant into "oyster"-shaped cakes. Dip these into the beaten egg and then roll them in the breadcrumbs. Arrange on the prepared baking sheet. Bake in the preheated oven for 10 minutes on each side, until golden brown. Serve immediately.

Sweet-Sour Borsht-Fish

Serves 12

A fish recipe that I cherish! This was shared with me by Abby Belkin, wife of the late Dr. Samuel Belkin, president of Yeshiva University. The recipe was passed on to her by her grandmother, and it was published in my *Complete Passover Cookbook*. It warrants repetition. It can be used the year-round.

Coarse salt
12 slices striped bass or any white-meated
    fish (½- to ¾-inch thick)
2 medium-sized onions, sliced
2 small lemons, peeled and sliced
¾ teaspoon cinnamon
Scant ½ teaspoon ginger

⟶

> **1 teaspoon salt**
> **¼ teaspoon white pepper**
> **2 tablespoons sugar**
> **1 jar (32 ounces) beet borsht**
> **Water**
> **1 egg (graded large), beaten**

Salt the fish, place in a dish, cover, and refrigerate for several hours. Rinse off the salt and drain. Line the bottom of a 2½- to 3-quart saucepan with the onion and lemon slices. Arrange the sliced fish on top.

In a small bowl, combine the dry seasonings. Sprinkle portions of the mixture over each slice. Strain the jar of borsht. Combine some of the borsht liquid with an equal amount of water. (Start with 1 cup each of borsht and water.) Pour it over the fish in the saucepan. If necessary, make more of the borsht-water combination and add it to the saucepan until you have completely covered the fish. Cover the saucepan and bring to a boil over medium heat. Reduce the heat and simmer for 1 hour. Taste frequently and adjust the seasoning, adding additional sugar, salt, and pepper as needed to arrive at the desired sweet-sour balance.

Carefully lift the slices of fish with a wide-slotted spatula. Place in a pan large enough to accommodate the fish slices arranged in a single layer. Strain the fish broth. Reserve ½ cup. Pour the remainder back into the saucepan. Cool the reserved broth. Gradually add it to the beaten egg. Beat well. Slowly pour the combined mixture into the saucepan. Bring to a rapid boil over medium high heat. Boil for 1 minute. Pour the hot broth over the fish slices. Refrigerate. Serve cold.

Kulebyaka

(Couilibiac)

Makes 2 loaves
each serving 8

Kulebyaka, or *couilibiac* as it generally is known in English-speaking countries, is a traditional Russian fish pie. Unlike most pies, it is baked in a leavened dough that is oblong-shaped. This is a favorite party dish most frequently featuring fresh salmon teamed with rice and mushrooms. Here is a modern, easy version that uses canned salmon. The salmon is prepared the night before by adding one-quarter teaspoon of liquid smoke to a one-pound can of salmon. Cover with plastic wrap and refrigerate overnight.

Dough:

> 2½ to 3½ cups unsifted flour
> 1 tablespoon sugar
> 1 teaspoon salt
> 2 envelopes active dry yeast
> 1 cup very warm tap water (120 to 130
>   degrees F.)
> 2 tablespoons oil
> 1 egg (graded large), beaten

To prepare the dough, in the bowl of an electric mixer thoroughly combine 1 cup of the flour with the sugar, salt, and undissolved active dry yeast. Gradually add the water and oil to the dry ingredients. Beat at medium speed for 1 minute, scraping the bowl occasionally. Add the egg. Increase the speed and continue to beat for an additional minute before beginning to stir in additional flour to make a soft dough. Turn out onto a lightly floured board and knead until smooth and elastic, at least 10 minutes. Transfer the dough to a lightly greased bowl; turn to grease all sides. Cover and let rise in a warm draft-free place until doubled in bulk, 30 to 45 minutes.

Filling:

> 1 can (1 pound) salmon, prepared with
>   ¼ teaspoon liquid smoke (see recipe
>   introduction)
> 2 tablespoons unsalted butter or margarine
> 1 small onion, finely diced
> ¼ pound fresh mushrooms, thinly sliced, or
>   1 can (4 ounces) sliced mushrooms,
>   drained
> 1 generous tablespoon unsalted butter or
>   margarine if using fresh mushrooms ⟶

      2 tablespoons flour
      ¾ cup dairy or pareve milk
      ¼ teaspoon dried tarragon or oregano
      1 tablespoon dry white wine
      2 cups cooked rice
      Salt and black pepper to taste

Drain the liquid from the prepared canned salmon and reserve. Remove the skin and bones from the fish. Flake the salmon and set aside.

In a medium-sized saucepan, melt the butter or margarine. Add the onion and sauté until golden. If using fresh mushrooms, sauté them in the tablespoon of butter or margarine in a small saucepan; cook until no more liquid is given off. Stir the flour into the onions; cook and stir until all the flour is absorbed by the fat. Gradually stir in the dairy or pareve milk, stirring constantly until the sauce is smooth and very thick. Stir in the tarragon or oregano, the wine, and the reserved liquid from the can of salmon. Add the salmon. Stir in the mushrooms and the rice. Season to taste with salt and pepper, then let the mixture cool. (When adding salt, be conservative. Remember that canned salmon already contains salt.)

Preheat the oven to 350 degrees F.

To assemble the pie, punch down the risen dough and divide in half. Transfer one portion of the dough to a lightly greased 12 x 15-inch baking sheet. Roll out the dough to a 10 x 14-inch rectangle. Spread half of the prepared filling mixture down the center third of the rectangle. With a sharp knife, cut the dough on both sides of the filling into 1-inch-wide strips. Fold the strips at an angle across the filling, alternating sides to give a braided effect. Brush the dough with the beaten egg. Repeat with remaining dough and filling. Bake in the preheated oven for 25 to 30 minutes or until golden brown.

Tuna-Cheese Pizza Roll-ups

Makes 12 roll-ups

    To create another intriguing flavor combination, substitute salmon bits for the tuna. Both are lucious. Or, better yet, prepare one crust with tuna and one with salmon.

1 package active dry yeast
¼ cup warm water (110 to 115 degrees F.)
1 cup water
1 tablespoon sugar
1 tablespoon oil
1 teaspoon salt
3 cups sifted all-purpose flour,
   approximately
3 tablespoons unsalted butter or margarine
¼ cup all-purpose flour
1 tablespoon dried oregano
1½ teaspoons garlic powder
1 cup milk
2½ cups (10 ounces) mozzarella cheese,
   divided
2 cans (7 ounces each) tuna, drained and
   flaked
1 medium-sized green pepper, cut into thin
   strips

Dissolve the yeast in the ¼ cup of warm water. In a small saucepan, heat the cup of water until almost simmering. In a medium-sized mixing bowl, combine the sugar, oil, and salt. Add the water and stir until the sugar dissolves. Cool to lukewarm.

Now stir in 1 cup of the flour and beat until smooth. Beat in the yeast. Stir in enough additional flour to make a moderately stiff dough. Turn out onto a lightly floured board or pastry cloth and knead until the dough is smooth and satiny, 5 to 8 minutes. Shape the dough into a ball and place in a lightly greased bowl, turning to coat all sides. Cover and let rise in a warm draft-free place until doubled, about 1 hour. Punch down the dough. Divide it in half, shape each half into a ball, and let rest for 10 minutes.

While the dough is resting, melt the butter or margarine in a saucepan over low heat. Stir in the flour, oregano, and garlic powder. Gradually blend in the milk. Increase the heat and bring to a boil, stirring constantly. Remove from the heat and stir in 1½ cups of the cheese. Cool.

Preheat the oven to 425 degrees F.

Pat or roll each half of dough onto a greased 13-inch pizza pan. Spread half of the milk-cheese mixture on each circle, leaving a ½-inch border. Sprinkle each dough circle with half of the tuna, then with ½ cup of cheese. Top with strips of green pepper. Bake for 15 to 20 minutes, until the edges of the crust are golden brown. Cut each circle into 6 wedges. Beginning at the narrow end of each wedge, roll up the wedges jelly-roll-fashion. Secure with wooden picks and serve warm.

7

Garden Bounty

Vegetable Specialties

"We remember . . . the cucumbers, and the melons, the leeks, the onions, and the garlic." (Numbers 11:5).

Vegetable Pâté

Serves 8 or more

This is painstaking work, but the result is very elegant and impressive and, I think, well worth the trouble. Make it ahead and reheat when needed.

> 1 cup puréed cooked carrots (6 to 8)
> 1 cup puréed cooked cauliflower (about
>   1½ pounds)
> 1 package (10 ounces) frozen chopped
>   broccoli, cooked and well drained
> 3 eggs (graded large), divided
> 6 tablespoons pareve milk, divided
> 6 tablespoons all-purpose flour, divided
> 1 tablespoon firmly packed brown sugar
> ⅛ teaspoon cinnamon
> Grated nutmeg
> 1 to 2 tablespoons dry onion soup mix,
>   to taste
> Salt and black pepper to taste
> Grease for the pan

Line an 8 x 4-inch loaf pan with aluminum foil. Grease the bottom and sides of the lined pan. Set aside.

Put the prepared vegetables in separate bowls. Add 1 egg, 2 tablespoons pareve milk, and 2 tablespoons flour to each bowl. Season each bowl individually as follows: add the brown sugar, cinnamon, and a pinch of nutmeg to the carrots; the onion soup to the chopped broccoli; the salt, pepper, and a pinch of nutmeg to the cauliflower.

Preheat the oven to 350 degrees F. Spoon the broccoli mixture into the pan. Spread evenly. Carefully spoon the cauliflower mixture over the broccoli layer. Top carefully with a layer of the remaining carrots. Cover the pan with greased aluminum foil. Place the pan in a hot water bath. The hot water should come at least half way up the sides of the inner pan. Bake for 40 minutes, then remove the foil cover and continue baking for an additional 20 minutes. Remove from the hot water and let rest for 10 minutes. Holding the aluminum foil, carefully lift the pâté up and out of the pan. Invert and unmold onto a serving platter. Serve warm, cut into slices.

Variation:

Create your own attractive pâté. Substitute other vegetables. You might consider pumpkin, sweet potato, rutabaga, squash, or chopped spinach. Be mindful of color contrast when selecting vegetables.

Sweet-and-Sour Tofu

Serves 4 to 6

Tofu (bean curd) is very versatile. Neutral in flavor, it absorbs the flavors of what it is combined with. Here, the tofu is pan-fried until golden then doused and heated together with a sweet-sour sauce.

> 1 pound firm tofu
> 6 tablespoons oil, divided
> 1 large green pepper, cut into 2-inch-long
>   strips
> 1 large carrot, thinly sliced
> 1 large onion, finely diced

The tofu must be drained before being fried. Wrap the tofu in cheesecloth or in a clean kitchen towel. Place on a slanted cutting board. Weight it down with a dinner plate or two. Allow to drain for about 10 minutes. Pat dry and cut the block of tofu into fourths lengthwise, then cut crosswise into 10 slices.

Heat 3 tablespoons of oil in a large skillet over medium-high heat. Add the tofu and sauté for about 10 minutes, until golden. Simultaneously, in another skillet, sauté the pepper strips, carrot slices, and diced onion in the remaining 3 tablespoons oil. Cook until the vegetables are crisp-tender. Cool.

Sweet-Sour Sauce:

> 1 can (20 ounces) pineapple chunks in unsweetened juice, drained and juice reserved
> ⅛ cup soy sauce
> ¼ cup molasses or honey
> ¼ cup vinegar
> 3 tablespoons catsup
> 1 garlic clove, minced
> ¼ cup cornstarch dissolved in ⅓ cup water
> ¾ to 1 teaspoon ginger, to taste

To prepare the sauce, in a separate bowl combine 1 cup of the reserved pineapple juice with the remaining sauce ingredients. Make sure the starch is completely dissolved. Stir until blended.

Now, to the tofu in the large skillet, add the vegetables, pineapple chunks, and the sauce mixture. Cook and stir until thick, about 5 minutes. Nice to serve over rice. Chow mein noodles are an optional garnish.

Variations:

• Slice the tofu into 1-inch cubes.
• For sweet-and-sour chicken, substitute 1 pound boneless chicken breasts, cubed, for the tofu.
• For a spicier sauce, increase the soy sauce to ¼ cup and add a dash to ⅛ teaspoon of cayenne pepper.

Carrot Mold

Serve 6 or more

Grated carrots plus a few extra ingredients take on a special flavor in this molded delight that is sure to please the entire family.

> ½ cup unsalted margarine, softened
> 1 cup firmly packed brown sugar
> 1½ cups grated carrots
> 1 egg (graded large), well beaten
> 1 cup all-purpose flour
> ½ teaspoon baking powder
> ½ teaspoon salt

Preheat the oven to 350 degrees F.

In a mixing bowl, cream the margarine with the brown sugar. Add the grated carrots and the well-beaten egg. Sift together the dry ingredients. Add to the creamed mixture. Mix well. Spoon the mixture into a greased 5½-cup ring mold. Bake for 45 minutes, until done.

Scalloped Carrots and Celery

Serves 4

> 1 package (10 ounces) frozen diced carrots
> ¾ cup diced celery
> ¼ cup water
> ½ teaspoon salt (optional)

Topping:

> 2 tablespoons unsalted butter
> 2 tablespoons flour
> ½ teaspoon salt
> 1 cup milk
> ½ cup grated American cheese
> 2 tablespoons unsalted butter or margarine
> ⅓ cup breadcrumbs

Cook the vegetables in the water until tender. Drain.

Prepare a white sauce with the butter, flour, salt, and milk. In a small saucepan over low heat, melt the butter. Stir in the flour. When the mixture begins to bubble, gradually whisk in the milk. Cook, stirring until thick and smooth. Add the grated cheese. Stir and remove from the heat.

Preheat the oven to 450 degrees F. Place the vegetables in a 1½-quart casserole in alternate layers with the sauce. Melt the butter or margarine in a small skillet. Add the breadcrumbs and mix well. Sprinkle the buttered breadcrumbs on the vegetables. Bake for 15 minutes.

Carrot and Walnut Timbale

Serves 6

At a luncheon, I once was served a festive carrot timbale, and it did give the meal an air of celebration. The dish was baked and served in a small drum-shaped timbale mold. I use custard cups, which do the job well.

> 3 tablespoons unsalted margarine
> 2 tablespoons all-purpose flour
> 1 cup pareve milk
> 2 cups mashed cooked carrots
> 2 eggs (graded large), well beaten
> ¼ teaspoon cinnamon
> ½ teaspoon salt (optional)
> Margarine for the custard cups
> 6 teaspoons firmly packed brown sugar,
>   scant
> 3 to 4 teaspoons chopped walnuts

In a small saucepan over low heat, melt the margarine. Add the flour and blend well. Slowly add the pareve milk, whisking until smooth. Simmer for 5 minutes. Set aside.

Preheat the oven to 350 degrees F.

Place the mashed carrots in a mixing bowl. Add the eggs, cinnamon, and salt. Stir. Add the white sauce; blend all together very well. Grease 6 custard cups with margarine. Place a scant teaspoon of brown sugar in the bottom of each of the custard cups. Sprinkle with a portion of the chopped nuts. Spoon the carrot mixture into the dishes. Place the custard cups in a shallow baking pan half-filled with hot water. Bake for 30 minutes. Let the timbales rest for a few minutes before inverting and unmolding onto serving dishes.

Stuffed Cut Carrots

Serves 6

Peanut butter isn't only for sandwiches. Imaginative cooks have used it in many unexpected ways. Here, it is combined with carrots to add additional flavor and texture.

> 3 large carrots, peeled
> 3 tablespoons peanut butter of your choice,
>   creamy or chunky
> 2 cups soft breadcrumbs
> 1 small onion, finely minced
> 1 stalk celery, finely minced
> 1 tablespoon unsalted margarine
> Salt and black pepper to taste
> Dry breadcrumbs
> Grease for the pan

Preheat the oven to 350 degrees F. Lightly grease a baking sheet; set aside.

Cut the carrots in half lengthwise. Cook them in a small amount of boiling water until tender. Drain and let cool until they can be handled. Scoop out the centers of the carrots, leaving a shell. Mash the scooped-out carrot. Blend with the peanut butter and soft breadcrumbs.

In a small saucepan over medium heat, sauté the onion and celery in the tablespoon of margarine until soft but not browned. Add this to the carrot mixture. Season to taste with salt and pepper. Heap the filling into the prepared carrot shells. Sprinkle the tops with dry breadcrumbs. Arrange the carrots on the prepared baking sheets. Bake until the top is nicely browned.

Stuffed Beets

Serves 6

Two vegetables are twice as appealing as one—at least in this recipe. Here, beets share their red color with tiny succulent green peas, making a very attractive vegetable side dish.

>6 medium-sized beets
>Half of a 10-ounce package frozen petite
>   green peas
>1 tablespoon unsalted margarine, at room
>   temperature
>Salt and black pepper to taste

Wash the beets carefully. Don't break the skin. In a large pot, bring the water to a boil. Add the beets and cook until tender, anywhere from 30 minutes upward. Cool for a few moments, then slip off the skins. Cut the beets in half crosswise.

Cook the peas according to package directions. While the peas are cooking, hollow out the pulp from the beet halves, leaving a shell ¼-inch thick. (A grapefruit knife with a curved blade is ideal for scooping out the pulp of beets—or, for that matter, of tomatoes or any vegetable that is to be filled.) Coarsely chop the pulp. Drain the cooked peas and add 1 cup of peas to the chopped beets. Stir in the tablespoon of margarine. Season with salt and pepper. Spoon the filling into the beet shells. Serve hot.

Corn Pudding

Serves 9

Canned creamed corn makes this pudding quick and easy to prepare. I line my baking pan with aluminum foil, grease it, and then pour in the batter. It facilitates removing the pudding for packaging for the freezer.

>4 eggs (graded large)
>½ stick (¼ cup) unsalted margarine,
>   softened
>1 tablespoon sugar

3 heaping teaspoons flour
1 teaspoon baking powder
½ cup water
1 can (17 ounces) creamed corn

Preheat the oven to 425 degrees F. Grease a 9-inch-square baking pan; set aside.

In a mixing bowl, beat the eggs with the margarine. Add the sugar, flour, baking powder, and water. Lastly, beat in the corn. Pour the batter into the prepared pan. Bake for 1 hour, until the top is golden.

Eggplant Steaks

Serves 4 to 6

Slices of eggplant with an Italian topping are easy to prepare. Excellent with spaghetti and tomato sauce.

1 clove garlic, cut
Grease for the pan
1 large eggplant (1½ pounds)
¼ cup bottled Italian dressing
¼ to ½ teaspoon oregano or Italian
**   seasoning, to taste**
Garlic powder (optional)
Salt and freshly ground black pepper, to
**   taste**

Prepare a baking sheet by rubbing the cut clove of garlic over the pan and then greasing the pan lightly. Preheat the oven broiler.

Peel the eggplant and slice it lengthwise into ½-inch slices. Brush liberally on both sides with the Italian dressing. Sprinkle the top of each slice with the oregano or Italian seasoning. Arrange on the prepared baking sheet.

Broil on one side, then turn and broil the other side. The steaks should be nice and soft but not charred. Sprinkle with garlic powder, salt, and freshly ground pepper.

Vegetable-filled Eggplant Crêpes

Makes 8 to 10 crepes

Eggplant crêpes are filled with a vegetable stuffing and slices of cheese and then baked in a tomato sauce.

> 1 medium-sized eggplant (1 to 1¼ pounds)
> ½ cup oil, or more if necessary
> 1 cup all-purpose flour seasoned to taste
>   with salt and black pepper
> 3 eggs (graded large), beaten to mix
> ⅓ cup finely grated carrot
> ½ cup breadcrumbs
> ¼ cup chopped fresh parsley
> ¼ teaspoon onion powder
> ¼ cup water
> Mozzarella cheese, thinly sliced (1 slice per
>   crêpe)
> Italian seasoning
> 1 tablespoon grated mozzarella cheese
> 1 can (14¼ ounces) salt-free stewed
>   tomatoes or small peeled whole tomatoes
> ⅓ cup water

Peel the eggplant. Cut lengthwise into ¼-inch slices. In a large teflon-coated skillet over medium-high heat, heat a few tablespoons of the oil. Dredge a slice of eggplant in the flour seasoned with the salt and pepper; shake off excess. Dip in the egg, allowing the excees to drip back into the bowl. Dredge the eggplant in flour a second time, shaking off the excess. Add the coated eggplant slices to the skillet, a few at a time, and brown on both sides, adding more oil if necessary. Using a slotted spatula, remove the eggplant crêpes from the skillet and drain on paper towels. Repeat until all the eggplant has been cooked.

While the crêpes are draining and cooling, prepare the stuffing. Put the finely grated carrot in a bowl. Add the breadcrumbs, parsley, and onion powder. Mix together. Add the remaining beaten egg and ¼ cup of water. Stir well to blend. If too dry, add an additional teaspoon or more of water; the mixture should be spreadable.

Preheat the oven to 350 degrees F. Divide the filling among the eggplant slices. Spread the filling evenly over two-thirds of each slice, then top the filling with a thin slice of mozzarella cheese. Starting at a filled edge, roll up each crêpe into a cylinder. Arrange the rolls seam side down in a 6½ x 10¼-inch baking pan. Sprinkle with Italian seasoning and the grated mozzarella cheese. Pour the stewed tomatoes over and around the rolls. If using whole tomatoes, cut them into quarters or eighths. Add the ⅓ cup of water. Cover with foil and bake for 15 minutes, then uncover and continue baking for an additional 15 minutes, until hot and bubbly.

Variation:

Use seasoned breadcrumbs. After uncovering, arrange a thin slice of mozzarella cheese on each roll, then continue baking for an additional 15 minutes.

Stuffed Acorn Squash

Serves 4

Baked hidden within the shells of acorn squash is a delicious combination of three types of squash. The mixture is richly sweetened with brown sugar and sprinkled with chopped nuts for character. An unusual accompaniment for baked fish fillets.

>   2 small acorn squash
>   Boiling water
>   1 small butternut squash
>   3 tablespoons unsalted margarine, divided
>   1 small zucchini
>   2 to 4 tablespoons firmly packed brown
>   sugar
>   ¼ teaspoon cinnamon
>   ⅛ teaspoon nutmeg
>   3 tablespoons chopped pecans or walnuts

Preheat the oven to 375 degrees F.

Cut each acorn squash in half and remove the seeds. Place each half cut side down in a shallow baking dish. Pour in ½ inch of boiling water. Bake uncovered for 35 minutes. Drain the water. Turn over the squash, cut sides facing up. Let the squash cool, then carefully scoop out the pulp, leaving 4 firm shells intact. Mash the pulp and set aside.

Peel the butternut squash. Cut in half and remove the seeds. Cut into large cubes and steam or cook in boiling water over medium-high heat until fork-tender. Drain well. Mash the butternut pulp with 1 tablespoon of the margarine until smooth. Combine the acorn squash pulp with the mashed butternut pulp. Season with brown sugar to taste. Add the cinnamon and nutmeg. Set aside.

Preheat the oven to 375 degrees F. Peel and slice the zucchini squash. Sauté it in the 2 remaining tablespoons of margarine until tender.

Line each acorn squash shell with a few slices of the sautéed zucchini. Spoon the mashed mixture into the squash cavities lined with the zucchini. Sprinkle with chopped pecans or walnuts. Arrange on a baking sheet and bake uncovered for 30 minutes.

Pineapple Acorn Squash

Serves 6

A perfect accompaniment for a roast. A side dish that is at once sweet and savory.

> 3 medium-sized acorn squash (about 4
>   pounds)
> Salt (optional)
> 1 can (8¾ ounces) crushed pineapple,
>   drained
> 1 medium-sized apple, unpeeled and
>   chopped (1¼ cups)
> 2 tablespoons firmly packed brown sugar
> 2 tablespoons unsalted butter or margarine
> ⅛ teaspoon nutmeg

Preheat the oven to 350 degrees F.

Wash the squash. Cut in half and remove the seeds. Place the halves cut side down in a shallow baking pan. Pour in boiling water ½ inch deep. Bake for 40 to 45 minutes. Drain the water. Turn the halves cut side up. Sprinkle with a little salt if desired.

In a small mixing bowl, combine the pineapple, apple, and brown sugar. Divide the filling among the squash halves. Dot each with butter or margarine and sprinkle with nutmeg. Return to the oven and bake 30 minutes longer, until the squash is tender.

Glazed Squash Cubes

Serves 4

Whether you use butternut, hubbard, turban, or pumpkin squash, it is the glaze that gives this recipe its unique character, either sweet or savory.

> **2 to 2½ pounds butternut, hubbard, turban,**
>   **or pumpkin squash**
> **1 small onion, sliced (optional)**
> **½ teaspoon salt (optional)**
> **Hot water**
> **Sweet Cinnamon Glaze or Savory Garlic**
>   **Glaze**

With a sharp heavy knife, cut the squash in half. Remove the seeds and stringy portions. Cut into large pieces, peel, then cut into 1½-inch cubes. In a saucepan, place the squash cubes, onion, salt, and hot water to measure about ½-inch deep. Cover tightly and simmer until fork-tender, 12 to 15 minutes. While the squash is cooking, prepare the glaze of your choice.

Sweet Cinnamon Glaze:

> **3 tablespoons unsalted margarine or butter**
> **3 tablespoons firmly packed dark brown**
>   **sugar**
> **¼ teaspoon cinnamon**
> **Dash of nutmeg**
> **Salt and black pepper to taste**

In a small saucepan, combine all the ingredients. Cook over

medium heat until the margarine or butter are blended with other ingredients and the glaze is hot.

Savory Garlic Glaze:

> 1 to 2 large cloves garlic, minced
> ¼ cup oil
> 2 tablespoons minced fresh parsley
> 2 teaspoons lemon juice
> Salt and black pepper to taste

In a small saucepan, sauté the garlic in the oil until golden, stirring constantly. Do not let the garlic brown too much. Stir in the parsley, lemon juice, salt, and pepper. Blend together. When the squash is done, drain well. Arrange the squash cubes on a serving dish and spoon the glaze over all.

Baked Potato Accordion

You may think of the potato as just an everyday vegetable. Here the "lowly" potato is served in party dress and suddenly it is fancy fare.

> Baking potatoes, 1 per serving
> Melted butter, margarine, or oil
> Salt and white pepper to taste

Preheat the oven to 400 degrees F.

Select potatoes that are uniform in size. Peel them. Slice each potato crosswise into ¼-inch-thick slices, almost to the bottom, so that the slices are held together by a base of uncut potato. Wash thoroughly under cold water, dry well, then brush the cut surfaces with melted shortening and arrange in a well-greased baking pan. Bake for 1 to 1½ hours, depending on the size of the potatoes. Brush once or twice with the melted shortening during the baking. Sprinkle with salt and pepper toward the end of the baking.

Variation:

Cut the potato with a sectional apple corer and slicer, then proceed as above. If the potato is cut almost to the bottom, leaving a base to hold the "petals" together, the result will be very appealing. Prepare sweet potatoes the same way.

Chantilly Potatoes

Serves 4 to 6

In French culinary parlance, *chantilly* refers to sweetened whipped cream that has been flavored with vanilla. Here, however, the whipped cream is not sweetened, and it is flavored with grated cheese, salt, and pepper. Excellent with fish.

> **Butter or margarine for the pan**
> **3 cups mashed potatoes**
> **½ cup heavy cream**
> **½ cup grated Swiss cheese**
> **Salt and black pepper**

Preheat the oven to 350 degrees F.

Grease a shallow 1½-quart baking dish. Spread the mashed potatoes evenly over the bottom of the dish. In a chilled bowl with chilled beaters, whip the cream until stiff. Fold in the cheese. Add salt and pepper to taste. Spread the whipped cream over the potatoes. Bake for 25 to 30 minutes, until the top is delicately browned.

Vegetable Quiche

Serves 6 to 8

A quiche is essentially a pastry shell filled with a savory egg custard to which various ingredients are added. This is a marvelous one made with vegetables of your own choosing.

Dough:

> **1 teaspoon active dry yeast**
> **¼ cup milk, at room temperature**
> **1½ cups all-purpose flour**
> **1½ sticks (¾ cup) unsalted butter or margarine**
> **2 egg yolks (from eggs graded large)** ⟶

Custard:

> Vegetables of your choice: tomatoes, peeled
>   and sliced; green pepper rounds or strips;
>   onion rounds; mushrooms, sliced
> Flour and butter or margarine for
>   browning
> 1¼ cups milk
> 3 eggs (graded large)
> 1 cup grated cheese of your choice, such as
>   Swiss, mozzarella, or American
> 1 tablespoon flour

Dissolve the yeast in the milk. Place the flour in a large bowl and with a pastry blender cut the butter or margarine into the flour. Add the egg yolks and dissolved yeast. Mix well. Press the dough onto the bottom and 1 inch up the sides of a 9-inch spring-form pan. Set aside. Preheat the oven to 350 degrees F.

Prepare the vegetables by sautéing them in butter or margarine. Dip the tomatoes in flour before browning. Onions should be cooked until soft and translucent, not browned. The mushrooms should be cooked until their liquid is released. The vegetables and amount used is a matter of personal choice. When the vegetables have been browned, arrange them attractively in the shell.

In a large bowl, prepare the custard by combining the milk, eggs, cheese, and flour until well blended. Pour this mixture over the vegetables. Bake the quiche for 1 hour, until set. Serve with crusty bread and a salad.

Crustless Vegetable Casserole

Serves 6 to 8

If you are looking for something new to do with vegetables, try this crustless casserole. Made with eggs, pareve milk, and vegetables, it is eye-catching for meatless meals. It's quiche-related but not truly a quiche.

> Grease for the pan
> Cornflake crumbs

1½ tablespoons oil
1½ tablespoons all-purpose flour
1 cup pareve milk
½ cup mayonnaise
1½ tablespoons dry onion soup mix
3 eggs (graded large)
1 bag (20 ounces) frozen mixed vegetables,
    thawed

Preheat the oven to 350 degrees F. Grease and sprinkle with cornflake crumbs a 9 x 9-inch baking pan; set aside.

In a large mixing bowl, combine the oil, flour, pareve milk, mayonnaise, onion soup mix, and eggs. Mix well until all ingredients are thoroughly blended. Stir in the thawed, uncooked frozen vegetables. Transfer the vegetable mixture to the prepared pan. Sprinkle the top with cornflake crumbs. Bake for 40 to 45 minutes, until the top is golden brown.

Variations:

• For dairy meals, substitute dairy milk for the pareve milk and add ½ cup shredded mozzarella cheese to the vegetable mixture before transferring it to the baking pan.

• Bake in a deep 9-inch pastry crust. Sprinkle with ½ cup shredded mozzarella cheese before baking.

Green Bean Bake

Serves 8

The vegetable dish to serve when the meal calls for something different. Green beans prepared with water chestnuts, baked in a cheese sauce, and dressed with almonds and breadcrumbs makes an elegant oven vegetable dish.

3 packages (9 ounces each) frozen French-
    style green beans
½ stick (¼ cup) unsalted butter
2 tablespoons all-purpose flour
2 teaspoons minced onion
1½ teaspoons salt

———————→

⅛ teaspoon black pepper
2 cups milk
¼ cup grated Muenster or mozzarella
   cheese
1 teaspoon Worcestershire sauce
1 can (5 ounces) water chestnuts, drained
   and sliced
1 cup breadcrumbs
1 tablespoon butter, melted
¼ cup slivered almonds

Preheat the oven to 325 degrees F.

Cook the string beans according to package directions. Do not overcook. Drain. In a large saucepan, melt the butter. Add the flour, onion, salt, and pepper. Mix until smooth. Add the milk and cook over medium heat, stirring constantly until the mixture is thick and bubbly. Stir in the cheese and Worcestershire sauce. Remove from the heat. Blend in the beans and chestnuts. Transfer to a 2-quart casserole. Combine the breadcrumbs with the melted butter. Add the slivered almonds. Sprinkle the mixture on top. Bake uncovered for 50 to 60 minutes, until the top is nicely browned.

Split Pea Purée

Serves 4

This very popular European accompaniment has not achieved great popularity here, yet it is extraordinarily simple to prepare. Nice to serve with fowl or meat. I was once served an appetizer of sliced tongue on a background of green pea purée. A lovely color contrast.

1 heaping cup of split green peas
1 onion
1 dried mushroom (optional)
1 teaspoon sugar
1 tablespoon unsalted margarine, softened
1 tablespoon flour
Salt and black pepper to taste

In a 2-quart saucepan, place the split peas. Add cold water to cover by 2 inches. Soak overnight. The next day, drain and cover with fresh water, adding the onion, dried mushroom, and teaspoon of sugar. Bring to a boil, then simmer until tender and thick, about 1¼ hours. Transfer to a food processor or blender and purée. Return to the saucepan. Blend the softened margarine with the flour and add to the peas. Season to taste. Reheat, stirring gently.

Mushrooms Florentine

Serves 8

Spinach and sautéed mushrooms, under an umbrella of grated cheese, combine to make a marvelous nonmeat entrée.

> Grease for the pan
> 1 pound fresh mushrooms
> 2 packages (10 ounces each) frozen chopped
>   spinach, thawed
> 1 onion, finely chopped
> ½ stick (¼ cup) unsalted butter, divided
> 1 cup grated Cheddar cheese
> Garlic powder (optional)

Preheat the oven to 350 degrees F. Lightly grease a shallow 10-inch casserole; set aside.

Clean the mushrooms. Slice off the stems. In a skillet, sauté the stems and caps in 2 tablespoons of melted butter until brown. Brown the cap side of the mushrooms first. Drain the thawed spinach well. Season with the onion and remaining butter. Line the prepared casserole with the seasoned spinach. Sprinkle with ½ cup of the cheese. Arrange the mushrooms over the spinach, cap side up. Sprinkle with the remaining cheese. Season with garlic powder. Bake for 20 minutes, until the cheeese is melted.

Bavarian Red Cabbage

Serves 6 to 8

This sweet-sour cabbage-and-apple combo may be served either warm as a vegetable or at room temperature as a relish.

1 small head red cabbage (approximately
   2½ pounds)
2 tablespoons oil
1 medium-sized onion, diced
3 apples, peeled, cored, and sliced
¼ cup white vinegar
¼ cup firmly packed brown sugar
¼ cup water
½ teaspoon salt
Dash of freshly ground black pepper
½ teaspoon allspice (optional)

Shred the cabbage. Place in a colander and rinse. Drain well.
In a large saucepan or Dutch oven, heat the oil. Add the onion
and sauté until soft. Add the cabbage and cook over low heat for
about 10 minutes, stirring often until the cabbage begins to
wilt. Add the apples, vinegar, sugar, water, and seasonings. Mix
well. Cover the pot; lower the heat. Stir occasionally. Cook for
25 to 30 minutes. Taste and adjust the seasoning.

Rice-stuffed Green Peppers

Serves 6

Who says green peppers have to be stuffed with meat? These
green peppers filled with a tasty rice filling make an attractive
entrée as they rest on a bed of red tomato sauce.

1 cup raw rice
2 cups boiling water
1 large onion, diced
3 tablespoons unsalted margarine
2 eggs (graded large)
1 to 2 tablespoons sugar, to taste
Dash of black pepper
6 large green bell peppers, wide and chunky
1 can (15 ounces) tomato sauce
1 can water
1 tablespoon sugar

Cook the rice in the boiling water over low heat for about 20 minutes, until all the water is absorbed. While the rice is cooking, in a medium-sized skillet sauté the diced onion in the margarine until golden brown. Stir the onions into the cooked rice. Add the eggs and stir until well blended. Add the sugar and dash of pepper. Set aside while preparing the peppers.

Cut a "lid" off the stem end of each pepper; reserve the lids. Remove the seeds and whitish ribs. A curved grapefruit knife will serve you well to seed and derib the green pepper. Wash inside and out. In a large saucepan, parboil the peppers for 5 minutes. Drain well upside down before filling.

Fill the peppers with the rice mixture. Cover with the pepper lids. Arrange in a medium-sized saucepan. Any remaining filling can be spooned into the pot. Pour the can of tomato sauce into the pot. Rinse the can with water and pour around peppers. Cover and bring to a boil over medium heat. Correct the seasoning. Turn down the heat and simmer for about 45 minutes, until the peppers are tender and the sauce thickens.

Neat Balls

Serves 6

These are an excellent substitute for meatballs. Served on spaghetti with tomato sauce ladled over them, they look like the real thing.

> 1 pound firm tofu, drained and patted dry
> ½ cup seasoned or plain breadcrumbs
> ⅛ cup finely minced onion
> 1 clove garlic, finely minced, or ½ teaspoon
>   garlic powder
> 1 tablespoon chopped fresh parsley
> ⅛ teaspoon black pepper
> 1 tablespoon oil
> Grease for the baking sheet

Preheat the oven to 350 degrees F. Grease a baking sheet; set aside.

In a large bowl, combine all the ingredients. Using a blending fork, mix thoroughly. Then, in an electric blender, process one-fourth of the mixture at a time. Form the mixture into 1-inch balls. Arrange them on the greased baking sheet. Bake, turning them over once, for 20 to 30 minutes, until firm. Serve with spaghetti and topped with tomato sauce.

Spaghetti all' Olio e Aglio con Broccoli
(Spaghetti With Oil, Garlic, and Broccoli)

Serves 4 to 6

This Italian pasta recipe, given to my daughter Rena, is very generous in its use of garlic. A whole garlic bulb is sliced, simmered in oil, and then mixed with pasta and broccoli. It delights everyone, even those who proclaim a dislike for garlic.

> 1 whole bulb garlic
> ¾ cup oil
> 1 pound spaghetti #9
> 1 bag (21 ounces) frozen broccoli cuts (not chopped)
> 2 tablespoons chopped fresh parsley (optional)

Peel the garlic cloves and slice thinly. In a small skillet over low heat, heat the oil until hot. Add the garlic and sauté until golden. Do not let them get too brown. Remove from the heat.

Into a large pot with boiling water, place both the spaghetti and the frozen broccoli. Cook together until the spaghetti is *al dente* (tender but still firm to the tooth). Drain the spaghetti and broccoli mixture, reserving 1½ cups of the cooking liquid. Do not rinse under cool water.

Return the spaghetti to the pot or transfer to a large serving bowl. Immediately add the oil and garlic. Mix thoroughly and serve. If the mixture seems dry, add a small amount of the reserved cooking liquid. Serve at once, garnished with chopped parsley if desired.

Variation:
• To use fresh broccoli, cut the broccoli into small pieces.

Parboil for 3 minutes. Add the broccoli to the spaghetti to continue its cooking.

• For dairy meals, sprinkle your favorite grated cheese as a topping on each serving.

• To add additional color, cook one-cup bias-sliced carrots (thinly cut) in boiling water for 10 minutes. Drain and add to the cooked spaghetti.

Note: Two to 3 cloves of coarsely chopped garlic sautéed in ½ cup olive oil until golden brown and seasoned with salt and freshly ground black pepper makes a very nice sauce to serve with broiled fish. When I vacationed in Acapulco, this dressing was always served with broiled red snapper. It is a good substitute for the egg-rich *aioli*, a mayonnaise-like sauce redolent of garlic.

Zucchini Italiano

Serves 8

Here, zucchini are baked together with tomatoes and spicy Italian seasonings, resulting in a succulent side dish.

> **Grease for the pan**
> **¼ cup onion flakes or 1 medium-sized onion, minced**
> **¼ cup water**
> **2 pounds zucchini**
> **4 medium-sized tomatoes (about 1½ pounds)**
> **1 to 2 teaspoons salt, to taste**
> **1 teaspoon dried oregano**
> **½ teaspoon freshly ground black pepper**
> **½ to 1 teaspoon garlic powder or 1 clove garlic, minced, to taste**
> **2 tablespoons oil**

Preheat the oven to 350 degrees F. Grease a 6 x 10 x 2-inch casserole; set aside.

Combine the onion flakes with the water and let stand for 8 minutes. In the meantime, slice the zucchini crosswise into ½-inch slices. Cut the tomatoes into ½-inch slices. Arrange a layer of zucchini in the prepared casserole. Cover with a layer of the tomatoes. Combine the reconstituted onions with the seasonings and sprinkle half over the zucchini and tomatoes. Top with the remaining zucchini and tomato slices. Brush with oil and sprinkle with the remaining seasonings. Cover and bake for 25 to 30 minutes.

Variation:

Bake for 20 minutes, uncover, and sprinkle with grated cheese. Cover, return to the oven, and continue baking for an additional 10 to 15 minutes.

Zucchini Squares

Serves 8 or more

Zucchini baked in an Italian-seasoned biscuit mix. Serve as an hors d'oeuvre or as a vegetable sidedish.

> **Grease for the pan**
> **4 eggs (graded large)**
> **3 tablespoons oil**
> **½ cup finely chopped onion**
> **2 tablespoons chopped fresh parsley**
> **½ teaspoon onion powder**
> **½ teaspoon Italian seasoning**
> **1 clove garlic, minced**
> **Dash of black pepper**
> **1 cup biscuit mix**
> **3 cups thinly sliced zucchini**

Preheat the oven to 350 degrees F. Lightly grease a 9 x 13 x 2-inch baking pan; set aside.

In a mixing bowl, beat the eggs with the oil. Add the chopped onions, parsley, and seasonings. Beat in the biscuit mix. Stir in the zucchini. Spread the batter evenly in the prepared pan. Bake for 40 minutes or until the top is golden. Cut into small squares to serve as hors d'oeuvres or into larger squares to serve as a side dish.

Variation:

Add ½ cup grated parmesan or other cheese of your choice to the batter before adding the zucchini. Mix well.

Pasta-free Noodle and Cottage Cheese Custard

Serves 12

Here, strands of spaghetti squash give the illusion of noodles. When I worked as Passover food stylist for a very large New England dairy company, I developed this recipe. It was very well received and is especially good throughout the year.

> **Grease for the pan**
> **1 large spaghetti squash (about 4 pounds)**
> **¼ cup raisins**
> **¼ cup orange juice**
> **2 teaspoons grated orange rind**
> **4 eggs (graded large)**
> **½ to ⅔ cup sugar, to taste**
> **½ teaspoon salt**
> **2 cups milk**
> **1½ pounds cottage cheese**

Preheat the oven to 375 degrees F. Grease a 9 x 13 x 2-inch baking pan; set aside.

Boil the spaghetti squash for about 45 minutes, until a fork will pierce the flesh easily. Set aside to cool while preparing the cheese mixture.

In a small cup, combine the raisins, orange juice, and orange rind; set aside. In a large mixing bowl, beat the eggs well. Add the sugar (amount depending on personal preference), salt, and milk. Stir together the cheese and the plumped-up raisins with the orange juice and rind. Beat until blended.

Cut the squash in half. Discard the seeds and center fibers. Gently pull out the strands of squash from half of the squash and arrange the strands to cover the bottom of the baking pan. Pour the cheese mixture over the squash. Arrange the squash strands from the remaining half on top of the cheese batter. Bake for about 1 hour, until puffed and brown. Serve warm. A dollop of sour cream makes a nice accompaniment.

Pizza in a Tomato Shell

Serves 4

A very imaginative way to prepare tomatoes. A lower-in-calories substitute for the traditional pizza.

> **Grease for the pan**
> **4 medium-sized tomatoes, at room**
> **   temperature**
> **1 cup diced mozzarella cheese**
> **3 tablespoons dry breadcrumbs, divided**
> **¾ teaspoon dried basil**
> **¼ teaspoon dried oregano**
> **½ teaspoon salt (optional)**
> **⅛ teaspoon black pepper**
> **2 teaspoons vegetable oil**

Grease an 8-inch-square baking pan and set aside. Preheat the oven to 350 degrees F.

Cut a thin slice from the stem end of each tomato. With a grapefruit knife or spoon, scoop out the tomato pulp, leaving a ¼-inch-thick shell. Coarsely chop ½ cup of the pulp; discard the rest. Arrange the tomato shells, blossom end down, in the prepared pan. In a small bowl, combine the chopped tomatoes, cheese, and 2 tablespoons of the breadcrumbs. Add the herbs and the salt and pepper. Stir to blend. Spoon into the tomato shells. Combine the oil with the remaining tablespoon of breadcrumbs. Sprinkle over each tomato. Bake uncovered until the cheese melts, about 15 minutes.

8

Hearty Accompaniments

Kugels, Casseroles & Other Sidelights

"*Thou shalt eat bread without scarceness; thou shalt not lack anything. . . . Thou shalt eat and be satisfied*" (Deuteronomy 8:9-10).

Vine-ick Kugel

Serves 8 or more

A *kugel* (pudding) may be made from a wide variety of ingredients. Countless hours were spent trying to duplicate the "vine-ick [winery] kugel" that was one of my mother-in-law's notorious recipes. To this day I fail to see why this family favorite was so named but, the name notwithstanding, the kugel is delicious and makes a tasteful alternative to pastry. To be appreciated, it must be eaten warm.

Filling:

6 ounces pitted prunes, cut into small
    pieces
¼ to ⅓ cup raisins
⅓ cup breadcrumbs, scant
½ cup finely chopped nuts
¾ cup sugar
Dash of ginger
½ cup oil, divided

Dough:

1 egg (graded large)

2 tablespoons oil
1 tablespoon vinegar
¾ to 1 cup all-purpose flour

Measure the filling ingredients into individual dishes. Set aside.

Pour 3 tablespoons of oil into an 8-inch round pyrex baking dish. Set aside.

To prepare the dough, beat the egg with the 2 tablespoons of oil and the vinegar. Add enough flour to make a soft dough that can be rolled out. Remove about ⅛ of the dough and set aside. On a lightly floured pastry cloth, roll out the remaining dough into a very thin rectangle measuring 10 x 16 inches.

Brush the dough with 2 tablespoons of the oil. Spread the cut prunes and raisins over the dough. Sprinkle with the bread-crumbs, chopped nuts, sugar, and a light sprinkling of ginger. Drizzle a generous tablespoon of oil over the filling. Lift up the end of the cloth nearest you and make the dough fold over the filling. Continue raising the cloth so that the dough continues to fold over itself but only until the filled dough is about 1½ inches high. Cut the roll of filled dough off from the remaining dough. Cut the roll diagonally into sections that will fit across the prepared baking dish.

Continue this process until all the dough has been rolled up. When all the rolls have been arranged in the pan, score the tops at equal intervals. Brush the tops with 1 tablespoon of oil. It may be necessary to layer the rolls so they will all fit in the baking dish. Now roll the reserved piece of dough into a large circle and place it over the cut rolls in the pan to serve as a cover. Place the baking pan in the oven at the lowest setting for 2 or more hours, until nicely brown. Remove the pastry cover and enjoy eating the cover as well as the baked kugel beneath it.

Zucchini Kugel

Serves 6 to 8

My daughter Naomi, who is always experimenting, made this zucchini kugel and added a commercial matzo ball mix. It resulted in a very interesting side dish. Matzo meal was merely sprinkled on top. A nice kugel for Passover.

Grease for the pan
4 medium-sized zucchini, about 2½ pounds
1 medium-sized onion
¼ cup oil
4 eggs (graded large)
1 envelope (2½ ounces) matzo ball mix
Salt and black pepper to taste
Matzo meal

Preheat the oven to 350 degrees F. Lightly grease a 7½ x 11½-inch baking pan; set aside.

On the coarse side of the grater, grate the zucchini and onion into a bowl. Add the oil. Beat in the eggs. Lastly, stir in the matzo ball mix and seasonings. Transfer to the prepared baking pan. Sprinkle matzo meal on top. Bake for 30 to 40 minutes, until golden.

Spinach Kugel

Serves 6 or more

A meatless, protein-rich main dish. It's made with two cheeses: cottage cheese and Cheddar.

Grease for the pan
1 pound uncreamed cottage cheese
6 eggs (graded large)
2 packages (10 ounces each) frozen chopped
spinach, thawed
3 tablespoons farina
½ pound Cheddar cheese, grated
Salt and black pepper to taste

Preheat the oven to 350 degrees F. Grease a 7½ x 11½-inch baking pan; set aside.

Pass the cottage cheese through a sieve. Beat in the eggs. Drain the chopped spinach well. Add it to the cheese and eggs. Stir in the farina and the grated cheese. Transfer the mixture to the prepared pan. Bake for 45 minutes, until done.

Potatonik

There are many variations on the potato kugel. There are those made with raw potatoes, cooked potatoes, or a combination of both. The potatonik, a heavy-textured Old World dish, is really a mixture of a bread dough and a potato kugel made from raw potatoes. To serve, it is often cut into thick slices, and the crust is rubbed with cloves of fresh garlic. Wonderful with meat in place of potatoes or bread.

> 1 package active dry yeast
> ¼ cup warm water (110 to 115 degrees F.)
> 3 eggs (graded large)
> ½ to 1 teaspoon salt, to taste
> ¼ teaspoon white pepper
> ⅓ cup oil
> 4 pounds potatoes
> 1 large onion
> ¼ teaspoon cream of tartar
> 2½ cups all-purpose flour
> Oil for baking pan

Dissolve the yeast in the water and set aside. In a large mixing bowl, beat the eggs well. Add the salt, pepper, and oil. Beat together. With a hand grater or a food processor, grate the potatoes along with the onion. Sprinkle with the cream of tartar. Mix. Add the grated potatoes and onion to the beaten egg mixture. Blend very well. Beat in the flour. Lastly, add the yeast. Mix vigorously to blend very well. Cover the bowl and set aside in a warm draft-free place for 1 hour.

Preheat the oven to 400 degrees F. Coat a 9 x 13-inch baking pan with oil. Set the pan in the oven to heat. When hot, pour the potato mixture into the heated oil in the pan. Bake for 30 minutes, then turn the heat down to 350 degrees F. Continue baking for an additional 30 minutes, until a lovely golden brown. Remove from the oven, pour off any excess oil and remove the potatonik from the pan. Set on a rack to permit air to circulate around it.

Note: I line my baking pan with aluminum foil and then oil the foil. I find that this makes it easier to remove the potatonik from the pan. Peel down the foil from the sides and bottom.

Kluski Noodle Kugel

Serves 6 to 8

Sadie Schoen, a member of the committee that plans menus and prepares the food that is served at various Agudas Achim Sisterhood functions, once recommended this kluski noodle pudding instead of an ordinary noodle kugel. It received rounds of applause at a donor dinner.

This pasta and vegetable kugel is delicious served with baked fish or roasted meat.

> **8 ounces kluski noodles**
> **1 package (10 ounces) frozen chopped broccoli**
> **½ stick (¼ cup) unsalted margarine, divided**
> **3 eggs (graded large)**
> **1 cup pareve cream**
> **1 package dry onion soup mix**

Preheat the oven to 350 degrees F.

Cook the noodles according to package directions; drain. Cook the chopped broccoli; drain. In a medium-sized mixing bowl, beat together the eggs, cream, and onion soup mix. Add the drained noodles and broccoli. Stir to blend.

Melt half of the margarine in a 7 x 11-inch baking pan. Add to the noodle mixture and stir. Pour the mixture into the pan. Dot the mixture with the remaining margarine. Bake covered for 30 minutes. Uncover and continue baking for an additional 30 minutes. Freezes very well.

Jerusalem Noodle Kugel

Serves 6 to 8

Those who have spent time in Israel will recognize this as a popular Israeli noodle pudding. It is referred to as a Jerusalem kugel because it is popular among the chassidic Jews of Jerusalem. The liberal seasoning is an enjoyable contrast to the subtle sweetness of the caramelized sugar used.

Grease for the pan
½ pound thin eggs noodles
⅓ cup sugar
⅓ cup oil
3 eggs (graded large), lightly beaten
Salt, and black pepper, onion powder, and
    garlic powder

Preheat the oven to 350 degrees F. Lightly grease a 9 x 13-inch baking pan; set aside.

Cook the noodles according to package directions. Drain and set aside. In a small saucepan, combine the sugar and oil. Cook over low heat until caramelized. Watch carefully—the sugar burns easily. As soon as it is a nice deep caramel color, add the caramelized sugar to the noodles and stir until all the noodles are coated. Add the beaten eggs and season liberally with salt, pepper, onion powder, and garlic powder. Pour the noodles into the prepared pan and bake for about 45 minutes, until the top is golden brown and crispy.

Soufflé-like Broccoli Bake

Serves 8 to 10

No need to worry about this Broccoli Bake falling when removed from the oven. The very well beaten eggs combined with a roux and mayonnaise make for a dish whose texture is very similar to a soufflé.

1 deep 9-inch pie shell
2 packages (10 ounces each) frozen chopped
    broccoli
1½ tablespoons unsalted margarine
1½ tablespoons flour
½ cup pareve milk
½ cup mayonnaise
1 tablespoon dry onion soup mix
3 eggs (graded large), well beaten
Salt and black pepper to taste

Prebake the pie shell for 5 to 6 minutes in a preheated 350-degree F. oven. Cool.

Cook the frozen chopped broccoli according to package directions. Set into a strainer to drain well while preparing the roux. In a heavy saucepan, melt the margarine. Mix in the flour well. Gradually add the pareve milk until the mixture is quite smooth. Boil gently until thick, stirring all the time. Remove the pan from the heat. Add the mayonnaise, onion soup mix, and beaten eggs. Season with salt and pepper, bearing in mind that the onion soup mix has salt in it. Lastly, fold in the well-drained chopped broccoli. Put half of the mixture into a blender jar. Cover and process until smooth. Empty into a bowl. Repeat with the remaining mixture. Combine with the first mixture.

Transfer the broccoli mixture into the prepared pie shell and bake for 40 minutes, until set.

Variations:

• Lightly grease a 7½ x 11½-inch baking pan. Coat with a thin layer of cornflake crumbs. Transfer the chopped broccoli mixture to the greased pan. Sprinkle cornflake crumbs lightly on top. Processing the broccoli mixture in the blender may be eliminated, but the texture will not be the same.

• Bake the mixture in individually greased muffin pans. Yields 12 muffins.

• Bake in individual 3½-inch tart shells. Yields 14 to 16.

• Chopped spinach may be substituted for chopped broccoli

Prune and Potato Tzimmes

Serves 6 to 8

Tzimmes is a traditional Jewish holiday dish. In many homes, it is served as a side dish at Sabbath meals.

A tzimmes (a vegetable or fruit stew) can consist of a variety of ingredients. These may include meat, carrots, sweet potatoes, white potatoes, a dumpling, or a dried fruit, notably prunes.

The traditional tzimmes is usually sweet and may be sweetened with sugar or honey. A canned fruit, such as crushed pineapple with its juice, adds to the sweetness of the dish.

2 tablespoons vegetable shortening or oil
3 pounds meat (brisket, flanken, or
   chicken)
1 onion, diced
1 teaspoon salt
¼ teaspoon black pepper
Water
5 large carrots
5 medium-sized sweet potatoes (optional)
3 small white potatoes (optional)
1 pound prunes, pitted and rinsed
¼ cup honey (optional)
½ cup firmly packed brown sugar
½ teaspoon cinnamon

In a Dutch oven or heavy pot, melt the shortening or heat the oil. Cut the meat into 6 or 8 pieces. Sear the meat with the onions until the meat is nicely browned. Sprinkle with the salt and pepper. Add water to cover and cook over low heat for 1 hour.

Pare and cut the carrots and potatoes into thick slices. Add the vegetables and rinsed prunes. Season with the honey, brown sugar, and cinnamon. Cover the pot with lid askew and cook over low heat for 2 hours or until the meat is tender. Taste and adjust the seasoning, adding more brown sugar for a sweeter tzimmes. Check occasionally during the cooking to see if more water is needed. Small amounts of boiling water may be added as required to prevent scorching. The tzimmes should not be soupy. Do not stir it, just gently shake the pot occasionally to prevent sticking.

Variations:

• For a vegetarian dish, omit the meat.
• After cooking the tzimmes as above, it may then be baked, but first it should be thickened. To do so, prepare an *einbren* (roux), as follows: In a skillet, brown 2 tablespoons of flour in 2 tablespoons of melted fat. Stir in about ½ cup of liquid from the cooking pot with the meat. Stir to make a smooth mixture. Pour the mixture over the tzimmes and shake the pot gently to distribute the *einbren*. Then turn into a casserole and bake at 350 degrees F. till brown on top.

Carrot-Pineapple Tzimmes

Serves 4 to 6

An easy-to-prepare tzimmes pairing carrots with Hawaiian pineapple.

> 2 cups sliced carrots (see method)
> 2 tablespoons seedless raisins
> 2 cups water
> ¼ teaspoon salt
> 1 tablespoon sugar
> 1/16 teaspoon ginger
> 1 can (8 ounces) Hawaiian pineapple tidbits
>   in heavy syrup, drained, ¼ cup syrup
>   reserved
> 2 tablespoons cornstarch
> 2 tablespoons honey

Use large carrots. Scrape and slice ¼-inch thick. In a medium-sized saucepan with a cover, combine the carrots and raisins with the water. Add the salt, sugar, and ginger. Cover and cook until the carrots are soft, about 20 minutes. Mix the cornstarch with the pineapple syrup. Add to the carrots. Cook until thickened, then stir in the drained pineapple and honey. Heat through.

Cranberry-Sweet Potato Tzimmes

Serves 12

Cranberries seem to be as much a part of Thanksgiving as turkey. For an unusual accompaniment, prepare this cranberry tzimmes. It is a large recipe that will adequately serve many guests. Freezes well.

> 1 can (16 ounces) sliced cling peaches
> 1 tablespoon cornstarch
> 1/3 cup liquid brown sugar or ½ cup firmly
>   packed brown sugar and ¼ cup water
> 1 can (8 ounces) whole cranberry sauce
> ½ teaspoon cinnamon
> 2 tablespoon unsalted margarine
> 2 cans (16 ounces each) yams, drained

Drain the peaches, reserving the syrup. Dissolve the cornstarch in ¼ cup of the peach syrup; set aside. In a large skillet, combine the remaining peach syrup with the brown sugar, cranberry sauce, cinnamon, and margarine. Heat over medium heat until the margarine has melted. Add the cornstarch mixture. Cook and stir until the mixture thickens.

Arrange the peaches and yams in a 9 x 13-inch baking pan. Pour the cranberry mixture over all. Cover and let marinate overnight in the refrigerator. Heat covered in a 325-degree F. oven until thoroughly warmed through.

Hungarian Cabbage and Noodle Flakes
Serves 4 to 6

Hungarians love noodles. They eat them plain; in combination with meat (as in Hungarian goulash, which is served on a bed of broad noodles); tossed with sour cream and cottage cheese; or in combination with a vegetable (such as cabbage or potatoes).

> **Grease for the pan**
> **1 medium-sized head of cabbage (about 2 pounds)**
> **1 teaspoon salt**
> **½ stick (¼ cup) unsalted butter or margarine**
> **½ to 1 cup minced onion**
> **8 ounces noodle flakes**
> **Dash of black pepper**

Preheat the oven to 375 degrees F. Grease a 2-quart casserole and set aside.

Core and wash the cabbage. In a food processor coarsely chop the cabbage; or grate it by hand using the large holes of the grater. Sprinkle with salt and set aside, covered, for 1 to 2 hours. Drain and squeeze out excess liquid.

In a large skillet over medium heat, melt the butter or margarine. Add the minced onion and cook until limp. Add the cabbage and sauté until golden brown.

Cook the noodles according to package directions. Drain and

rinse, then combine the noodles with the cabbage. Season with black pepper. Transfer to the prepared casserole and set into the oven until brown on top, approximately 20 to 30 minutes. Serve hot.

Fasolyes Mit Tayglach
(Beans and Noodle Flakes)

Serves 6

This interesting blend of beans and pasta would never have occurred to me, but it was a combination my mother would occasionally serve as a substitute for potatoes. I have subsequently learned that beans and a grain make a good protein combination. Interestingly, *fagioli e pasta*, beans and a pasta, is a favorite Italian dish.

> 1 cup navy beans
> ½ teaspoon salt
> 4 ounces tayglach (noodle flakes)
> 2 onions, finely diced
> 3 tablespoons unsalted margarine
> Salt and black pepper to taste

Sort and rinse the beans. Place them in a 2-quart saucepan. Cover with cold water by 2 inches; soak overnight. The next day, drain and add water to cover; add the ½ teaspoon of salt to the water. Simmer covered (do not boil) from 30 minutes up to as long as 1 hour, until tender. Drain.

In a medium-sized saucepan, cook the noodle flakes according to the package directions. Simultaneously, in a medium-sized skillet over medium heat, sauté the onions in the margarine until golden brown.

Drain the cooked flakes and combine with the cooked beans and sautéed onions. Mix well. Adjust the seasoning, adding pepper and additional salt if necessary.

Beans 'n Barley

Serves 4 to 6

As a child, I recall singing, "Oats, peas, beans, and barley." Here is a side dish of peas, beans, and barley—but no oats. This is a hearty side dish for any roast meat.

> ½ cup kidney or pinto beans
> 4½ cups water, divided
> ½ cup barley
> 2 tablespoons olive oil
> ½ cup chopped onions
> ½ cup sliced mushrooms
> 1 cup frozen green peas or chopped broccoli
>   or spinach
> Salt to taste
> 2 teaspoons lemon juice
> ⅛ teaspoon dried rosemary
> ½ cup water

Wash and sort the beans. Place in a 2-quart saucepan. Cover with cold water by 2 inches and soak overnight. Alternatively, cover the pot and bring to a boil. Let boil for 1 minute; remove from the heat and let soak for 2 hours. Bring to a boil again, reduce the heat, and simmer with the lid ajar for 1 hour. Add the barley and continue simmering.

Meanwhile, heat the oil in a skillet over medium heat. Add the onions and mushrooms and sauté until the onions are golden. Add the green peas or chopped broccoli or spinach. Add the salt. Stir for a few minutes. Add the lemon juice, rosemary, and ½ cup water. Cover and simmer for about 15 minutes.

After the barley has been cooking for 40 minutes, check to see if the beans are tender. Add the vegetable mixture and a bit more water if necessary. Stir well and cook for about 10 minutes to blend the flavors.

Rice and Noodle Casserole

Serves 6 to 8

Browning the noodles first gives the casserole a superb flavor. Just as you would purchase thin noodles to cook as an accompaniment to chicken soup or stroganoff noodles for beef stroganoff, be sure to purchase kluski noodles for this recipe. You will note that their cut and texture is different.

> 1 bag (8 ounces) kluski noodles
> ½ stick (¼ cup) unsalted margarine
> ½ cup raw rice
> 1 package dry onion soup mix
> 2¼ cups hot water
> 1 can (4 ounces) sliced mushrooms, drained

Preheat the oven to 350 degrees F.

In a skillet, melt the margarine. Add the uncooked noodles and stir constantly until lightly browned. Mix the onion soup with the water. Combine the rice with the onion soup mixture; add the drained mushrooms. Stir. Add the mixture to the browned noodles. Transfer to a 2-quart casserole. Cover and bake for 1 hour. Stir once during baking time.

Variations:

•One cup of chicken broth may be substituted for 1 cup of the water. Serve garnished with paprika or parsley flakes.

•Omit the noodles and increase the rice to 1 cup. Add a few grains of freshly ground black pepper.

Orzo and Rice Pilaf

Serves 5 or 6

Orzo, a Greek pasta that resembles rice, is combined with actual rice. The two mingle together as they are sautéed to a toasty golden brown.

> 2 tablespoons unsalted margarine
> 1 onion, finely diced
> ⅔ cup raw rice
> ½ cup orzo

3 cups water
1 teaspoon dry onion soup mix, or more to
    taste

In a medium-sized saucepan, melt the margarine. Add the onion, rice, and orzo. Sauté, stirring often until toasty golden. Bring the water to a boil. Add to the rice-orzo combination. Add the onion soup mix. Cover tightly and simmer for 20 minutes or until all the liquid is absorbed.

Variations:

•For variety, add ¼ pound fresh mushrooms that have been sliced and sautéed in margarine. Or add a 4-ounce can of sliced mushrooms, drained.

•For a meat meal, chicken broth may be substituted for the water.

•For a dairy meal, serve the pilaf richly sprinkled with the grated cheese of your choice.

•Serve cloaked with tomato sauce.

Orange Rice

Serves 4 to 6

Rice simmered in orange juice serves as a flavorful alternative to pasta or potatoes.

½ stick (¼ cup) unsalted margarine
⅔ cup thinly sliced celery
3 tablespoons finely cut onion
1¼ cups water
1 cup orange juice
2 tablespoons grated orange rind
Salt and black pepper to taste
1 cup raw rice

In a medium-sized saucepan over medium heat, melt the margarine. Add the celery and onion. Stir and sauté until the celery is tender and the onion translucent. Add the water, orange juice, orange rind, salt, and pepper. Bring to a boil. Stir in the rice. Lower the heat, cover the saucepan, and simmer for 20 to 25 minutes.

Kasha Italienne

Serves 6 or more

When I was introduced to the macrobiotic diet, I was delighted to learn that it stresses the use of whole grains, kasha (buckwheat groats) among them. Kasha is closely identified with Russian cooking. In Jewish cooking, kasha has long been considered a fine substitute for rice, potatoes, and pasta. Its versatility knows no bounds.

Kasha Italienne is a savory dish featuring kasha, or course, and a host of vegetables.

> 1 large onion
> 1 medium-sized green pepper
> 2 stalks celery
> 3 tablespoons unsalted margarine
> ½ pound mushrooms, sliced
> 1 clove garlic, mashed
> 4 medium-sized zucchini, scraped and sliced
> 2 medium-sized tomatoes
> 3 cups cooked kasha

Dice the onion. Seed, derib, then dice the green pepper. Slice the celery stalks. In a medium-sized skillet, melt the margarine. Sauté the cut vegetables until translucent, not browned. Add the mushrooms, mashed garlic, and sliced zucchini. Cook until the squash is soft, stirring and turning several times. Add the chopped tomatoes and cook for 5 minutes. Stir in the cooked kasha. Mix well. Taste-check for seasoning.

Variation:

Add ½ cup of grated cheese to the mixture. Pour into a greased 2-quart casserole. Sprinkle the top with a little more cheese and dot with butter or margarine. Cover and bake in a 350-degree F. oven for 30 to 40 minutes.

Carrot Stuffing

Makes 3 cups

Roast chicken or roast turkey just isn't complete without a delicious flavorful stuffing. Try this very different carrot stuffing.

> 1 cup sifted all-purpose flour
> 1 teaspoon baking powder
> ½ teaspoon salt
> ½ teaspoon ginger
> ½ teaspoon nutmeg
> ½ cup wheat germ
> 1 cup dry breadcrumbs
> ½ cup chopped pecans or walnuts
> ½ stick (¼ cup) unsalted margarine
> ½ cup firmly packed brown sugar
> 1 egg (graded large)
> 1 cup finely shredded carrots
> 3 tablespoons finely chopped parsley
>   (optional)

Into a medium-sized bowl, sift together the flour, baking powder, salt, ginger, and nutmeg. Stir in the wheat germ, breadcrumbs, and nuts. In a separate mixing bowl, cream together the margarine and brown sugar; add the egg and mix well. Add the carrots and parsley. Blend together. Lightly stir in the sifted dry ingredients until combined. Stuff the bird.

Or you may bake this stuffing as a kugel in a greased 9-inch-square pan. Bake covered at 350 degrees F. for 20 minutes. Uncover and bake for an additional 10 minutes, until nicely browned.

Mamaliga

(Yellow Cornmeal Mush)

Serves 4 to 6

Mamaliga is to the Rumanians what pasta is to the Italians or potatoes are to the Irish. Having been brought up by Rumanian parents, it is not surprising that the famous cornmeal dish made frequent appearances at our table—whether at breakfast as a cereal or at lunch partnered with sour cream and brinza (the Rumanian equivalent of feta cheese). At supper, mamaliga was served as a substitute for potatoes or pasta. It is a fine accompaniment to a fricassee or stew.

> **4 cups cold water**
> **1 cup yellow cornmeal**
> **1 teaspoon salt**

In a heavy 2-quart saucepan, bring the water and salt to a boil over high heat. Pour in the cornmeal very slowly, stirring constantly to prevent lumps. Reduce the heat. Cover partially and simmer for 10 to 12 minutes, stirring occasionally until all the water has been absorbed and the mamaliga is very thick. Add additional salt if desired. Serve with butter.

Or you may proceed as follows: Pour the cooked mamaliga into a well-buttered 8-inch-square pan. Refrigerate until cold. Turn out onto a piece of wax paper. Cut into ½-inch slices. Arrange a layer of the mamaliga slices in the buttered pan, drizzle with ¼ cup melted unsalted margarine or butter, sprinkle with ⅛ to ¼ cup of grated Swiss or parmesan cheese. Cover with a second layer of mamaliga slices and sprinkle the top with an additional ⅛ to ¼ cup grated cheese. Bake in a 375-degree F. oven until thoroughly heated through and nicely browned.

Alternate Method:

Stir the cornmeal into 1 cup of cold water until smooth. Bring 3 cups of water and 1 teaspoon salt to a boil. Gradually pour in the cornmeal mixture, stirring constantly. Cook over low heat until the mamaliga is thoroughly cooked.

Israeli Vegetable Couscous

Serves 6 to 8

Couscous, the national dish of Morocco, finds itself just as comfortable in the Israeli kitchen. Couscous (grain made from semolina), can be served in a variety of ways. This side-dish version is prepared with carrots, green peas, and mushrooms. It makes an eye-appealing accompaniment for fish, chicken, or meat and is a superb stand-in for potatoes.

> **3 tablespoons unsalted margarine**
> **1 medium-sized onion, finely chopped**
> **2 small carrots, peeled and finely diced**
> **Half of a 10-ounce package of frozen tiny**
>   **green peas**
> **Boiling water**
> **1 package (8 ounces) toasted Israeli couscous**
> **½ teaspoon dried parsley flakes**
> **½ teaspoon Mrs. Dash seasoning**
> **Salt and black pepper to taste**
> **1 can (4 ounces) tiny button mushrooms,**
>   **drained**

In a medium-sized saucepan, melt the margarine. Add the finely chopped onion and sauté until golden. Simultaneously, in a small saucepan cook the chopped carrots and peas in boiling water to cover. Cook until tender, but do not overcook. Drain and set aside. Add the couscous to the golden onions and sauté until browned. Add boiling water to cover plus 1 extra cup. Add the seasonings. Simmer covered for 6 to 8 minutes, until most of the water is absorbed. Combine the drained carrots, peas, and mushrooms with the couscous. Stir to blend over low heat until heated through.

Traditional Kishka

Serves 6 to 8

Kishka, often referred to as stuffed derma, is beef casing (the intestine of the animal) that is filled with a savory filling and is then parboiled and roasted. This classic delicacy is most frequently served as an appetizer or alongside roast meat or chicken as a side dish.

Today, kishka is more often than not prepared in a much simpler fashion. A filling is simply encased in plastic or wrapped in aluminum foil and then cooked or baked. Here is the real thing.

> 1 beef casing, approximately 12 inches long
>   (available from your butcher)
> 1 cup sifted all-purpose flour
> 2 tablespoons matzo meal or fine
>   breadcrumbs
> ¼ teaspoon salt
> ¼ teaspoon black pepper
> ½ teaspoon paprika
> 1 onion, grated
> ½ cup melted vegetable shortening or ½
>   cup finely chopped beef suet (fat from
>   the casing may be used)
> Oil for roasting

Wash the beef casing well with cold water. Turn it inside out and scrape off the excess fat. Wash again, this time with warm water. Dry the casing thoroughly. Sew up one end of the tube. The casing is stuffed inside out.

In a medium-sized mixing bowl, combine the filling ingredients. Blend thoroughly. Spoon the stuffing into the casing, gradually easing it down. Fill the casing loosely because the filling expands and the casing shrinks during cooking. Sew up the open end. Rinse off any filling that has clung to the outer surface. Drop the filled kishka into a large pot of boiling water for 2 minutes to shrink the casing.

To cook, massage the kishka with oil and roast it alongside poultry or a beef roast until nicely browned, turning occasionally. Slice to serve.

Alternate Method:

Cook in a pot of boiling water for 1 hour. Transfer to a bed of sliced onions in a shallow roasting pan to which fat has been added. Roast in a 325-degree F. oven until nicely browned, about 1½ hours. Baste frequently. It may be necessary to add a little hot water to the roasting pan to have adequate drippings with which to baste.

Pareve Kishka

Makes 2 rolls,
10 to 12 slices each

This makes a nice stuffing for a breast of veal.

> 1 cup matzo meal
> 1 cup sifted all-purpose flour
> ½ cup farina
> 2 large carrots, peeled
> 2 stalks celery
> 1 large onion
> 2 eggs (graded large)
> ½ cup oil
> 1 teaspoon salt
> ¼ teaspoon white pepper

Preheat the oven to 350 degrees F.

In a medium-sized mixing bowl, blend together the matzo meal, flour, and farina. Set aside. Dice the carrots, celery, and onion into the blender container. Add the eggs, oil, and seasoning. Blend until smooth.

Combine the vegetable mixture with the dry ingredients in the mixing bowl. Blend well. Divide in half. Form the mixture into 2 rolls about 12 inches long and place each on a piece of very lightly greased aluminum foil. Wrap each roll in the foil securely. Place the rolls on a baking sheet. Bake for 45 minutes. Serve hot.

Alternate Method:

Combine the dry ingredients in a bowl and set aside. Put the carrots, celery, and onion through a grinder or process in a food processor. In a mixing bowl, with a rotary beater, beat together the eggs, oil, and seasoning. Combine the ground vegetables with the beaten eggs. Pour over the dry ingredients. Mix well and proceed as above.

Cracker Kishka

Serves 10 to 12

A modern version of an old favorite. Determine how you wish to serve this Cracker Kishka. Slice it and present it as an accompaniment to meat or chicken, or cut it into squares and serve it as a kugel or an unusual hors d'oeuvre. Prepare and bake accordingly.

> 1 box (8 ounces) crackers (preferably Tam Tams)
> 2 carrots, peeled
> 2 stalks celery
> 1 medium-sized onion
> Salt and white pepper to taste
> 1 stick (½ cup) unsalted margarine, melted

Preheat the oven to 350 degrees F.

Grind the crackers into very fine crumbs. Place in a mixing bowl. Dice the carrots, celery, and onion into a blender container or food processor; blend until finely chopped. Or run the vegetables through a grinder. Combine the chopped vegetables with the cracker crumbs, salt and pepper, and melted margarine. A pastry blender will serve you well.

Divide the mixture in half and form into 2 rolls on 2 pieces of ungreased, unwrinkled aluminum foil. Wrap and seal each tightly. Bake for about 1 hour. Slice and serve hot. For a browner kishka, open the foil for the last 15 minutes of baking.

Variations:

• For a delicious hors d'oeuvre, divide the dough into very lightly greased or vegetable-sprayed tea muffin-size baking cups. Cover the baking pans and bake for approximately 30 minutes.

• May be baked as a kugel in a lightly greased 8-inch-square pan. Cover with aluminum foil during the baking period.

Gefilte Helzel
(Stuffed Poultry Neck)

Serves 3 or 4

In order to prepare a stuffed poultry neck skin *(helzel)* it would be advantageous if the skin were not slit, then you would be able to sew just one end of the helzel, creating a little sack. If the skin has been slit, sew the sides and bottom together to create a sack, leaving the top open for filling. Once cooked and browned, it is an excellent substitute for stuffed derma.

> 1 large poultry neck skin (chicken, turkey,
>   or goose)
> 1 cup sifted all-purpose flour
> ¼ teaspoon salt
> Dash of black pepper
> ½ teaspoon paprika
> 1 to 2 tablespoons matzo meal or
>   breadcrumbs
> ¼ cup diced unrendered poultry fat
> 1 small onion (optional)

Wash and clean the poultry neck. Sew it so as to create a little sack, leaving the top open for filling. Sift together the dry ingredients. Cut in the fat so the mixture is crumbly. A small onion may be grated in. Stuff the poultry neck and sew up securely. The neck may be cooked covered in chicken soup or boiling water. Cook at a slow boil for 2 hours. When the helzel has been cooked, roast it together with chicken to brown.

Gefilte Hoete
(Stuffed Flank Skin)

Serves 8 to 10

Stuffed *hoete* is a nice variation on stuffed kishka (intestine) or stuffed helzel (neck). Request from your butcher that he remove the flank skin all in one piece so that you can prepare it for stuffing.

    1 hoete (flank skin), about 2¼ pounds
    2¾ cups sifted all-purpose flour
    1 teaspoon salt
    ¼ teaspoon black pepper
    1½ teaspoons paprika
    ¼ cup matzo meal or dry breadcrumbs
    ½ cup minced onion
    ½ teaspoon chopped parsley
    ⅔ cup solid white vegetable shortening
    Boiling water
    2 to 3 cloves garlic
    1 teaspoon paprika
    ½ teaspoon salt
    ⅛ teaspoon black pepper
    ¼ cup solid white shortening or oil

Wash the hoete and remove the excess fat. Sew the sides of the skin together to form a sack, with the fat side kept on the inside of the sack. Leave one end open for filling.

Sift the flour and seasonings into a large mixing bowl. Add the matzo meal or breadcrumbs, minced onion, and parsley. Cut in the shortening until the mixture looks crumbly. Stuff the hoete with this mixture and sew up the end securely.

Place the filled hoete in a large pot. Prick gently with a fork twice. Cover with boiling water. Cover the pot and simmer for 2½ hours, adding more boiling water as necessary. Turn the hoete frequently during the cooking period.

Preheat the oven to 400 degrees F. Crush the garlic and combine with the seasonings. Melt the shortening in a roasting pan. Add the cooked hoete. Brush the skin with the melted shortening and spread with the prepared seasonings. Bake for 30 minutes or until golden brown. Turn frequently during baking. Slice to serve. Serve hot.

Alternate Method:

Place the hoete flat on a sheet of wax paper. Spread the filling on the hoete. Roll up jelly-roll-fashion. Then sew up all open ends securely. Place in a large pot and proceed as above.

9

The Griddle & the Oven

Blintzes, Latkes, Kreplach & Such

"And if thy offering be a meal offering baked on a griddle . . ." (Leviticus 2:5-6).

The Basic Bletl

(Blintz Pancake)

Makes about 14 pancakes

A *blintz* is made by filling a *bletl*, a thin pancake, with one of a variety of fillings. Depending on the filling used, the blintz may be served as a tantalizing appetizer, a magnificent main dish, an interesting side dish, or a sumptuous dessert.

Every nationality has its own variation on the bletl and the blintz. The French have the *crêpe*, used to make the famous Crêpes Suzette. The Russians have the *blini*, frequently served with caviar. The Italians fill bletl-type pancakes with meat or cheese to produce the popular *cannelloni* or *manicotti*; and, of course, the Chinese have the egg roll.

The following bletl recipe will serve you well. For sweet *bletlach* (plural), add a tablespoon of sugar to the batter.

> **4 eggs (graded large)**
> **1 cup liquid (water, milk, or juice)**
> **1 generous tablespoon oil or 1 generous tablespoon margarine or butter, melted**
> **1 cup sifted all-purpose flour**
> **Oil for frying**

In a medium-sized bowl, beat the eggs, liquid, and oil. Gradually add the flour, beating continuously until the mixture is completely smooth. Or place all the ingredients in a blender jar and blend until smooth.

Lightly grease a 7-inch skillet and heat it over medium-high heat. Measure ¼ cup of batter into the skillet and quickly tilt it in all directions to spread the batter in a thin even film that covers the bottom of the skillet. Pour off any excess batter. Return the pan to moderate heat. Cook until the batter sets and the edges of the pancake start to leave the sides of the pan. Invert the skillet over a clean cloth. The pancake will fall out cooked side up. Repeat until all the batter is used up.

The blintz pancakes are now ready to fill. Or you may refrigerate them for up to a week or freeze them for up to 2 months. To freeze, stack them with a sheet of waxed paper between each crêpe. Wrap in foil and freeze.

Shaping the Blintzes:

Blintz pancakes can be filled with any of the fillings in the next recipe, or you can create an interesting mixture of your own. Once the filling has been prepared, you are ready to assemble the blintzes, as follows:

• The *traditional blintz* is the most practical of all, because the way it is shaped prevents the filling from oozing out. Simply spread the filling on the third of the pancake nearest you, leaving a half-inch border all around. Fold the sides of the pancake toward the center, covering the filling. Starting at the filled edge of the bletl, fold that edge of the bletl over the filling and roll it up, making sure the folded sides are secure in the roll.

• For *blintz squares*, spoon the filling onto the center of each bletl. Fold 2 sides into the center so they overlap. Fold the other 2 sides into the center to make a square package with all the filling enclosed.

• For *blintz cups*, use the blintz pancakes as liners for greased muffin cups. Fill the cups as desired and bake. This is a unique way to prepare and serve quiche.

• For *"Italian cannelloni" blintzes*, spread the filling on ¾ of each bletl, leaving a small border, ¼ inch, all around. Starting on the filled side, roll up jelly-roll-fashion. This is appealing for appetizers or main dishes.

• For *dessert blintzes,* spoon the filling (perhaps a fruit mixture) along the center of the blintz. Fold one side over toward the center; fold the opposite side over to overlap the first side.

Cooking the Blintzes:

To cook the blintzes, in a large skillet melt a few tablespoons of butter (a generous amount) over medium-high heat. Fry the blintzes on both sides, starting with the seam side down, until lightly browned.

To bake the blintzes, grease a baking sheet with butter. Arrange the blintzes on the baking sheet and brush the tops with melted butter. Bake them seam side down in a preheated 375-degree F. oven for about 20 to 30 minutes, until browned. Frozen blintzes will require a longer baking time.

Blintz Fillings

What you use as a blintz filling is limited only by your imagination. Here are some recipes to get you started, but feel free to create.

Cheese Filling:

> 1½ pounds small-curd cottage cheese
> 2 eggs (grade large)
> Sugar to taste
> Dash of black pepper
> Pinch of cinnamon
> ⅓ cup golden raisins (optional)

Pass the cheese through a fine sieve or strainer and into a bowl. Add the eggs, sugar, seasonings, and optional raisins. Mix well and the filling is ready to use for main dish or dessert blintzes.

Meat Filling:

> 2 cups finely ground cooked meat
> 1 egg (grade large)
> Salt and black pepper to taste

Mix together all ingredients thoroughly and the filling is ready to use.

Blueberry Filling:

> 1½ cups blueberries, fresh or frozen
> 1 tablespoon cornstarch
> ¼ teaspoon grated lemon rind
> ¼ teaspoon nutmeg
> Sugar to taste

Place the berries in a small bowl. Add the remaining ingredients, toss everything together, and the filling is ready to use.

Easy Fruit Fillings:

To a 1-pound 5-ounce can of commercial pie filling of your choice, add your own spices or flavorings. Add the grated rind of an orange or lemon or perhaps some chopped nuts. Nutmeg makes a fine addition to apple pie filling.

Blintz Soup Garnish

> Batter for The Basic Bletl recipe (page 194)
> 3 tablespoons finely minced fresh parsley
> Oil for the skillet

Prepare the basic blintz pancake batter, adding the fresh parsley. In a lightly greased 7-inch skillet over medium-high heat, cook each bletl on both sides. Roll each cooked pancake into a tight cylinder. Slice each cylinder into noodles, thin or wide. Serve in hot chicken broth. Two or 3 blintz pancakes, 7 inches in diameter, will yield an adequate amount of noodles for 2 quarts of chicken broth.

Baked Blintzes

Serves 9

If you are intimidated by the thought of having to make the thin bletlach for blintzes, try this simple recipe.

The batter for these blintzes is not prepared as individual bletlach. Half of the batter is poured into a prepared baking pan and topped with the cheese filling. The remainder of the batter is poured over the filling. Once baked, the blintzes are cut into individual oblong shapes.

Serve these plain or with your choice of accompaniments: dollop of sour cream, sliced strawberries, or a combination of both: applesauce or any fruit sauce. A sprinkling of cinammon sugar adds flavor to blintzes served without a fruit accompaniment.

Batter:

Grease for the pan
2 eggs (graded large)
3 tablespoons sugar
¾ cup milk
1 stick (½ cup) unsalted butter or
margarine, at room temperature
1 teaspoon baking powder
1¼ cups unsifted all-purpose flour

Lightly grease with butter or margarine a 9 x 13-inch baking pan; set aside. Preheat the oven to 350 degrees F. In a blender or food processor, combine the eggs, sugar, milk, butter or margarine, and baking powder. Cover and blend thoroughly. Add the flour and blend until smooth. Set aside.

Filling:

1 pound farmer cheese or dry cottage
cheese
1 egg (graded large)
1 tablespoon unsalted butter or margarine,
melted
2 to 3 tablespoons sugar, to taste
⅛ teaspoon cinnamon
Dash of white pepper

Pass the farmer cheese or dry cottage cheese through a fine sieve and into a bowl. Beat in the egg and melted butter or margarine. Add the sugar to taste, then add the cinnamon and dash of white pepper. Mix thoroughly.

Pour half of the batter into the prepared pan. Spoon the cheese filling evenly over the batter, then pour the remainder of the batter on top of the cheese. Place the pan in the oven and bake for about 1 hour, until golden brown. Serve immediately or refrigerate or freeze and reheat for later use.

To serve, cut this one large baked blintz into 18 oblong-shaped blintzes, each approximately 1½ x 4½ inches. To make individual servings, cut in half lengthwise, then cut the long pieces crosswise into 1¼-inch portions.

French Blintzes

Serves 6

Surprise! These French Blintzes aren't difficult to make (nor are they really blintzes). They look like large kreplach and taste like filled French toast.

> **12 slices white bread**
> **1 pound pot cheese**
> **3 eggs (graded large)**
> **Sugar to taste**
> **Dash of cinnamon**
> **½ cup milk**
> **Butter or margarine for frying**

Decrust each slice of bread and flatten it with a rolling pin. Pass the cheese through a fine sieve. Beat one of the eggs well, then combine it well with the cheese. Add the sugar and cinnamon and mix thoroughly.

Place a tablespoon's worth of cheese mixture off-center on each slice of bread. Fold each slice of bread in half to form a triangle. Pinch the sides together so that each slice stays closed.

Beat the remaining eggs well with the milk. Dip each bread blintz into the egg mixture and, in a skillet over medium-high heat, fry in butter or margarine, as you would French toast. Serve at once with maple syrup or a sprinkling of cinnamon sugar.

Variation:

For Mock French Blintzes, place some of the cheese filling in a strip along one side of each flattened slice of bread. Roll up like a jelly roll. Dip into the beaten egg. Arrange the rolls seam side down in a well-buttered baking pan. Bake at 350 degrees F. for 10 to 15 minutes, turning once. Serve with cinnamon sugar or a flourish of sour cream. These may be prepared in advance and reheated in a slow oven.

Cheese Roulades

Makes about 18 roulades

The term *roulade* generally refers to meat that has been flattened, stuffed, and rolled before cooking. These "roulades" are really imitation blintzes. They are quick and easy because there are no crêpes to prepare and they are oven-baked, not fried. Sliced strawberries with or without sour cream make a nice accompaniment.

> Grease for the pan
> 1 pound farmer cheese
> 8 ounces cream cheese, at room
>   temperature
> ½ cup sugar
> 2 eggs (graded large)
> 1 teaspoon almond extract
> ½ teaspoon grated lemon rind
> Dash of cinnamon (optional)
> Cornflakes

Lightly grease a baking sheet or pan; set aside. Preheat the oven to 350 degrees F.

Mix together the farmer cheese, cream cheese, sugar, and eggs. Add the extract, rind, and the cinnamon if using, and stir until completely blended. Place the cornflakes in a deep dish. Place large spoonfuls of the cheese mixture into the cornflakes. Roll by hand to cover the mixture completely with flakes. Arrange on the baking sheet and bake uncovered for about 15 minutes, until the cheese is baked. These freeze very well. Defrost before heating.

Food Processor
Potato Latkes

Makes about 26

Latkes (pancakes) are the gastronomical symbol of Chanukah, though in Israel *sufganiyot* (see page 232), jelly doughnuts, rival latkes. There are many kinds of latkes, but potato latkes are the most popular.

If you have never made potato latkes, now is the time to start. With some effort they can be prepared with a hand grater, but using a food processor reduces the work enormously. Serve these crisp golden treats all year long. Serve plain or with sour cream or applesauce.

> **3 eggs (graded large)**
> **3 large potatoes, unpeeled**
> **1 medium-sized onion, peeled and**
>   **quartered**
> **1 teaspoon salt**
> **¼ teaspoon black pepper**
> **¼ teaspoon baking powder**
> **¼ cup all-purpose flour**
> **Oil for frying**

In the bowl of a food processor fitted with the steel blade, place the eggs. Process for a few seconds. Leaving the blade in the bowl, put the shredding disc in place. Under water, briskly scrub the potatoes with a stiff brush; dry well. Cut the potatoes into pieces that will fit into the feed tube. Shred the potatoes and continue to process until finely chopped. Process the onion in the same manner.

Transfer the mixture to a mixing bowl. Add the salt and pepper. Sprinkle on the flour and baking powder. Stir in.

In a large heavy skillet over medium-high heat, heat a scant quarter-inch of oil to 375 degrees F. Drop a large tablespoon's worth of potato mixture into the hot oil. Flatten slightly with the back of the spoon to make thin cakes. Fry slowly. Brown one side well; turn the pancake and brown the other side. Transfer the pancakes to paper towels to drain. Blot the top of the pancakes also. Adding oil as necessary, repeat the procedure until all the batter is used up.

Note: These latkes can be made in advance and refrigerated or frozen. To reheat, place in a single layer on an ungreased baking pan. Heat in a 350-degree F. oven till hot, about 5 to 10 minutes.

Variations:

• For a zesty flavor, add half a package of dry onion soup mix to the batter. Omit the salt.

• For herbed potato latkes, add ½ teaspoon parsley flakes, ½ teaspoon rosemary leaves, and ¼ teaspoon crushed sage to the batter. This makes an excellent accompaniment for poultry dishes.

• Substitute ¼ cup potato pancake mix for the flour.

Cheese Latkes

Makes about 12

Many of our traditional Chanukah dishes have their origin in legend. Cheese latkes, for example, can be traced to the story of Judith, the brave daughter of the Maccabees who fed large amounts of cheesecakes to the enemy's leader (Assyrian Captain Holofernes) to make him thirsty. This made him drink too much wine, making it possible to capture him. These pancakes are served to commemorate Judith's bravery.

> 3 eggs (graded large), lightly beaten
> 1 cup milk
> 1 cup dry pot cheese
> 1 cup unsifted all-purpose flour
> 1 teaspoon baking powder
> ½ teaspoon salt (optional)
> 1 teaspoon sugar
> 1 teaspoon cinnamon (optional)
> Oil or butter for frying

In a large mixing bowl, beat the eggs until frothy. Add the milk and cheese. Beat until well blended. Sift together the dry ingredients and stir into the cheese mixture. Blend well. Drop by the tablespoonful into a large hot frying pan greased with the oil or butter. Fry until brown on both sides. Serve with jam, syrup, sour cream, or a sprinkling of cinnamon sugar.

Fanny Brice Latkes

Serves 2

On one occasion, when I delivered a lecture entitled "Cooking for Passover," one of the guests gave me a latke recipe that she assured me was a Fanny Brice original. The recipe calls for one-quarter cup of matzo meal for every two eggs.

> **2 eggs (graded large), separated**
> **¼ cup matzo meal**
> **Salt and pepper to taste**
> **Oil for frying**

Separate the eggs. Beat the yolks until light. Add the matzo meal and salt and pepper. Blend well. Beat the egg whites until stiff. Fold them into the yolk mixture. In a deep skillet, heat ½ inch of oil to 375 degrees F. By the tablespoonful, drop the batter into the hot oil and fry until golden. Remove with a slotted spatula. Drain on paper towels. Serve with cinnamon and sugar.

Potato-Apple Latkes

Makes 36 to 40

The ordinary potato latke gets special treatment. Grated apples are added to the grated potatoes, transforming the plain latke to one with a built-in garnish.

> **3 pounds red russet potatoes**
> **1 pound apples**
> **4 eggs (graded large), beaten**
> **¼ teaspoon salt**
> **Dash of black pepper**
> **¼ to ½ cup all-purpose flour**
> **Oil for frying**

Peel the potatoes and coarsely grate them into a mixing bowl. Peel the apples and grate them into the potatoes. Add the beaten eggs, salt, and pepper. Mix in ¼ cup of flour, adding more flour if the batter is too loose.

Coat a large teflon-coated skillet with a thin film of oil, or pour a scant quarter-inch of oil into a large heavy skillet. When the oil is hot, drop in a generous tablespoon's worth of the mixture. Flatten the pancakes slightly with the back of the spoon. Fry slowly. Brown well on one side, turn, and brown well on the other side. Transfer the pancakes to paper towels to drain. Blot the top of the pancakes also. Adding oil as necessary, repeat the procedure until all the batter is used up. Serve with applesauce or sour cream.

Chremslie

Makes about 28

My daughter Rena's Hungarian friend, Vera Barta, has an annual gathering during Passover when she prepares and serves her pièce de résistance: *chremslies.* She usually uses seven and one-half pounds of potatoes and twenty-six eggs. Here is a family-size version of the recipe.

> **6 medium-sized potatoes**
> **6 eggs (graded extra-large), beaten**
> **1 tablespoon sugar**
> **Salt and black pepper to taste**
> **Oil for frying**

Peel and cook the potatoes in salted water until tender. Drain, dice, and pass the potatoes through a food mill or sieve. Add the beaten eggs, sugar, salt, and pepper. Beat until very smooth.

In a deep skillet, heat 2 inches of oil to 375 degrees F. Drop in ¼ cup's worth of batter for each chremslie. Cook until golden brown. Turn once. Drain on paper towels. Serve hot with or without fruit sauce.

Variation:

Use only 3 potatoes. Separate the eggs. Beat the potatoes smooth with the yolks and sugar. Fold in the beaten egg whites. Fry as above. Cool slightly. If desired, cut a pocket in each and insert jam, jelly, or the sweet filling of your choice.

Vegetable Latkes

Makes 22 to 24 pancakes

A colorful combination of vegetables: white potatoes, orange carrots, and green zucchini.

> **2 medium-sized zucchini**
> **2 medium-sized carrots, peeled**
> **2 large potatoes, peeled**
> **½ teaspoon salt**
> **Dash of black pepper**
> **3 eggs (graded large)**
> **½ to ¾ cup matzo meal**
> **Oil for frying**

Scrape the zucchini, but do not peel completely. Shred them and set in a colander to drain while you shred the peeled carrots and peeled potatoes. Squeeze out excess water from the zucchini. In a large mixing bowl, combine the zucchini with the potatoes and carrots. Add the salt, pepper, and the eggs. Mix to combine. Stir in enough matzo meal to achieve a good batter consistency.

Lightly coat with oil the bottom of a large teflon-coated skillet, or pour about ¼ inch of oil into a large heavy skillet.

Shape the vegetable mixture into flat pancakes. Heat the skillet and arrange a few pancakes in the skillet at a time. With the back of a large serving spoon, flatten each pancake. Cook until golden brown on each side. Add additional oil as needed. Drain both sides on paper towels.

Tofu Latkes

Makes 18

These highly nutritious, protein-rich latkes are a combination of tofu and carrots bound together with vitamin-rich wheat germ. They freeze very well.

> **1 large carrot, peeled**
> **1 pound soft tofu**
> **2 eggs (graded large)**
> **½ teaspoon salt**

¼ teaspoon black pepper
1 tablespoon sugar
½ cup wheat germ
Vegetable oil for frying

In a food processor, with the steel blade in the bottom of the bowl and the shredder disk in place, shred the carrots and process until chopped fine. Transfer the shredded carrots to a mixing bowl. Drain the tofu well and process in the food processor with the steel blade, or mash very well with a fork. Combine the tofu with the grated carrot. Beat in the eggs, pepper, and sugar. Lastly, stir in the wheat germ.

Lightly coat a large teflon-coated skillet with oil. Or, pour a scant ¼-inch of oil in a heavy skillet. Heat the oil and drop in the batter by the tablespoonful. Cook until golden brown, then turn and brown the other side. Drain on paper towels. Blot the top of each pancake with paper towels as well. Serve hot.

Viennese Layer Latkes

Makes eight 8-inch pancakes

There are as many variations on the latke as there are imaginative cooks to invent them. Although we most often think of the latke as a side dish or main dish, it can make a most glamorous dessert. Here, cottage cheese pancakes are spread with a spicy applesauce filling and layered one on top of the other. They are served hot in pie-shaped wedges.

Pancakes:

6 eggs (graded large)
2 cups uncreamed small-curd cottage
    cheese, passed through a sieve
½ stick (¼ cup) unsalted butter or
    margarine, melted
6 tablespoons all-purpose flour
½ teaspoon salt
1 teaspoon sugar (optional)
Butter or oil for the skillet

In the large bowl of an electric mixer, beat the eggs until light and foamy. Mix in the sieved cottage cheese and melted butter or margarine. Add the flour and salt. Mix well. The batter should be smooth. Use ½ cup batter for each pancake. Lightly grease an 8-inch skillet or griddle. Fry the pancakes until golden, turning once.

Filling:

> 4 cups applesauce
> ½ teaspoon cinnamon
> ½ teaspoon nutmeg
> ¼ cup firmly packed brown sugar

In a medium-sized saucepan, combine the applesauce, cinnamon, nutmeg, and sugar. Bring to a boil over medium heat, stirring often.

To Assemble the Dessert:

Preheat the oven to 350 degrees F. Spread some of the applesauce on a latke, and place it on the bottom of an 8-inch spring-form pan. Continue until all the latkes and sauce have been used up. Bake for about 10 minutes, until the pancakes are hot. Remove the sides of the spring-form and place the layered latkes on a serving dish. Sprinkle with confectioners' sugar and cut into pie-shaped wedges to serve.

Note: These latkes may be made a day ahead if desired. Just prepare the filling as above and layer the hot filling with the prepared latkes and heat in a moderate oven.

Basic Noodle Dough

Makes about ¾ pound

On the Sabbath, a dish of clear chicken soup is enhanced by the addition of thin cooked noodles. On *Erev* Yom Kippur (the eve preceding the Day of Atonement) kreplach are traditionally served in chicken soup at the prefast meal.

This noodle dough will come in very handy, whether making simple noodles or the slightly more complicated *kreplach.* The dough should be soft and very workable.

> **2 eggs (graded large)**
> **¼ teaspoon salt**
> **1½ to 2 cups sifted all-purpose flour,**
> **approximately**

In a medium-sized bowl, beat the eggs until frothy. Add the salt. Gradually work in the flour to make a stiff dough, then knead for about 5 minutes, until soft and elastic. You now have your Basic Noodle Dough.

To make noodles, divide the dough in half. On a lightly floured surface, roll out one piece of dough very thin and even. Let the dough dry enough that it will not stick when rolled up, but not until it is brittle. Drying will take about 15 minutes.

Fold or tightly roll up the dough jelly-roll-fashion. Using a sharp knife, cut the dough crosswise into very thin strips. Toss lightly to separate the strips and then let them dry thoroughly till brittle. The noodles are cooked in boiling salted water for about 10 minutes then drained and served in soup.

Note: You can cut the dough differently, depending on how it is to be used. Cut wide strips for lasagna, medium for kugel, and so on.

For farfel (also referred to as egg barley), do not roll out the prepared dough. Let the dough dry for at least an hour. Grate the ball of dough on a coarse grater and spread out the particles to dry.

Kreplach

Makes about 3 dozen

Kreplach, like Italian *ravioli* or Chinese *wontons*, are made from a noodle dough that is cut into squares and stuffed with any of a variety of fillings. Poached in salted water, they may be immediately served in soup as a garnish. Poached and sautéed until golden, they are served as a side dish or main dish depending on the filling and the size of the serving.

According to Jewish folklore, kreplach are eaten when *men shlugt* (there is beating): namely, on *Erev* Yom Kippur, when we beat our breasts as we say *Al chet* (the confessional prayer); on Purim, when Haman's name is "beaten out"; and on Hoshanah Rabbah, when the willows are beaten.

Basic Noodle Dough recipe (page 207)

Prepare the dough according to the instructions in the preceding recipe. When the dough is soft and elastic, roll it out on a floured surface until very thin. Cut the dough into 2½- to 3-inch squares. Prepare your favorite filling. Ground meat, mashed potatoes, cheese, kasha, or fruit are among the fillings you might consider. Place a teaspoon of filling in the center of each square. Take a corner of the square and fold it diagonally over the filling to form a triangle. Seal the edges by pressing firmly together. Let the kreplach dry for at least an hour before cooking. Drop them into boiling salted water and cook for 15 minutes. When done, they will rise to the top. Drain well and serve in soup, or sauté until golden. Or brown them in the oven in a greased baking pan.

Liver Filling for Kreplach

Makes 36 to 40

A marvelously tasty filling for kreplach.

> 2 to 3 tablespoons oil or unsalted
>   margarine
> 2 to 3 medium-sized onions
> ½ pound liver, broiled, deveined and
>   skinned
> Salt and black pepper
> 1 egg (graded large)

To prepare the filling, heat the oil or margarine in a small skillet. Dice the onions into the skillet and sauté over medium heat until the onions are golden. Grind the liver and onions together. Season to taste with salt and pepper. Add the unbeaten egg and mix. Set aside.

Variations:

• For a filling shortcut, use a 7-ounce container of commercially prepared chopped liver, or substitute ½ pound ground cooked meat for the liver.

• Liver kreplach served before the Yom Kippur fast are frequently shaped into little caps. Before letting the kreplach dry, hold the folded side of the triangle against your finger and bring the 2 points of the triangle around your finger. Pinch together to seal the ends. The Italians refer to these as *cappelletti*.

Gourmet Cheese Kreplach

Makes about 36 squares

Whereas traditional kreplach are made with a basic noodle dough, these are made with a sour cream dough that is extraordinarily light and flaky when baked, similar to puff pastry.

An alternative way of filling these elegant pastries is to place one-half to one teaspoon of filling diagonally on each square. Pull two opposite corners of the square into the center. Overlap them and press firmly together to seal, leaving the filling exposed on both ends.

Dough:

2 sticks (½ pound) unsalted butter or
   margarine, at room temperature
1 cup sour cream
2 cups unsifted all-purpose flour
⅛ cup sugar (optional)
Grease for the pan
Sugar and cinnamon mix to sprinkle on the
   shaped pastries (optional)

In a large bowl, thoroughly blend together the butter and sour cream. Work in the flour and the optional sugar. Knead to blend well. Wrap in wax paper and refrigerate overnight.

Filling:

1 pound farmer cheese
1 egg (graded large), slightly beaten
1 tablespoon sugar, or to taste
¼ teaspoon cinnamon
Dash of white pepper
¼ cup golden raisins (optional)

To prepare the filling, press the farmer cheese through a sieve. Add the egg, sugar, cinnamon, and pepper and stir till well blended. Add the raisins if desired. Set aside. Grease a

10½ x 15½-inch baking pan and set aside. Preheat the oven to 350 degrees F.

To shape the kreplach, cut the chilled dough in half. Place half of the dough on a floured surface, and return the remaining dough to the refrigerator until ready to use. Roll out the dough to ¼-inch thickness. Cut the dough into 2½-inch squares. Place a heaping teaspoonful of filling in the center of each square. Bring together the opposite corner to form a triangle. Press the edges firmly together to seal. Arrange the kreplach in the greased baking pan. Sprinkle the tops with sugar and cinnamon. Repeat with the remaining dough. Bake the kreplach until golden brown, 25 to 35 minutes.

Variation:

This dough can be used to make a *milchig* (dairy) strudel. Roll portions of the dough into a rectangle. The dough should be thin. Sprinkle the dough with your favorite strudel filling. Roll carefully, jelly-roll-fashion, being sure to seal the ends. Bake on a lightly greased cookie sheet in a preheated 350-degree F. oven until golden brown. Cut with a sharp knife. Serve sprinkled with powdered sugar. Cut into 1- or 1½-inch slices. Yields approximately 40 to 45 slices.

Calzone

Makes 8 pastries

Calzones, filled crescent-shaped pastries made with pizza dough, are really a "meal-in-a-pocket." They can be shaped any size you wish. A large, family-sized calzone is served in slices; medium-sized may be served as a luncheon main course; and small calzones are ideal to serve as snacks or hors d'oeuvres.

This recipe makes medium-sized luncheon pastries. Vary the fillings as you wish. Create interesting combinations of ingredients—dairy, meat, or pareve.

Dough:

    1 cup warm water (110 to 115 degrees F.)
    1 package active dry yeast
    1 teaspoon sugar

⟶

    2 tablespoons vegetable oil
    2½ to 3 cups all-purpose flour
    Egg wash (1 egg lightly beaten with 1
        teaspoon water)

Spinach-Cheese Filling:

    ¼ cup finely diced onion
    1 generous tablespoon unsalted butter or
        margarine
    1 package (10 ounces) frozen chopped
        spinach
    8 ounces mozzarella cheese, shredded
    ¼ teaspoon salt
    ⅛ teaspoon black pepper
    ⅛ teaspoon nutmeg

To prepare the dough, pour the water into a large mixing bowl. Add the yeast and sugar and let stand for 10 to 15 minutes, until foamy. Stir in the salt and vegetable oil. Gradually add 2½ cups of the flour, blending until a dough is formed. Turn out onto a floured surface. Knead the dough until smooth and elastic, about 10 to 15 minutes, adding more flour as necessary. Roll into a ball.

Lightly oil a 2-quart bowl. Roll the ball of dough in the bowl to coat it all around with oil. Cover the bowl with plastic wrap, and set it in a warm draft-free place to rise until doubled in bulk.

To prepare the filling, in a small skillet sauté the diced onion in the butter or margarine until translucent. Thaw the chopped spinach and drain well. In a mixing bowl, combine the drained spinach with the sautéed onions and shredded cheese. Add the seasonings and stir to blend. Divide the filling into 8 portions.

Preheat the oven to 425 degrees F.

To shape the pastries, punch down the dough and divide it into 8 portions. On a lightly floured surface, roll out each portion into a 6-inch circle. Spoon a portion of the filling on the lower half of each circle, leaving a border all around. Bring the top half of the circle over the filling. Pinch the edges together securely (or crimp the edges together with the tines of a fork) to prevent the filling from leaking out. Transfer the pastries to a lightly greased baking sheet. Prick the top of each once or twice with the tines of a fork to allow steam to escape. Lightly brush the top and sides of each pastry with the egg wash. Bake for about 15 minutes, until lightly browned.

Filling Variations:

•One-quarter cup mushrooms sautéed with the onions complements the spinach and cheese in the filling.

•The spinach in the recipe may be replaced with chopped broccoli.

Size Variations:

•For snack calzones, divide into ten 4-inch circles.

•For main dish servings, divide the dough into 6 portions and roll out into 8-inch circles.

•For family size, use the entire ball of dough to make one 15-inch calzone.

Quick Calzone:

Thaw one package of frozen challah dough. Divide the dough in half, and roll each half into a 10-inch circle. Divide the filling, and spread over each round of dough. Prepare as above, pinching the edges tightly to seal. Prick the top of the pastries. Bake at 350 degrees F. for about 30 minutes. Each calzone serves 3 or 4.

Pirogen

Makes 32 to 36

Ethel Katz, a friend of longstanding, shared with me a treasured family recipe for meat-filled *pirogen*. These were pastries that her grandmother made nigh fifty years ago. The recipe is extravagant in the time required to prepare it, but I guarantee that it is well worth the effort. The working time can be spread over two days. Prepare the filling one day; prepare the dough, assemble, and bake the next day.

Filling:

> 2 pounds ground meat
> ¾ cup water or clear broth
> 2 eggs (graded large)

———————————➤

        ½ to 1 package dry onion soup mix
        ½ cup cornflake crumbs
        1 can (8 ounces) tomato sauce

Preheat the oven to 325 degrees F.

The method of preparing the filling is the most unusual one I have ever used: Combine the chopped meat with the water or broth, eggs, and onion soup mix. Mix thoroughly. Stir in the crumbs. Blend well. Shape the meat into 2 loaves in a vegetable-sprayed 9 x 13-inch baking pan. Spoon the tomato sauce over both loaves, covering them completely. Cover the pan securely with aluminum foil. Bake for 1½ hours. Cool and refrigerate.

When completely cold, degrease. Remove all the congealed fat. Mash the meat loaves and spoon the mixture into a bowl. The filling is now ready to be used. Set aside.

My friend keeps the filling warm by suspending the bowl containing the filling in a larger pot containing about 2 inches of water that is kept warm over very low heat. I have found no difficulty in using the meat cold.

Dough:

        1 envelope active dry yeast
        ½ cup warm water (110 to 115 degrees F.)
        2 tablespoons solid white shortening or oil
        2 tablespoons sugar
        1 teaspoon salt
        ½ cup boiling water
        1 egg (graded large), lightly beaten
        3½ to 4 cups sifted all-purpose flour
        1 egg beaten with 1 teaspoon water
        Sesame or poppy seeds (optional)
        Oil for the pan

In a small bowl, dissolve the yeast in the warm water. Set aside. In a medium-sized bowl, combine the shortening or oil, sugar, salt, and boiling water. Stir to dissolve the sugar and salt. Cool to lukewarm. Add the yeast and beaten egg. Gradually add the flour to make a soft dough that is no longer sticky. Turn out the dough onto a floured surface and knead until smooth and satiny. Transfer the dough to a large greased bowl. Turn to coat all sides. Cover and let rise in warm draft-free place until doubled in bulk. Then punch down the dough and allow it to rise again until doubled in bulk. Then punch down again.

Divide the dough into 4 equal portions. Keep 3 portions covered and warm while working with the fourth. On a well-floured surface, roll out the dough as large and thin as possible. Cut into 5-inch circles.

Place 2 tablespoons' worth of filling in the center of each circle. Gather up the edges of the dough, pulling and pinching them together around the filling but leaving about 1 inch opening in the center so the steam can escape. Place the filled pirogen on a greased 10½ x 15½-inch baking sheet. Gather up the scraps of dough and set aside in a bowl to reuse.

Repeat with the remaining 3 portions of dough. Combine all the scraps of dough and proceed as above. Preheat the oven to 375 degrees F.

When all the pirogen have been made, brush each pastry with the egg wash. Sprinkle with poppy or sesame seeds if desired. Let rise for 15 minutes, then bake for about 15 minutes, until delicately browned.

Note: These freeze very well. They may also be prepared in a much larger size. Pirogen, soup, and a salad make a very adequate lunch.

Spinach-Cheese Dumplings

Serves 6 as a main dish,
10 as a side dish

Dumplings, tender and cheesy, rich in spinach flavor and color, and bathed with a robust cheese sauce.

Dumplings:

> 2 cups ricotta cheese
> 1 package (10 ounces) frozen spinach,
>   thawed and squeezed dry
> ½ cup grated parmesan cheese
> ½ teaspoon salt
> 1 egg (graded large)
> 1 small clove garlic, minced
> ¾ cup plus 2 tablespoons all-purpose flour
> Water

In a large mixing bowl, combine the first 6 ingredients. Add the ¾ cup of flour and mix well. Spread the 2 tablespoons of flour onto a piece of wax paper. With floured hands, shape the spinach mixture into 1-inch balls. Gently roll the balls in the flour to coat lightly.

In a large 6-quart saucepan, over high heat, bring 3 quarts of water to a boil. Add the spinach balls one at a time to the boiling water. Cook for 10 minutes or until slightly puffed and set. With a slotted spoon, remove the spinach balls to paper towels to drain. Preheat the oven broiler (about 450 degrees F.)

Cheese Sauce:

> 2 tablespoons unsalted butter
> 2 tablespoons all-purpose flour
> ⅛ teaspoon salt
> ⅛ teaspoon black pepper
> 2 cups milk
> ½ cup shredded Swiss cheese

To prepare the cheese sauce, melt the butter in a 2-quart saucepan over medium heat. Stir in the flour, salt, and pepper. Cook for 1 minute. Slowly add the milk, stirring constantly, and cook until the sauce is smooth and slightly thickened. Add the shredded cheese and cook until it melts.

Spoon a small amount of the cheese sauce into an 8 x 12-inch baking pan. Arrange the drained spinach balls in the sauce. Spoon the remaining sauce over and around the balls. Place the baking pan in the broiler, about 7 to 9 inches away from the source of heat. Broil for 10 to 15 minutes, until hot and bubbly.

Shakshouka

(Eggs in Tomato Sauce)

When a Yemenite young lady from Israel was my houseguest, she shared with me her favorite egg dish. She said each cook has his or her own version of the dish. I find it comparable to a vegetable-laden Spanish omelette.

1 large onion, coarsely chopped
3 tablespoons vegetable oil
6 medium-sized tomatoes, cubed
1 large green pepper, cubed or cut into thin
   strips
2 to 5 large garlic cloves, peeled and sliced
   (to taste)
Salt and pepper to taste
1 or 2 eggs per serving

In a large skillet with a cover, sauté the onion in the oil until golden brown. Add the tomatoes, green pepper, garlic, and seasonings. Cover the skillet and simmer over low heat, stirring occasionally until the tomatoes are very soft and break apart. Pour in the eggs, either whole or slightly beaten, and continue simmering without stirring until the eggs are set. Serve on toast for breakfast or with pita or French bread for a luncheon dish. A nice crisp green salad is the perfect accompaniment.

10

For a Festive Holiday

Specialties of the Season

"*Come this day unto the banquet I have prepared*"
(Esther 5:4).

Bible Fruit Cake

Serves 16 or more

"And they gave him a piece of cake" (I Samuel 30:12).

This recipe makes a deliciously fragrant and refreshing fruit cake destined to make any of your holidays festive. The cake is so named because the ingredients called for are referred to in various passages in the Bible.

¾ cup Proverbs 30:33 *"bringeth forth curd"* **butter**

1 cup Jeremiah 6:20 *"and the sweet cane"* **sugar**

1 tablespoon I Samuel 14:25 *"there was honey"* **honey**

4 Isaiah 59:5 *"eateth of their eggs"* **eggs**

2 cups Leviticus 2:2 *"handful of fine flour"* **flour**

1 teaspoon Amos 4:5 *"that which is leavened"* **baking powder**

A pinch Leviticus 2:13 *"season with salt"* **salt**

1 teaspoon Exodus 20:23 *"of sweet cinnamon"* **cinnamon**

Season to taste II Chronicles 9:9 *"and spices in great abundance"*: ¼ **teaspoon cloves,** ½ **teaspoon nutmeg,** ½ **teaspoon allspice,** ½ **teaspoon vanilla extract**

½ cup Judges 5:25 *"water he asked, milk she gave him"* **water or milk**

1 cup II Samuel 16:1 *"cluster of raisins"* **raisins**

1 cup chopped Nahum 3:12 *"the first ripe figs"* **figs**

½ cup chopped Numbers 17:23—*"bore ripe almonds"* **almonds**

Preheat the oven to 300 degrees F. Follow method of Solomon: *"Beat him with the rod"* (Proverbs 23:14).

In a large mixing bowl, cream the butter, gradually adding the sugar and beating until light. Add the honey and egg yolks. Beat for at least 3 minutes, until very light.

While the eggs are beating, sift together the flour, baking powder, salt, cinnamon, cloves, nutmeg, and allspice. Add the vanilla to the water or milk.

In a separate bowl, combine the raisins, figs, and chopped nuts. Add the dry ingredients to the batter, alternating with the liquid flavored with vanilla. Beat until well blended. Stir in the fruit-nut mixture. In a clean bowl, beat the egg whites until stiff but not dry. Fold into the batter.

Spoon the batter into a well-greased 10-inch tube pan and bake at 300 degrees F. for about 1 hour, until tested done. Cool completely as the cake slices best when cold. Keeps well in the refrigerator for a few days. Freezes well.

Variation:

Psalms 92:14 *"bring forth fruit"*: Substitute 1 cup mixed dried fruit for the chopped figs.

Note: For pareve, substitute vegetable shortening for the butter. Combine ½ cup water with ½ cup pareve milk to make the 1 cup of milk. Or use all water or apple juice.

Lekach

(Honey Cake)

Serves 12 or more

Honey cake is traditionally served on Rosh Hashanah and during the weeks that follow, until Simchat Torah. However, the popularity of honey cake, with its countless variations, is not limited to the holidays. Lekach is apreciated throughout the year, particularly at the synagogue Kiddush (reception following services, when the blessing over wine is recited).

Warm the honey (set the jar in a pan of hot water) before adding it to the mixing bowl. Note how easily the honey combines with the other ingredients.

½ cup oil
1 cup sugar
1 cup honey
4 eggs (graded large)
4 cups sifted all-purpose flour
1 teaspoon baking soda
2 teaspoons baking powder
1 scant teaspoon salt
1 teaspoon cloves
½ teaspoon nutmeg
2 teaspoons cinnamon
1 cup brewed black coffee, cooled
1 large or 2 small apples, peeled
½ cup chopped nuts (optional)

Preheat the oven to 325 degrees F. Line a 9 x 13 x 2-inch pan with wax paper; set aside.

In a large mixing bowl, beat together the oil, sugar, and honey. Add the eggs, one at a time, beating well after each addition.

Into a medium-sized bowl, sift together the dry ingredients. Add the dry mixture to the egg-honey mixture alternately with the cup of cooled coffee. Then grate the apple(s) into the batter. Transfer the batter to the prepared pan and bake for 1 hour, until the cake springs back when touched with a finger. The ground nuts may be sprinkled on the batter before baking.

Variations:

• One-half cup chopped nuts and/or ½ cup raisins can be added to the batter.

• Two tablespoons of brandy can replace 2 tablespoons of the brewed coffee.

• This can be baked in 2 loaf pans, though I always use a 9 x 13 x 2-inch pan.

Tayglach

Makes about 48

In Yiddish, *tayglach* means "dough pieces," and that's exactly what this New Year (and other holiday) confection consists of:

pieces of dough bathed in a hot honey syrup. Tayglach are similar to *stufoli,* an Italian treat, but the latter are deep-fried before being cloaked with a honey syrup.

Syrup:

> 1 pound honey (1⅓ cups)
> 2 cups sugar
> 1 cup cold water
> ½ cup boiling water
> Chopped nuts or coconut

Dough:

> 4 eggs (graded large)
> 1 tablespoon oil
> ¼ teaspoon salt
> ¼ teaspoon ginger
> 2 to 2½ cups all-purpose flour

In a large deep pot, combine the honey, sugar, and cup of cold water. Cover and place over very low heat.

To prepare the dough, in a medium-sized mixing bowl beat together the eggs, oil, salt, and ginger. Gradually add enough flour to make a soft, pliable dough. Add just enough flour so the dough can be handled. Transfer a small portion of the dough to a floured surface and roll it out to form a long rope about ½ inch in diameter. Cut the rope into pieces about 2½ inches long. Tie each segment of dough into a knot. Continue in this fashion until all the dough has been rolled out and shaped.

Increase the heat under the honey mixture. Bring to a rolling boil. Gradually drop the "knots" into the syrup. Add only a few at a time to prevent lowering the temperature of the syrup. Cook uncovered, without stirring, for 10 minutes.

Cover the pot and simmer, shaking occasionally. After 15 minutes, stir carefully. Continue to cook for 45 minutes to an hour, until all tayglach are a golden brown. When ready, the tayglach will sound hollow when tapped with the back of a spoon. Before removing from the heat, add ½ cup boiling water. Stir gently. Let stand for 1 minute. With a slotted spoon, remove the tayglach from the syrup. Enhance the appearance of the tayglach by rolling them in coconut or chopped nuts. Cool and store like cookies.

Variations:

• Sprinkle with additional ginger before rolling in coconut or nuts.

• Form the dough into small balls and cook in the honey syrup.

• Encase a nut or raisin in each small ball of dough before cooking in the syrup.

• Mix cooked round tayglach with honey, nuts, and candied fruits and form into a pyramid shape. Guests pull off tayglach with fingers. Provide napkins!

Note: You may recycle the honey syrup. Use it in a tzimmes, candied sweet potatoes, or as a syrup over waffles.

Sukkah Centerpiece

Sukkot, known as the Festival of Booths, is observed for a week in commemoration of the days our forefathers lived in *sukkot* (booths) while traveling in the desert. It is also considered the Festival of Thanksgiving.

One of the unique features of this holiday is the tradition of building temporary dwellings reminiscent of the sukkot built in the desert. For the most part, Jews today who erect sukkot do not actually live in them, but they do take their meals there for the duration of the holiday.

What's more fitting as a table centerpiece on Sukkot than an edible *sukkah* (singular)? The structure is made from a delicious spice dough that is very easy to work with. When baked, it becomes hard, so that once the sukkah has been assembled, it requires no additional support.

I concede that preparing this dramatic centerpiece is rather time-consuming, but it is eminently worth the time and trouble. A bonus is that after the holiday is over, the gingerbread sukkah can be eaten and enjoyed.

    5 cups sifted all-purpose flour
    1¼ teaspoons salt
    4 teaspoons cinnamon

1 teaspoon ginger
1 tablespoon cloves
1 tablespoon mace
1½ cups unsalted margarine
1½ cups sugar
2 eggs (graded large)
2 teaspoons vanilla extract
1 teaspoon lemon extract
½ cup sugar for gluing
Shredded coconut
Green food coloring

Preparing the Dough:

Into a large mixing bowl, sift together the flour, salt, and spices; set aside. In a medium-sized mixing bowl, cream together the margarine and sugar until very light. Stir in the eggs and extracts. Beat well. Stir the flour mixture into the creamed mixture. Mix until the ingredients are well combined. Cover the bowl with wax paper. Refrigerate the dough for at least 1 hour.

Making a Cardboard Pattern:

While the dough is chilling, cut a sukkah pattern from cardboard as follows: Cut 2 rectangles, each 4½ inches high x 8¾ inches long. One piece will be the back, the other the front. Cut one side piece measuring 4½ inches high x 5½ inches wide. Now, in the back piece, cut 2 windows, each 1 inch high x 1½ inches wide. Each window should be cut 1½ inches in from the side and 1⅝ inches up from the bottom.

The front piece has 2 windows and a door. The door is cut 3⅜ inches in from the side; cut it 2 inches wide x 3 inches high. The front windows are the same size as the back windows, 1 x 1½ inches, but cut them ¾ inch from the side and the same distance from the bottom of the front. Cut out a window in each side; cut them 2 inches in from the side and 1⅝ inches up from the bottom. Cut a piece of cardboard measuring ⅝ inch wide x 9¾ to 10 inches long or 7¾ inches long for supports from which to suspend foliage and decorations. The length of the supports will be determined by how you wish to set them atop the sukkah (either diagonally or straight across); cut 5 or 6 pieces.

Sukkah Centerpiece

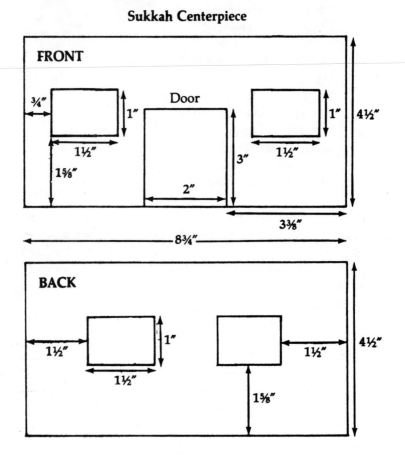

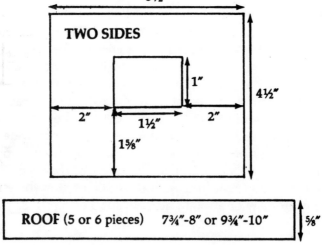

Back — cut 1 piece

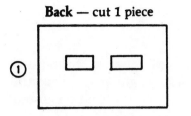

Front — cut 1 piece

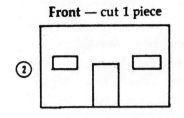

Side — cut 2 pieces

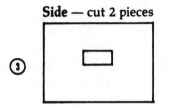

Top — cut 5 pieces

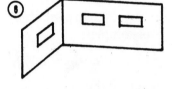

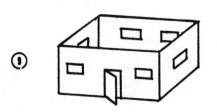

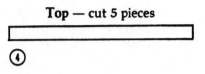

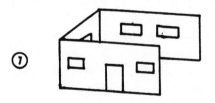

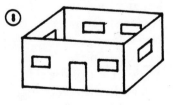

Cutting and Baking the Dough:

Preheat the oven to 375 degrees F. Have 2 or 3 ungreased baking sheets available.

If the dough is not stiff enough to roll out after chilling, add more flour, a few tablespoons at a time, and mix. Divide the dough into 4 equal parts. Place one part of dough on an ungreased baking sheet; roll it out ⅛- to ¼-inch thick. Place the cardboard pattern for the back of the sukkah directly on the dough. Cut around the pattern; remove the windows. Remove excess dough from the baking sheet; set aside. Roll out another portion of the dough on another baking sheet. Place the cardboard pattern piece for the front of the sukkah on the dough; cut around the pattern. The piece cut out from the door is baked separately as a door. Continue rolling out and cutting the balance of the dough. Make sure you cut 2 sides.

Combine all the excess dough into a ball. Roll it out and use the appropriate pattern to cut out 5 or 6 supports that will be placed on top of the sukkah.

Bake the cut dough in the preheated oven for about 10 minutes, until golden brown. Remove the baked cutouts to wire racks to cool completely.

Assembling the Sukkah:

When all the pieces have been baked and cooled, they are ready to be glued together with melted sugar. Melt ½ cup granulated sugar in a heavy skillet, being careful not to scorch it. Use a cookie sheet or large tray as the foundation for the sukkah. Dip one side edge of the back piece into the melted sugar. Then immediately place the edge with the melted sugar on it at a right angle to one of the side pieces. *Work quickly because the sugar hardens fast.* Hold the pieces together until the sugar hardens. Next, dip a side edge of the front piece into the melted sugar; hold it at a right angle to the side piece that has been glued to the back. Dip both edges of the second side piece into the melted sugar, and glue it to the front and back pieces. Now, dip the side of the door into the sugar and hold it to the door opening at any angle you desire, until the sugar hardens.

Before setting the supports across the top of the sukkah furnish the structure with a doll house table and chairs if available. Doll house people are welcome to sit on the chairs. A 3½-inch round paper doily serves as an elegant lace tablecloth. Tiny candlesticks and birthday candles ready the sukkah for the holiday meal. Set the supports across the sukkah top, and suspend from them, into the sukkah, miniature plastic fruits and vegetables. Or, string together cranberries, raisins, and popcorn and hang them inside the sukkah. A package of mermaid fern is excellent to use as foliage. Otherwise, substitute small tree branches or small boughs of evergreen leaves. Green coconut may be spread around the base of the sukkah to simulate green grass. To tint coconut green, place 1⅓ cups coconut in a jar, filling the jar no more than half full. Mix several drops of green food coloring diluted in ¼ to ½ teaspoon of water and sprinkle over the coconut. Cover the jar and shake vigorously until the coconut is evenly tinted.

Variations:

•Using this dough, a square Chanukah *dreidel* (top) can be constructed. First, cut the dreidel pattern from cardboard, then proceed to bake, cool, and glue the sides together. This makes an eye-appealing centerpiece. If made large, it can be filled with a variety of cookies. Small ones can serve as place-card holders (names are iced on each dreidel).

•Letters—Hebrew or English—can be made out of the dough and be used to spell out names or initials. To form letters, roll small amounts of the dough in the palms of the hands until pencil thin. Press the dough on ungreased baking sheets to form letters 2 to 3 inches high.

Simchat Torah
Lollipop Apples

As a child on Simchat Torah, I recall carrying a flag on a stick. A candied apple was inserted onto the part of the stick that protruded above the flag, and a candle was inserted into the top of the apple, which had been hollowed out to accommodate it.

If you decide to hollow out these Lollipop Apples so that

candles can be inserted, be sure to do so only after the candying process has been finished. It may be necessary to crack through the hardened candy with a nut pick or other sharp instrument.

> **8 medium-sized red apples**
> **8 lollipop sticks**
> **2 cups sugar**
> **⅔ cup light corn syrup**
> **1 cup water**
> **16 to 18 drops red food coloring**
> **½ teaspoon cinnamon flavoring**

Wash and dry the apples. Remove the stems. Insert a lollipop stick into each apple.

In a medium-sized saucepan, stir together the sugar, corn syrup, and water. Place over medium heat and continue stirring until the sugar has dissolved. Cover and bring slowly to a boil. Remove the cover, insert a candy thermometer, and boil rapidly without stirring until the mixture reaches 300 degrees F. or until a teaspoon of syrup separates into hard, brittle threads when dropped into cold water. During the cooking, remove any sugar crystals that may still cling to the sides of the pan by wiping the sides with wet cheesecloth wrapped around the tines of a fork. *Do not stir the syrup.* Add flavoring and coloring to tint the syrup a bright red. Remove from the heat and stir until blended.

Tip the saucepan to form a deep well of syrup. Dip the apples, one at a time, into the syrup, twisting until covered completely. Work quickly. If necessary, place the saucepan over low heat or boiling water to keep the syrup thin enough to coat the apples easily. Reserve excess syrup to be used as glue to attach any decorations you may desire.

On a lightly greased baking sheet, place the coated apples, stick up, to harden. Apples can be decorated with faces. Use your imagination. Try using lifesavers for eyes, gumdrops for nose and mouth, coconut for beard or hair, and so on. Use the reserved syrup to secure the features.

"Candle" Salad

The character of the food served on Chanukah can enhance the spirit of the holiday. These "candles" are symbolic of the Chanukah lights. They can serve as the focal point of your holiday table. On occasion, I serve these candles as a fruit dish before the appetizer at the Friday night dinner or at a birthday or anniversary get-together. Don't rule out the possibility of serving them as a fruit dessert.

> **Bananas**
> **Canned pineapple rings**
> **Lettuce**
> **Maraschino cherries**
> **Mayonnaise, whipping cream (pareve for**
> **meat), or Creamy Mayonnaise (whip**
> **½ cup cream and fold into 1 cup**
> **mayonnaise)**

Select straight rather than curved bananas. For each serving, place 1 or 2 pineapple rings on a ruffle of lettuce as a base. For the candle, insert half a peeled banana in the center of the pineapple. (To prevent the bananas from darkening, dip them into pineapple or lemon juice before assembling.) Mayonnaise, whipped cream, or creamy mayonnaise may be drizzled down the banana to simulate wax dripping down the side of the candle. With a toothpick, affix a red cherry atop each.

Chanukah Cranberry Candles

Serves 8

In order to prepare this attractive Chanukah accompaniment, one must accumulate eight empty six-ounce fruit juice cans. A dramatic way to serve cranberries. May also be served as a dessert.

> **1 can (1 pound) whole cranberry sauce**
> **1 cup boiling water**
> **1 package (3 ounces) red, yellow, or orange**
> **fruit-flavored gel**

————————▶

> ¼ teaspoon salt
> 1 tablespoon lemon juice
> ½ cup mayonnaise
> 1 apple, peeled, cored, and diced; or 1
>   orange, peeled, seeded, and diced
> ¼ cup chopped walnuts
> 8 baby carrots, peeled

In a small saucepan over medium heat, heat the cranberry sauce. Strain the hot juice into a mixing bowl and set the berries aside. Add the hot water to the hot juice. Dissolve the gel in the hot liquid mixture. Add the salt and lemon juice. Chill until thickened enough to mound slightly when dropped from a spoon. With a rotary beater, beat in the mayonnaise until light and fluffy. Fold in the cranberries, fruit, and nuts. Divide the mixture evenly into eight 6-ounce fruit juice cans. Chill for 4 hours or longer. With a vegetable parer, shave down each baby carrot to simulate a candle wick. When ready to serve, unmold the candles and insert a carrot wick into the top of each candle.

Sufganiyot

(Doughnuts)

Makes about 24

In Europe and America, on Chanukah it is traditional to eat *latkes* (pancakes). In Israel, it is the custom to eat *sufganiyot*, doughnuts fried in oil. These pareve doughnuts may be served plain, sugared, filled with jelly, or glazed.

> ½ cup plus 2 tablespoons pareve milk
> ½ cup plus 2 tablespoons water
> ⅓ cup unsalted margarine, cut up
> 5 cups unsifted all-purpose flour
> 2 envelopes active dry yeast
> ½ cup sugar
> 1 teaspoon salt
> 1 teaspoon nutmeg (optional)
> 2 eggs (graded large)
> Vegetable oil for frying

1 cup cherry jelly, or the flavor of your
   choice
Confectioners' sugar, granulated sugar, or
   cinnamon sugar

In a small saucepan, combine the pareve milk with the water and margarine. Cook over low heat until very warm; do not boil. The margarine does not have to melt.

In a large mixing bowl, combine 2 cups of the flour with the yeast, sugar, salt, and nutmeg. Mix well. Stir in the warm milk-margarine mixture; blend until smooth. Beat with an electric mixer at low speed for 2 minutes. Add the eggs and an additional ½ cup of flour. Beat until well blended. By hand, gradually stir in part of the remaining flour (about 1½ cups) to make a soft dough. Turn out onto a lightly floured surface; knead until smooth and elastic, about 8 minutes, adding only enough of the remaining cup of flour to keep the dough from sticking.

Place the dough in an oiled bowl, turning to grease all sides. Cover and let rise in a warm draft-free place until doubled in bulk, about 1 to 1½ hours.

Punch down the dough. Return to a floured surface and knead for about a minute to remove any air bubbles. Let rest under an inverted bowl for 15 minutes.

Divide the dough in half. Roll out the dough into a ¼-inch-thick circle. With a 3-inch cutter, cut out dough rounds. Arrange these on a lightly greased baking sheet. Lightly brush the tops with oil to prevent a skin from forming. Cover with plastic wrap. Repeat the procedure with the second piece of dough. Press the trimmings together, reroll and cut. Transfer these to a lightly greased baking sheet, brush with oil, and cover with plastic wrap. Set to rise in a warm draft-free place for about 45 minutes, until doubled in bulk.

In a deep fryer or a skillet at least 3 inches deep, heat a minimum of 1½ inches of oil to 375 degrees F. Fry the doughnuts, a few at a time, until golden brown, turning once. Remove and drain on absorbent paper.

When cool, with a sharp knife cut a small slit in one side of each doughnut. Force jelly into the doughnuts using a pastry bag, cookie press, or the tip of a teaspoon. Before serving, dust with confectioners' sugar, dip into granulated sugar or cinnamon sugar, or glaze as desired.

Doughnut Glazes:

Each glaze recipe makes ¾ to 1 cup of glaze.

• *Vanilla:*

In a small bowl, combine 2 cups of confectioners' sugar with 2 tablespoons water and 1 teaspoon vanilla extract. Stir until smooth. If the glaze is too thick to dip or drizzle, stir in more water, a teaspoon at a time.

• *Lemon:*

In a small bowl, combine 2 cups of confectioners' sugar with 2 tablespoons water, 1 teaspoon grated lemon rind, and 2 teaspoons lemon juice. Stir until smooth.

• *Orange:*

In a small bowl, combine 2 cups confectioners' sugar with 1 teaspoon grated orange rind and 2 to 3 tablespoons orange juice. Stir until smooth.

• *Maple:*

Place 2 cups of confectioners' sugar in a saucepan with ¼ cup maple-flavored syrup and 1 to 2 tablespoons water. Stir. Heat to boiling. Best used while still warm.

• *Chocolate I:*

In a small saucepan over low heat, melt 2 squares semisweet chocolate with 2 tablespoons unsalted margarine. Stir in 1 cup of confectioners' sugar and 3 to 4 tablespoons water. Stir until smooth.

• *Chocolate II:*

In a small bowl, combine 2 cups of confectioners' sugar with 2 to 3 tablespoons cocoa. Mix well. Gradually stir in ¼ cup of boiling water. Stir until the mixture is smooth.

• *Honey:*

In a small saucepan over low heat, combine ½ cup honey with 1 cup of confectioners' sugar. Heat just to boiling. Best used while still warm.

Menorah Upside-Down Cake

Serves 6 to 9

This is a traditional upside-down cake with a menorah design in the topping. Be sure to allow the baked cake to cool on a rack for five to ten minutes before turning it out. The menorah will then have a chance to set and the cake will slip out nicely.

Menorah Topping:

> 3 tablespoons unsalted margarine
> ½ cup firmly packed brown sugar
> 1 can (20 ounces) pineapple spears, drained,
>   reserve the juice
> 9 maraschino cherries

Cake Batter:

> ⅓ cup solid white vegetable shortening
> ½ cup sugar
> 1 egg (graded large)
> 1 teaspoon vanilla extract
> ½ teaspoon lemon rind
> 1½ cups sifted all-purpose flour
> 2 teaspoons baking powder
> ¼ teaspoon salt
> ½ cup reserved pineapple juice

Melt the margarine in a 9-inch-square pan. Add the brown sugar. Pat the mixture evenly over the bottom of the cake pan. Using the pineapple spears and cherries, arrange a menorah design on the brown sugar. Place 2 spears end to end across the pan for the menorah base. Then place a single spear in the center of the base at a right angle to it; this will be the *shamash* (the "servant" candle with which the others are lighted). Cut 8 pineapple spears one inch shorter than the *shamash*. Position these parallel to the *shamash*, 4 on either side, to represent the candles. Under the *shamash* spear and under the base, place 2 half-pieces of pineapple spear side by side; these are the menorah stand. Two more half-pieces may be placed end-to-end under the stand. Place a cherry over each vertical spear to represent the flames.

Preheat the oven to 375 degrees F.

Now prepare the cake batter. In a medium-sized mixing bowl, cream the shortening. Gradually add the sugar. Beat until light and fluffly. Add the egg, vanilla, and lemon rind.

Into a bowl, sift together the dry ingredients. Alternately add the dry ingredients and the pineapple juice to the creamed mixture, beating after each addition until blended and smooth.

Carefully spoon the batter over the menorah topping in the pan. Bake for 45 minutes, until the top springs back when lightly pressed. Let the cake cool in the pan for 5 to 10 minutes. Invert it onto a serving dish. Allow 2 to 3 minutes before removing the pan.

Variation:

For a shortcut, prepare the batter from a white or yellow cake mix (you will only need half of a regular-size package). Spoon this over the menorah topping.

Passover Sponge Cake

Serves 8 or more

Typical Passover sponge cake is not among my favorites. This recipe, however, makes one of the best sponge cakes I have come across. Although a classic sponge cake does not contain any shortening at all, this cake does contain a small amount of oil. It is delicately flavored with orange juice and vanilla sugar.

> 7 eggs (graded large), separated
> 1 cup sugar
> ¾ cup potato starch
> ¼ cup orange juice
> 1 envelope (.43 ounces) vanilla sugar
> 1 tablespoon oil

Preheat the oven to 325 degrees F.

In a large mixing bowl, beat the egg yolks with the cup of sugar until fluffy thick. Add the potato starch and orange juice. Beat until well combined.

In a clean bowl, with clean beaters, beat the egg whites until stiff, gradually adding the vanilla sugar. Just before folding the egg whites into the yolk mixture, stir the oil into the yolks. Fold in the stiffly beaten egg whites.

Bake in an ungreased 9-inch tube pan with a removable bottom for 45 minutes or until tested done. Consider the time given only as a guide. Check for doneness by piercing the cake at the center with a toothpick or fine skewer. If it comes out clean, the cake is done. The cake will also pull away slightly from the sides of the pan. Invert to cool.

Note: A steel knitting needle makes the perfect tool for loosening a cake baked in a tube pan. It will slip easily around the center of the tube and rim of the pan without tearing into the tender baked crust. Run a metal spatula or thin-bladed knife under the cake.

Purim Koilitch

(Very Large Challah Twist)

One of my fondest memories of Purim is the aroma emanating from my mother's kitchen as she was baking challah for the Purim *seudah* (dinner). She referred to it as a Purim *koilitch*. I tried to determine how she arrived at the name koilitch. I came to the conclusion that it was her version of *kulech* or *kolachy*, a traditional Russian Easter cake which originated in Bohemia and is made from a sweetened yeast-raised dough containing eggs.

Challah, a soft and delicious egg-rich white bread, is traditionally served at the Sabbath and holiday table. For holidays, it may be formed into many symbolic shapes. Rosh Hashanah and Yom Kippur challahs are shaped round, symbolizing continuity. For Yom Kippur, ladder and hand shapes are sometimes formed, the ladder symbolizing the hope that man's prayers will ascend to heaven, the hand expressing the hope that man will be inscribed for a good year.

> 2 envelopes active dry yeast
> 1 tablespoon sugar
> 1 cup warm water (110 to 115 degrees F.)
> 1 cup hot water

6 tablespoons oil
½ cup sugar
1 teaspoon salt
7 cups sifted all-purpose flour
4 eggs (graded large), divided
½ cup golden raisins
Oil for the bowl
1 tablespoon water

In a small mixing bowl, dissolve the yeast and tablespoon of sugar in the lukewarm water. In a large mixing bowl, combine the hot water with the oil, ½ cup sugar, and salt. Stir to dissolve the sugar and salt. Cool to lukewarm.

Add 2 cups of flour to the water to make a batter. Beat 3 of the eggs in a small bowl and add to the batter along with the yeast and raisins. Beat well. Add the remaining flour, or enough to make a soft dough. Knead lightly, gather into a ball, and place in an oiled bowl, turning to coat all sides. Cover and set in a warm draft-free place to rise until doubled in bulk, about 2 hours. When light, punch down the dough and shape the challah.

To make braids, cut the risen dough into 2 equal parts; then cut off a third of one part. These 3 pieces will make 3 braids of varying size.

Divide the largest piece of dough into thirds. Roll into 3 equal strips about 18 inches long. Align the strips next to each other on a large greased baking sheet. Braid the strips together; tuck each end in carefully. Divide the second piece into thirds. Roll into equal strips about 16 inches long, then form into a second braid and place on top of the first braid. With the remaining small piece of dough, make a third braid about 14 inches long and place on top of the second braid. Be sure to center each braid on the larger one below. Let rise for 1 hour or until doubled in bulk.

Preheat the oven to 350 degrees F. Beat the fourth egg with tablespoon of water until well blended. Brush the egg mixture over the entire challah. Bake for 35 to 45 minutes, until the bread is golden brown and sounds hollow when tapped with a knife handle, a spoon, or the knuckles. Remove the challah from the baking sheet and cool on a wire rack.

Variations:

• After glazing the challah with the egg wash, sprinkle with poppy seeds or sesame seeds.

• Divide the dough in half and make 2 smaller breads.

• For a less sweet bread, reduce the amount of sugar.

• Make individual challah rolls for the holidays. For Purim, form them as hamantaschen.

• Make miniature buns for hamburgers and miniature hot dog rolls for cocktail franks. To shape the buns, roll the dough ¼ inch thick on a lightly floured board. Cut out rounds with a small round cookie cutter or the top of an empty pill bottle. For the cocktail franks, an empty spice can or the top of an empty band-aid box (about 2¾ x 1½ inches) make excellent cutters. Round off the oblong ends by cutting away corners with a knife. Let the buns rise on a greased baking sheet. Brush with beaten egg. Bake in a 400-degree F. oven for 5 to 10 minutes, until done.

• Omit the raisins and you have a basic sweet dough from which a variety of dessert breads can be made. Try kneading in a generous amount of cut-up dried apricots, dates, and prunes. Bake in a mold or a bread pan and *voilà!* A delicious fruit bread.

Hamantaschen

The food most associated with Purim is the *hamantasch*, a filled triangular-shaped pastry. The traditional fillings are made with poppy seeds (*mohn*) or prunes, but you are free to make a filling out of the dried fruits, nuts, or jams or jellies of your choice.

Just as personal preference dictates the filling used for hamantaschen, so too does it dictate the dough used to hold the filling. The next several recipes give some popular options.

Cookie Dough:

Makes 60 or more

> 4 eggs (graded large)
> ¾ cup melted shortening or oil
> ¾ cup sugar
> Juice and grated rind of 1 lemon

———➤

4½ cups sifted all-purpose flour
3 teaspoons baking powder
½ teaspoon salt
1 egg (graded large) beaten with 1 teaspoon
    water

Preheat the oven to 350 degrees F. Grease baking sheets; set aside.

In a deep bowl, combine the eggs, shortening or oil, sugar, and lemon juice and rind. Beat until smooth.

Sift together the flour, baking powder, and salt. Combine with the egg mixture; mix until a dough is formed. Turn out the dough onto a floured surface. Knead for several minutes, until smooth. Wrap in plastic wrap and refrigerate for about 1 hour.

On a lightly floured board, roll out the dough to ⅛-inch thickness. With a 2½- or 3-inch cookie cutter, cut out rounds of dough. Place a half-tablespoon of filling in the center of each circle. Fold up the edges of the circle to form an equilateral triangle, a three-cornered packet. Brush with the egg wash. Place the hamantaschen about 1 inch apart on the prepared baking sheets. Bake for 25 to 30 minutes, until nicely browned. Transfer to racks to cool.

Yeast Dough:

Makes about 40

1 envelope active dry yeast
½ teaspoon sugar
½ cup warm water (110 to 115 degrees F.)
1 cup all-purpose flour
2 eggs (graded large)
2 teaspoons salt
2 tablespoons melted shortening or oil
¾ cup warm milk or pareve milk
⅓ cup sugar
3½ to 4 cups all-purpose flour
Honey
1 egg (graded large), beaten

In a large mixing bowl, proof the yeast and sugar in the warm water for about 5 minutes. Beat in the cup of flour. Set aside to rise for 30 minutes in a warm draft-free place. Beat in the eggs, salt, shortening or oil, warm milk, sugar, and 3½ cups of the flour. Knead for 5 minutes. Place the dough in a large bowl that has been lightly coated with oil. Cover and set in a warm draft-free place to rise for 1½ hours, until the dough is doubled in bulk. Punch down the dough and knead, adding a bit more flour if necessary.

Transfer the dough to a well-floured board and roll out to ¼-inch thickness. Cut into 3-inch rounds. Place a tablespoon of filling on each and top with a tiny bit of honey. Fold up the edges of each dough round to form an equilateral triangle. Pinch together the ends to seal. Place on greased baking sheets and allow to rise for at least 1 hour, until very light. When risen, preheat the oven to 400 degrees F. Brush with the beaten egg and bake for 20 minutes, until lightly browned. Cool on wire racks.

Honey Dough for Hamantaschen

Makes 30 to 36

When working with honey, it is always best to warm the honey before combining it with other ingredients. Do so by placing the jar of honey in a pan of hot water.

> 4 cups sifted all-purpose flour
> ½ teaspoon salt
> 1 teaspoon baking powder
> 4 eggs (graded large)
> ½ cup very soft solid white vegetable shortening or melted vegetable shortening
> 1 cup honey, warmed
> 1 tablespoon lemon juice

Sift together the flour, salt, and baking powder. Beat the eggs with the vegetable shortening. Beat in the honey and lemon juice. Stir in half of the sifted dry ingredients. Add the remaining dry ingredients to the mixture, mixing well until a dough is formed. It may be necessary to use your hands to get a smooth working dough. Divide the dough in half.

Preheat the oven to 350 degrees F. On a lightly floured surface, roll out half of the dough to ⅛-inch thickness. Cut into 3-inch rounds. Drop a heaping teaspoon of filling in the center of each circle. Fold up the edges of each round to form an equilateral triangle; pinch the seams together to seal. You may leave a slight opening in the center to expose the filling. Transfer the triangles to lightly greased baking sheets. Bake for 12 to 15 minutes, until lightly browned. Cool on wire racks.

Hamantasch Fillings

Prune:

> 1 pound prunes, washed, pitted and ground
>   fine
> ½ cup chopped nuts
> ¼ cup honey
> Grated rind of 1 orange
> 1 tablespoon lemon juice

Blend together all ingredients. The filling is now ready to use.

Easy Prune:

Purchase prune butter (lekvar), which is available in most supermarkets. Add your own nuts, raisins, orange or lemon rind, etc.

Poppy Seed:

> 1 cup poppy seeds
> ½ cup water
> ¼ cup honey
> ½ cup chopped almonds
> Grated rind of ½ lemon
> ¼ cup sugar
> 1 tart apple, peeled and grated

In a small saucepan, combine all ingredients except the apple. Cook over low heat until thick. Let cool. Add the grated apple. The filling is now ready to use.

Easy Poppy Seed:

To a can of ready-made poppy seed filling add ¾ cup chopped nuts and lemon juice to taste. Blend well.

Apricot:

> ½ pound dried apricots
> 1½ cups water
> ¾ to 1 cup sugar

In a small saucepan over medium-low heat, cook the apricots in the water until the apricots are very soft. Mash or process in a blender or food processor. Add sugar to taste and simmer over low heat until thick, about 10 minutes. Cool before using.

Appetizer Hamantaschen

Makes 9 or more

An unusual appetizer to serve at a Purim feast. These hamantaschen are somewhat on the order of *pirogen* or *peroshki*, small filled pastries. Prepared with a rich short pastry, they are filled with a savory chopped liver mixture and, if desired, sprinkled with poppy seeds.

Liver Filling:

> ¼ cup finely chopped onion
> 1 tablespoon unsalted margarine
> ¾ pound chicken livers
> Pinch of salt
> ⅛ teaspoon black pepper
> 2 tablespoons tomato sauce or ketchup
> ¼ cup green peas, cooked

Pastry:

> 3 cups sifted all-purpose flour
> 1 teaspoon baking powder
> ½ teaspoon salt
> 1 teaspoon onion powder
> 1 teaspoon poppy seeds
> 2 teaspoons crushed dried dill

→

2 teaspoons caraway seeds (optional)
1 cup solid white vegetable shortening
6 to 8 tablespoons cold water
1 egg (graded large), beaten
Poppy seeds

To Prepare the Filling:

In a small skillet over low heat, sauté the chopped onion in the margarine until translucent. Set aside. Broil the livers until no trace of redness remains, then chop fine or put through a food mill or food processor. Stir in the sautéed onions. Season with the salt, pepper, and tomato sauce. Finally, blend in the cooked green peas.

To Prepare the Pastry:

Into a large bowl, sift the flour, baking powder, salt, and onion powder. Stir in the dill and the seeds. With a pastry blender, cut in the shortening until the mixture resembles coarse meal. Sprinkle in the water a tablespoon at a time, mixing with a fork until all the flour is moistened and the dough leaves the sides of the bowl clean. Gather the dough together into a ball. Divide the dough into 2 parts and, on a floured surface, roll out the dough until ¼-inch thick. Preheat the oven to 400 degrees F.

To Shape the Hamantaschen:

Cut the pastry into 4-inch rounds. Brush with beaten egg. Place 2 tablespoons of liver filling in the center of each circle. Fold each into a triangle and seal the edges. Brush the tops with beaten egg. Sprinkle with poppy seeds if desired. Transfer to a lightly greased 10 x 15-inch baking sheet. Bake for about 20 minutes, until golden brown. These may be served with a mushroom or tomato sauce, but they make a more dramatic presentation if they are not cloaked in a sauce. A glass of tomato juice is a nice accompaniment to this appetizer.

Mohnlach

(Poppy Seed Candy)

Makes 18 to 24 pieces

Poppy seeds (*mohn*) are used in many desserts and pastries traditionally served on Purim. These candies are so easy to prepare.

> 1 cup mohn (poppy seeds)
> 1 cup honey
> ¼ cup sugar
> ¼ to ½ teaspoon ginger (optional)
> ½ cup chopped almonds or walnuts

Wash the mohn several times and drain overnight in a cheesecloth bag or in a cloth-lined sieve.

In a saucepan, combine the honey, sugar, and ginger. Cook over low heat until the sugar is dissolved. Remove from the heat. Stir in the mohn and chopped nuts. Return to the heat and bring to a slow boil, stirring constantly to prevent the honey from scorching. Cook for about 10 to 12 minutes, until a drop of the mixture forms a small ball when dropped into cold water.

Spread the mixture on a wet pastry board or baking sheet. With the back of a spoon moistened with cold water, flatten to the desired thickness, about ¼ inch. When slightly cool and hardened, cut into diamond shapes. When cooled completely, use a spatula to lift the candies off the board.

Variation:

Flatten out to desired thickness using the back of a tablespoon moistened with cold wine.

Sweet-and-Sour Meat Loaf

Serves 9 or more

While shopping in the supermarket one day, I was greeted by an acquaintance who raved about an unusual Passover meat loaf she had created. I tried it, and I pass it on to you for your eating pleasure.

> **2 pounds ground beef**
> **1 medium-sized onion, finely diced**
> **1 cup matzo farfel**
> **½ cup water**
> **2 eggs (graded large), beaten**
> **1 can (11 ounces) tomato and mushroom**
> **sauce**
> **¼ cup lemon juice**
> **¼ cup sugar, or more to taste**

Preheat the oven to 350 degrees F. Lightly grease a 9 x 13 x 2-inch baking pan; set aside.

In a large mixing bowl, combine the ground meat with the onion, matzo farfel, water, and eggs. In a large glass measuring cup, combine the tomato sauce, lemon juice, and sugar. Mix to blend well. Taste and adjust the balance of sweet-sour. Add half of the liquid mixture to the mixed meat. Blend together well. Place the meat in the baking pan and form into a loaf. Pour the remaining dressing over the meat. Bake for 1 hour. Slice to serve. (This makes a large loaf. It can be packed into a smaller 8½ x 10¾-inch utility pan and cut into squares to serve.)

Passover Carrot Kugel

Serves 6 to 8

Bite into a crisp raw carrot and you enjoy a crunchy vegetable rich in vitamin A. But if you'd rather have your carrots cooked, try this recipe.

One Passover I enjoyed the hospitality of Fran Gerber, a friend of my daughter Naomi. With the main dish I was served a piece of this carrot cake in place of a carrot tzimmes. Though it was referred to as a cake, I consider it a kugel. Once the carrots have been cooked, the cake is mixed together very quickly.

> **Oil for the pan**
> **10 carrots, cooked and mashed**
> **3 eggs (graded large)**
> **2 tablespoons oil**
> **½ cup sugar**

½ cup potato starch
1 teaspoon salt
1 teaspoon cinnamon

Preheat the oven to 350 degrees F. Grease with oil a 7 x 11-inch baking pan or an 8½-inch ring mold.

Place the mashed carrots in a mixing bowl. Beat in the eggs, oil, and sugar. Stir in the potato starch, salt, and cinnamon. Mix well. Transfer the batter to the prepared pan or mold. Bake for approximately 45 minutes, until the top is nicely browned.

Passover Granola Bars

Makes 40 bars

You can now enjoy granola bars during Passover.

Grease for the pan
3½ cups matzo farfel
1 cup shredded coconut
1 cup coarsely chopped blanched almonds
6 tablespoons unsalted margarine, melted
½ cup firmly packed brown sugar
⅓ cup honey
½ teaspoon salt
¾ cup raisins
2 eggs (graded large), well beaten

Preheat the oven to 325 degrees F. Lightly grease a baking sheet.

In a medium-sized bowl, combine the farfel, coconut, and chopped nuts. Spread the mixture on the baking sheet. Bake for 15 to 20 minutes, tossing several times, until the mixture is lightly toasted.

Increase the oven temperature to 350 degrees F. Generously grease a 10 x 15 x 1-inch jelly-roll pan; set aside. Meanwhile, in a 2-quart saucepan combine the margarine, brown sugar, honey, and salt. Bring to a simmer for a few minutes, stirring constantly. Remove from the heat.

Add the lightly toasted farfel-coconut-nut mixture to the syrup mixture. Add the raisins and mix well, tossing the ingredients as if you were making a tossed salad. Stir in the beaten eggs and mix well. Press the mixture firmly into the prepared jelly-roll pan. Bake for 15 to 20 minutes, until golden brown. Cool and cut into bars. Store in a cool dry place or refrigerator.

Cottage Cheese Brownies for Passover

Makes sixteen
2¼-inch squares

When I served as the Passover food stylist for a large New England dairy, I developed this cottage cheese brownie recipe for Passover. You and your friends will want to add it to your holiday repertoire.

Cheese Mixture:

> 1 egg (graded large), well beaten
> ¼ cup sugar
> 1 cup uncreamed cottage cheese
> 1 tablespoon potato starch
> ½ teaspoon lemon juice

Beat the egg well with the sugar. Thoroughly blend the cottage cheese, potato starch, and lemon juice with the beaten egg mixture. Set aside.

Brownie Batter:

> Grease for the pan
> 3 eggs (graded large)
> 1 cup sugar
> 1 stick (½ cup) unsalted butter or
>   margarine, melted
> 1 teaspoon lemon juice
> ⅓ cup unsweetened cocoa
> ½ cup matzo cake meal
> ½ cup chopped walnuts

Preheat the oven to 350 degrees F. Grease a 9-inch-square baking pan; set aside.

In the large bowl of an electric mixer, combine the eggs, sugar, melted butter or margarine, and lemon juice. Beat until smooth. Add the cocoa, matzo cake meal, and nuts. Beat until well blended.

Pour half of the batter into the prepared baking pan. Spread the batter evenly; top with the cheese blend. Add the rest of the batter. Draw a knife through the layers to create a marble effect. Bake for 35 minutes or until tested done. Pierce the cake at the center with a toothpick or fine skewer. If it comes out clean, the cake is done. Remove the pan to a wire rack. Let cool completely before cutting into 2¼-inch squares.

Shavuot Custard Pudding

Serves 10 or more

This large recipe, courtesy of Lillian Corr, is ideal as a Shavuot luncheon dessert. Noodles are baked in a sea of rich and creamy cheese custard, and the pudding may be served plain, with a dollop of cream atop each serving, or garnished with sliced strawberries.

Lillian is very enthusiastic about this dish, since she assembles the pudding a day ahead and bakes it just hours before serving time.

Pudding:

Grease for the pan
¾ pound medium egg noodles
¾ to 1 cup sugar, to taste
¼ cup unsalted butter or margarine, at
    room temperature
1 pint sour cream
7 eggs (graded large)
1 teaspoon vanilla extract
1 teaspoon lemon extract
1 teaspoon cinnamon
⅛ teaspoon nutmeg
3 cups milk
1 pound cottage cheese
1 cup golden raisins, cut

Topping:

> ½ cup cornflake crumbs
> 1 teaspoon sugar
> ½ teaspoon cinnamon

Grease an 11 x 15 x 2-inch baking pan; set aside. Cook the noodles according to package instructions. Meanwhile, in a large mixing bowl cream the sugar with the butter or margarine. Add the sour cream and eggs. Beat until blended. Add the extracts, spices, and milk. Beat together. Add the cottage cheese. Beat until the cheese is well blended into the mixture, but not until the curds of cheese are no longer discernible. Drain the cooked noodles. Fold the noodles and raisins into the custard mixture. Blend well.

Turn the mixture into the prepared pan. Set the pan in the refrigerator for 3 or more hours. Before baking, blend together the topping ingredients and sprinkle on top. Bake at 350 degrees F. for 1 to 1¼ hours, until the top is nicely browned.

Peach Glow Sponge

Serves 6

The compatibility of juicy cling peaches and cottage cheese has long been known to food fanciers. Here, cottage cheese is scooped into peach halves and baked in a richly satisfying sauce. A memorable three-layer dessert to serve on Shavuot.

> Grease for the pan
> 1 can (1 pound) cling peach halves
> ⅔ cup cottage cheese
> ¾ to 1 cup sugar, to taste
> ¼ cup all-purpose flour
> ¼ teaspoon salt (optional)
> 1 teaspoon grated lemon rind
> 2 tablespoons unsalted butter or margarine, melted
> 1 cup milk
> 3 eggs (graded large), separated
> ¼ cup lemon juice

Preheat the oven to 325 degrees F. Generously grease an 8 x 8 x 2-inch or 9 x 9 x 2-inch baking pan; set aside.

Drain the peaches very well. Mound the centers of each peach half with the cottage cheese. In a mixing bowl, combine the sugar, flour, salt, lemon rind, and butter or margarine. Beat until blended, then mix in the milk.

In a small mixing bowl, beat the egg yolks until thick and lemon-colored; blend into the sugar mixture along with the lemon juice. In a clean bowl, beat the egg whites until stiff but not dry; fold them into the sugar mixture. Pour the batter around the peaches. Place the pan in a hot water bath and bake for 45 to 50 minutes. Cool in the pan. Serve slightly warm.

Variations:

Substitute 1 can (1 pound) sliced cling peaches for the peach halves. Arrange them in the baking pan. Spread ⅔ cup small-curd creamed cottage cheese over the sliced peaches and proceed as above.

Three-cheese
Pinwheel Lasagna

Serves 6

Sometimes the hardest part of preparing a dairy meal for Shavuot or the Nine Days (the first nine days of the Hebrew month of Av, during which meat and wine are not served) is finding an interesting main course. This unusual version of lasagna saves the day. Whereas lasagna noodles are generally layered, here the noodles are coiled around a two-cheese mixture and baked topped with a spicy sauce and a third kind of cheese. A tossed salad is all that is necessary to complete the meal.

> 12 lasagna noodles
> 2 cups cream-style cottage cheese
> 4 ounces cream cheese
> 2 eggs (graded large)
> 1 tablespoon chopped pasley (optional)
> ½ teaspoon dried basil (optional)

➡

       ¼ teaspoon salt
       1 jar (16 ounces) marinara sauce
       8 ounces mozzarella cheese, shredded

Slide the noodles, one at a time, into a large kettle of boiling salted water (¼ teaspoon salt to each quart of water). Cook according to package directions; drain; cover with cold water. Preheat the oven to 350 degrees F.

In a medium-sized mixing bowl, combine the cottage cheese with the cream cheese; beat in the eggs and seasonings. Lift the noodles, one at a time, from the water; drain on paper towels. Spread each noodle with about 1 teaspoon of marinara sauce and ¼ cup of the cheese filling; roll up jelly-roll-fashion.

Place each rolled-up noodle seam side down in a 9 x 13 x 2-inch baking dish. Continue to roll up the remaining noodles in the same fashion until all noodles are used up and placed in the baking dish. Spoon the remaining sauce over the rolls. Cover the baking dish with foil and bake for 40 minutes. Uncover. Arrange the shredded mozzarella cheese over the rolls in the dish. Bake 5 minutes longer or until the cheese melts.

Note: For a reduced-salt diet, use salt-free cottage cheese and salt-free marinara sauce.

Fruity Noodles

Serves 7 or 8

Noodles and cheese is a favorite dish to serve on Shavuot or during the Nine Days. This combination of noodles and cheese plus fruit makes a delightful dessert. It is comparable to a glazed cheese pie but made in a noodle crust.

       Grease for the pan
       8 ounces broad egg noodles
       2 tablespoons unsalted butter or margarine
       8 ounces cream cheese, softened
       1 egg (graded large)
       2 tablespoons sugar
       1 can (21 ounces) fruit pie filling of your
          choice (or prepare your own—see below)

Crumb Topping:

        ½ cup all-purpose flour
        ⅓ cup firmly packed brown sugar
        3 tablespoons unsalted butter or margarine,
            melted

Preheat the oven to 375 degrees F. Grease an 8-inch-square baking pan; set aside.

Cook the noodles according to package directions. Toss the noodles with the butter or margarine and press evenly onto the bottom and sides of the prepared pan. Set aside.

In a medium-sized bowl, beat the cream cheese with the egg and sugar until blended. Spread evenly into the prepared baking dish; top with the filling and crumb topping. Bake for 30 minutes, then let stand for 30 minutes or until set.

Variations:

    You can prepare your own fruit filling.

Blueberry Fruit Filling:

        ⅓ cup sugar
        ¼ cup all-purpose flour
        ½ teaspoon cinnamon (optional)
        3 cups fresh blueberries
        1 teaspoon lemon juice
        1 tablespoon unsalted butter or margarine

Stir together the sugar, flour, and cinnamon. Mix lightly with the blueberries. Turn into the prepared baking dish. Top with crumb topping.

Pineapple Fruit Filling:

        1 can (15½ ounces) crushed pineapple
        ¾ cup sugar
        2½ tablespoons cornstarch
        2 tablespoons unsalted butter or margarine
        2 teaspoons lemon rind
        2 tablespoons lemon juice

Drain the pineapple, reserving ½ cup juice. In a medium-sized saucepan, combine the sugar and cornstarch. Stir well. Gradually add the reserved pineapple juice, and cook over medium heat, stirring constantly until thickened. Remove from the heat. Add drained pineapple, butter or margarine, lemon rind, and lemon juice. Stir until the butter melts.

Shavuot Dainties

Makes twenty-four
2-inch squares

Two favorites, malted milk and brownies, are combined to make these holiday treats. There is no chocolate to melt. The secret ingredient is the chocolate-flavored malted milk powder.

> **Grease for the pan**
> **1 cup sifted all-purpose flour**
> **⅓ cup solid white vegetable shortening**
> **½ cup firmly packed dark brown sugar**
> **2 tablespoons all-purpose flour**
> **½ cup chocolate malted milk powder**
> **½ teaspoon baking powder**
> **¼ teaspoon salt**
> **2 eggs (graded large)**
> **⅔ cup sugar**
> **1 cup grated coconut**
> **1 cup chopped nuts**

Preheat the oven to 375 degrees F. Lightly grease an 8 x 12-inch pan.

With a pastry blender, combine the cup of flour, shortening, and brown sugar until crumbly. Pat the mixture into the prepared pan. Bake for 10 minutes. Do not turn off the oven.

Into a small mixing bowl, sift together the 2 tablespoons flour, malted milk powder, baking powder, and salt. In a medium-sized bowl, with an electric mixer, beat the eggs very well. Gradually beat in the sugar. Toss the coconut and nuts with the sifted dry ingredients. Add to the beaten egg mixture. Blend well. Pour the batter into the baked crumb mixture. Bake for 25 minutes. Cool then cut into 2-inch squares.

Note: These dainties may be cut and served finger-fashion. Or cut into large squares and top with a dollop of whipped cream or a scoop of ice cream.

11

To Gild the Lily

Dressings, Sauces & Condiments

Poppy Seed Dressing

Makes 1½ cups

A dressing that can be used to complement fresh or canned fruits.

½ cup sugar
Dash of salt
Dash of dry mustard
¼ cup white salad vinegar
1 cup salad oil
½ teaspoon poppy seeds

In a small saucepan, combine the sugar, salt, mustard, and vinegar. Heat to boiling over medium-high heat. Cool completely. Transfer to a small mixing bowl. Add the oil slowly, beating constantly with an electric mixer. Stir in the poppy seeds.

Paulette Korn's Salad Dressing

Makes about 1 cup

Fresh romaine lettuce generously garnished with sliced fresh mushrooms and dressed with this salad dressing makes a gourmet delight.

2 teaspoons coarse salt
½ teaspoon freshly ground black pepper
1 teaspoon prepared mustard
1 clove garlic, minced
2 tablespoons lemon juice
½ cup salad oil
2 tablespoons olive oil
1 raw egg (graded large)
2 tablespoons parsley, minced
1 tablespoon wine vinegar

Combine all the ingredients in a screw-top jar with a tight-fitting lid. Shake well. Chill to blend flavors.

Variation:

Use all olive oil.

Lee's Secret Salad Dressing

Makes about 2¼ cups

My friend Lee Spector has shared with me many of her cherished recipes. Here is her secret salad dressing.

1 cup salad oil
2 teaspoons sugar
½ cup wine vinegar
½ cup ketchup
1 to 2 tablespoons soy sauce
1 tablespoon sherry
2 cloves garlic, sliced and reserved

In a blender jar, combine all the ingredients. Blend at high speed for 2 minutes. Or, combine all ingredients in a screw-top jar with a tight-fitting lid. Shake well to blend. Add the sliced garlic cloves and chill to blend flavors.

French Dressing

Makes ¾ cup

A popular salad dressing that is easy to make.

> ½ cup salad oil
> ¼ cup cider vinegar or wine vinegar
> ½ to 1 teaspoon sugar, to taste
> ½ teaspoon salt
> ¼ teaspoon paprika
> ⅛ teaspoon black pepper

In a blender jar, combine all the ingredients. Blend at high speed for 1 minute. Or, combine all ingredients in a screw-top jar with a tight-fitting lid. Shake well to blend.

Variation:

For an herbed French dressing, add ½ teaspoon dried basil and ½ teaspoon dried tarragon to the ingredients. Proceed as above.

Herbed Yogurt Dressing or Dip

Makes about 2 cups

Yogurt is a lower-in-calories alternative to sour cream. Here, it makes a pleasingly tart base for a dressing or dip.

> 1 container (16 ounces) plain yogurt
> ¼ cup mayonnaise
> 2 to 3 teaspoons lemon juice or vinegar, to
>   taste
> ¼ cup minced fresh celery leaves
> ¼ cup minced fresh parsley leaves
> Salt and freshly ground black pepper to
>   taste

In a bowl, combine the yogurt, mayonnaise, and juice. With a wire whisk or fork, beat until well blended. Add the minced celery and parsley leaves; season to taste. Stir well. Refrigerate for 1 to 2 hours to allow flavors to blend. Serve as a dressing for fish or as a dip with crudités (raw vegetables).

Variations:

- Add a minced clove of garlic or some garlic powder.
- Add 2 scallions, thinly sliced, or ¼ cup finely minced onion.
- Add a tablespoon of prepared horseradish and some sugar to taste.
- Add 2 tablespoons chopped green pepper.
- Add ¼ cup chopped fresh spinach or ¼ cup finely shredded carrot.
- Use minced dill or basil or other fresh herbs to taste.

Cheese 'n Herb Dip

Makes about 1 cup

A low-calorie cheese dip with a gourmet flavor. Try variations to suit your taste.

> **2 tablespoons lemon juice**
> **1 to 2 tablespoons milk**
> **1 cup cottage cheese**
> **⅛ to ¼ teaspoon dried basil**
> **2 teaspoons finely minced celery leaves**
> **2 teaspoons chopped fresh parsley**
> **Salt to taste**

Add the liquids to the cheese and stir until the mixture is smooth and creamy. Stir in the basil, celery leaves, parsley, and salt. Refrigerate for 1 to 2 hours to allow flavors to blend.

To serve, put the dip in a small bowl. Place the bowl in the center of a large plate. Arrange raw vegetables (and crackers if desired) around the outside. To preserve crispness, prepared vegetables of your choice cut into sticks and strips may be stored in plastic bags in the refrigerator until serving time.

Variations:

- Use sour cream or buttermilk in place of the lemon juice and milk.
- Use only 1 tablespoon of lemon juice and 1 tablespoon of mayonnaise. Omit the milk.
- Add a minced clove of garlic or a teaspoon minced onion or chives or half of a thinly sliced scallion.

• Use ½ to 1 teaspoon minced fresh basil in place of the dried herbs.

• Use other fresh or dried herbs to suit your taste.

Curry Dressing

Makes about 2¼ cups

This yields a large amount of dressing, but it keeps very well in the refrigerator if kept in a closed jar or covered bowl. An admirable substitute for French dressing.

> 2 cups (1 pint) mayonnaise
> 3 tablespoons ketchup
> 3 tablespoons grated onion
> 7 to 9 drops Tabasco sauce (optional)
> 1½ teaspoons curry powder (see next recipe)
> 3 tablespoons honey
> 1¼ teaspoons lemon juice

In a small bowl, with a rotary mixer, blend together all the ingredients. Transfer to a jar or bowl. Cover and refrigerate till ready to use.

Curry Powder

Makes about ⅜ cup

Several recipes in this book call for curry powder. Because commercially prepared curry powders are sometimes too hot, you may prefer to make your own and thereby be able to regulate the hotness. This is a basic mild curry powder formula from Mme. Gupta, wife of an Indian diplomat. You may have to vary the quantity of each ingredient until you arrive at a curry powder that has just the right proportions for your taste.

> 1 tablespoon turmeric
> 2 tablespoons ground coriander
> 2 tablespoons ground cumin
> 1 tablespoon chili powder, approximately
> Dash of allspice (optional)

In a bowl, combine all the ingredients. Blend well. It is the chili powder you must be wary of. Because one of its ingredients is hot pepper, it controls how hot the curry will be.

Note: If you are adventurous, try adding some spices or herbs not called for here. Cinnamon or cloves adds a sweet and spicy flavor. Try a bit of cayenne pepper for a bite or some crushed fennel seed for a hint of anise flavor. Experiment until you achieve just the right blend.

Curry Dip

Makes a scant 1¼ cups

> 1 cup mayonnaise
> 3 tablespoons applesauce
> 2 teaspoons curry powder

In a small bowl, combine the ingredients very well. Serve with fresh raw vegetables. An attractive way to serve is to hollow out the top of a cabbage and insert a dipping cup. The crudités can be skewered into the cabbage with colorful frill toothpicks.

Mushroom Sauce

Makes about 2 cups

Make a batch of the sauce and store in the refrigerator. Use it for vegetables or meat. Reheat as needed.

> ½ pound mushrooms, sliced
> 2 tablespoons unsalted margarine or butter
> 3 tablespoons flour
> ½ teaspoon salt
> ⅛ teaspoon black pepper
> 1½ cups pareve or dairy milk
> 1 tablespoon minced parsley (optional)

In a medium-sized saucepan over medium-high heat, sauté the mushrooms in the margarine until they are tender and all the liquid evaporates. Stir in the flour, salt, and pepper. Stir in the milk gradually until well blended. Stir over low heat until the mixture thickens and boils. Stir in the parsley. Taste and adjust the seasoning if necessary. The sauce can be covered well and refrigerated for up to 2 weeks. If the sauce thickens during storage, add liquid to dilute to the desired consistency.

Note: To slice the mushrooms uniformly, use an egg slicer.

Green Sauce

An excellent dressing to serve with fish.

> **1 cup mayonnaise**
> **¼ cup minced parsley**
> **¼ cup minced chives or scallions**
> **½ cup minced spinach**
> **½ teaspoon dried dill**

In a small bowl or blender jar, mix together all the sauce ingredients. Cover and refrigerate overnight to allow flavors to blend.

Easy Pizza Sauces

Whenever a pizza sauce is called for in a recipe, one has the choice of preparing a homemade sauce or of using a commercially prepared sauce or a canned tomato and mushroom sauce.

The two sauces below are subtly spiced. They can be made more zesty by adjusting the seasonings to suit your taste or adding any herbs or spices you desire.

Pizza Sauce I:

Makes a generous 1 cup

> **1 can (16 ounces) Italian plum tomatoes**
> **¼ teaspoon crushed oregano**
> **2 tablespoons olive oil or salad oil**
> **Onion powder**
> **Garlic powder**
> **Salt (optional)**
> **Dash of black pepper**

Drain the canned tomatoes and discard the juice or reserve it for another purpose. Break up the tomato solids with a fork, transfer it to a bowl, then add the oregano and oil. Season to taste with onion powder, garlic powder, salt, and pepper. Mix well until thoroughly blended. Taste to correct seasoning.

Pizza Sauce II:

Makes 1¾ cups

> 1 can (8 ounces) tomato sauce or 1 cup
>   homemade tomato sauce
> 1 can (6 ounces) tomato paste
> ¼ cup dry red wine or water
> 2 teaspoons dried minced onion
> ¼ teaspoon garlic powder
> Optional: ½ teaspoon each of dried basil,
>   dried oregano, and parsley flakes

Combine all the ingredients in a small saucepan. Bring to a boil, then reduce the heat, cover, and simmer for about 10 minutes. Keeps well in refrigerator.

Pareve Chicken Shmaltz

Makes approximately 2 cups

This may not be as flavorful nor have the aroma of freshly rendered chicken *shmaltz* (fat), but it is an admirable substitute for the real thing.

> 2 large onions
> 1 cup oil
> 2 sticks (½ pound) pareve margarine
> Few pieces of the outer brown skin of
>   onions (optional)
> 3 carrots, sliced or coarsely grated

Slice the onions into a 1-quart saucepan. Add the oil, margarine, onion skin pieces, and carrots. Cook over low heat until the onions are golden brown. Strain the mixture and refrigerate. Use in place of chicken shmaltz.

Shaped Butter or Margarine

Dairy foods play an important role in the kosher kitchen, for there are periods in the calendar when meat is not prepared or served. This recipe is for simple but elegant butter or margarine creations. Shaped butter or margarine adds a touch of class to many foods: morning toast, pancakes, waffles, or mashed potatoes.

Butter or margarine, softened

Press softened butter or margarine into small cookie cutters or small candy molds lined with plastic wrap. Freeze until firm. When firm, lift out the plastic wrap from the molds and *voilà*, you have very attractive shaped butters to dress up your table and tempt the appetite.

Flavored Butters

Before molding softened butter or margarine, feel free to flavor them with ground spices, chopped herbs, or other ingredients of your choice. Personal taste will determine the quantities of the ingredients to be added. Here are some guidelines.

Cream ½ cup softened butter or margarine.

For Garlic Butter, add 2 to 4 cloves minced garlic. This makes an excellent spread for Potatonik (see recipe, page 173).

For Curry Butter, add 1 to 2 teaspoons curry powder. A nice addition to fish or cooked rice.

For Spice Butter, add ¼ teaspoon cinnamon and ¼ teaspoon nutmeg. Perks up the morning toast.

For Honey Butter, add ⅓ cup honey, either plain or flavored, along with nutmeg, ginger, cinnamon, or allspice. A wonderful muffin enhancer.

Homemade Boursin

Makes ¾ pound of spread

Is there anyone who doesn't associate bagels with cream cheese and lox? Spread with this homemade Boursin-type spread, a seasoned cream cheese, the lox would not be missed.

> 8 ounces cream cheese, at room
> temperature
> 1 stick (½ cup) unsalted butter or
> margarine, at room temperature
> 2 cloves garlic
> ¼ cup chopped onion
> 1 tablespoon dried salad herbs (tarragon,
> parsley, thyme, chervil)

Thoroughly cream together the cream cheese and butter or margarine. A rotary beater will serve you well. Slice the garlic and put the slices through a garlic press directly into the cheese. Put the chopped onion through the garlic press as well; add it to the cheese. Rub the herbs in the palms of your hands to pulverize them and put back some of the moisture. Blend them into the cheese.

Note: To freshen bagels that are more than one-day old, split them crosswise, sprinkle the cut surfaces lightly with warm water, wrap in foil, and bake for 15 to 20 minutes at 325 degrees F. or until heated through. Serve warm. Or place the bagels in a brown paper bag, moisten the bag, and put into a 325-degree F. oven until the bag is thoroughly dry, approximately 15 to 20 minutes.

Coating Mixes

Makes enough mix
for 3 pounds of chicken

There are many commercially prepared coating mixes available. By preparing your own, you can blend together the seasonings and ingredients that please you most.

Cornflake Crumb Mix:

1 cup cornflake crumbs
1 teaspoon salt
¼ teaspoon white pepper
Dash of paprika or cayenne

Seasoned Flour Mix:

1 cup all-purpose flour
4 teaspoons onion powder
1 teaspoon salt
¼ teaspoon nutmeg
¼ teaspoon white pepper

Sesame Seed Mix:

1 cup all-purpose flour
¼ cup sesame seeds
1 teaspoon salt (optional)
½ teaspoon freshly ground black pepper
⅛ to ½ teaspoon garlic powder, to taste

Cornmeal Mix:

½ cup yellow cornmeal
½ cup matzo meal
½ teaspoon poultry seasoning
¼ to ½ teaspoon onion powder, to taste
1 teaspoon paprika

Blend the ingredients together very well before using as a coating mix.

Note: A mix can be altered by the elimination of one ingredient and the addition or substitution of other ingredients. Matzo meal, breadcrumbs, cornflake crumbs, and flour are interchangeable. Personalize the mix by adding favorite spices. Onion soup mix gives the crusty crumb coating a zesty flavor; if using, eliminate any salt called for in the recipe.

12

Finishing Touches

Fruit Desserts, Puddings, Sweets

Peach Melba

Serves 6

The melba sauce in this recipe is traditionally served over peaches and ice cream. It is equally good spooned over plain sponge cake and served with vanilla ice cream or another vanilla-flavored dessert.

> 1 box (10 ounces) frozen raspberries,
>   thawed
> ½ cup red currant jelly
> 1 tablespoon water
> 1 tablespoon Sabra or other orange-
>   flavored liqueur
> 1 tablespoon cornstarch
> 3 drops red food coloring (optional)
> 6 canned peach halves
> 6 scoops vanilla ice cream (dairy or pareve)

In a small saucepan, combine the raspberries and currant jelly. Place over medium heat, stirring constantly until the jelly melts. Stir well. Press the mixture through a food mill or sieve. Discard the seeds. Return the raspberry mixture to the pan.

In a measuring cup, combine the water and liqueur. Stir in the cornstarch, then add the cornstarch mixture to the raspberry mixture. Return to heat and cook, stirring until the mixture thickens, about 3 to 4 minutes. If desired, add the food coloring. Stir well. Pour the sauce into a small bowl, cover and chill.

At serving time, place each peach half, cut side up, in an individual dessert dish. Top each peach with a scoop of ice cream and pour raspberry sauce over the ice cream.

Peachy Pizza

Makes 2 pies, each serving 8 or more

The average American thinks of pizza as a yeast-raised crust with a savory topping. Here, however, is a far-out variation of pizza—a dessert. Pizza dough is strewn with a streusel topping. This is covered with a spiral arrangement of sliced cling peaches and sealed under more streusel topping.

Crust:

2 cups all-purpose flour
1 tablespoon sugar
2 teaspoons baking powder
1 teaspoon salt
⅓ cup solid white vegetable shortening
1 envelope active dry yeast
¾ cup warm water (110 to 115 degrees F.)

Streusel Topping:

1 cup firmly packed dark brown sugar
¼ cup all-purpose flour
½ teaspoon cinnamon
¼ cup unsalted margarine or butter, softened
2 cans (1 pound 13 ounces each) cling peach slices

Into a mixing bowl, sift together the dry ingredients. With a pastry blender or 2 knives, cut in the shortening. Dissolve the yeast in the warm water and stir into the flour mixture. Turn the mixture onto a floured board. Knead lightly. Let rest for 10 minutes.

While the dough is resting, prepare the streusel topping. Combine the brown sugar with the flour and cinnamon. Add the softened margarine and mix thoroughly with a fork or spoon until well mixed and crumbly. Divide the mixture in half. Drain the peaches, cutting any thick peach slices in half lengthwise. Save the juice for any other favorite recipe that may call for a sweetened liquid. Set aside.

Preheat the oven to 375 degrees F. Divide the dough into 2 equal parts. Roll each part into a 10-inch circle and transfer to cookie sheet or pizza pan. Pinch the dough to form a rim around the edges. Sprinkle a portion of topping on each crust. Arrange a can of the drained sliced peaches spoke fashion on each crust. Sprinkle with the remaining topping mixture. Bake for 25 to 30 minutes.

Prunewhip

Serves 4 to 6

A tasty treat for those who are cholesterol-conscious. This is a light and fluffy baked dessert, a pure pleasure to eat.

> **Grease for the casserole**
> **1 cup prune pulp (see method)**
> **¼ cup sugar**
> **⅛ teaspoon cinnamon**
> **¼ cup chopped walnuts**
> **Juice of ½ lemon**
> **2 egg whites, stiffly beaten**

Preheat the oven to 350 degrees F. Grease a 1-quart casserole and set aside.

Prepare prune pulp by cooking prunes in water to cover until they are soft but not mushy. Drain. Pit and press through a sieve. In a medium-sized bowl, combine the prune pulp, sugar, cinnamon, nuts, and lemon juice. Gently fold in the stiffly beaten egg whites. Transfer the mixture to the prepared casserole. Place the casserole in a larger baking pan and pour hot water into the baking pan so that it comes halfway up the sides of the casserole. Bake for 20 to 25 minutes.

Baked Apples

Serves 8

The apple introduced to us in the Garden of Eden story is one of America's favorite fruits, and the popular saying "An apple a day keeps the doctor away" attests to its high nutritive value. Unpared apples are also considered a good bulk food so necessary for digestion.

8 baking apples
2 cups water
¼ teaspoon salt
½ cup sugar
¼ teaspoon cinnamon
A few drops of red food coloring (optional)

Preheat the oven to 375 degrees F. Core the apples, then peel them about one-third inch down from the stem end. Prick the sides of the apples with a fork. Arrange in a 9 x 13-inch baking pan.

In a small saucepan, place the apple parings and cores and the salt, sugar, and cinnamon. Add the water and cook over medium heat. If desired, add a few drops of red food coloring. Cook until the parings are soft. Press the mixture through a food mill to remove the skins and seeds.

Pour the purée over the apples and bake for 30 to 45 minutes, until the apples are tender. Baste often with the syrup. Serve warm or cold.

Variations:

• Serve with sour cream.
• Use fruit juice in place of water to cook the parings and cores.
• Fill the center cavity of each apple with ⅓ cup apple purée and 3 to 4 cut-up prunes mixed with ¼ cup chopped walnuts.

Apple Crisp

Serves 6

An easy-to-prepare apple dessert that is equally delicious hot or cold. The flavor of the tart apples is enhanced by the cinnamon and nutmeg.

> **Grease for the pan**
> **4 cups peeled and sliced tart apples (about 4**
> **   medium)**
> **2 tablespoons sugar**
> **¼ teaspoon cinnamon**
> **¼ cup water**
> **½ cup all-purpose flour**
> **⅛ teaspoon salt (optional)**
> **¼ teaspoon nutmeg**
> **⅓ cup firmly packed dark brown sugar**
> **½ stick (¼ cup) unsalted butter or**
> **   margarine**

Grease an 8 x 8-inch baking pan and set aside. Preheat the oven to 325 degrees F.

In a mixing bowl, toss together the apples, sugar, and cinnamon. Spread the apples in the prepared pan. Sprinkle them with the water.

Using a pastry blender, prepare a streusel topping by blending the remaining ingredients until a crumbly mixture is formed. Spread the mixture over the apples. Bake uncovered for about 1 hour, until the top is lightly browned and the apples are tender.

Variations:

- Add ¼ cup chopped walnuts to the topping mixture.
- Add 2 tablespoons of raisins to the mixture.

Tutti Frutti Noodles

Serves 4

If you have just a cup of cooked noodles left over, turn it into a tasty dessert.

Grease for the casserole
1 cup leftover cooked egg noodles
1 apple, peeled, cored, and thinly sliced
1 can (9 ounces) crushed pineapple, drained
(reserve the juice)
½ cup raisins
¼ cup chopped walnuts (optional)
½ teaspoon cinnamon
½ teaspoon nutmeg
3 tablespoons firmly packed brown sugar
2 tablespoons unsalted butter or margarine

Preheat the oven to 350 degrees F. Grease a 1-quart casserole. Place a layer of cooked noodles in casserole; top with a layer each of apple, pineapple, raisins, and nuts. Sprinkle each layer with some of the cinnamon, nutmeg, and sugar. Repeat layering. Pour the reserved pineapple juice over all. Dot with the margarine. Bake for 15 minutes and the dessert is ready to serve.

Custard Noodle Pudding

Serves 12 or more

Admittedly, this luscious noodle pudding does not pamper the figure. But it is not difficult to prepare and is worth the extra calories.

Grease for the pan
8 ounces medium egg noodles
½ stick (¼ cup) unsalted butter or
margarine
8 ounces cream cheese, softened
½ to ¾ cup sugar, to taste
4 eggs (graded large), beaten
2 cups half-and-half or milk
1 tablespoon lemon juice
1 teaspoon vanilla extract
1 teaspoon cinnamon
½ cup golden raisins

         ½ cup chopped nuts (optional)
         ½ teaspoon salt (optional)
         2 apples, peeled, cored, and thinly sliced

Topping:

         2 tablespoons butter
         ½ cup graham cracker crumbs

Grease with butter or margarine one 9 x 13-inch or two 9-inch-square baking pans; set aside. Preheat the oven to 350 degrees.

Cook the noodles according to package instructions. While the noodles are cooking, cream together the butter or margarine, cream cheese, and sugar. Add the eggs and remaining ingredients. Mix well. Drain the cooked noodles in a colander. Toss the noodles into the batter. Stir to blend and distribute the fruit well. Pour the mixture into the baking pan(s).

For the topping, combine the butter with the graham cracker crumbs and sprinkle the mixture evenly over the batter. Bake for about 45 minutes, until golden brown on top. This pudding freezes well.

Macaroon Pudding

Serves 5 or 6

Puddings are usually a child's favorite dessert. Here is one that adults are sure to enjoy as well. Ideal for Passover, when macaroons are so plentiful.

         Grease for the pan
         10 to 12 macaroons (any flavor except
           chocolate)
         ¼ cup sweet red wine (divided)
         3 tablespoons potato starch
         ½ cup plus 2 tablespoons sugar
         2 eggs (graded large), separated
         2 cups milk

Preheat the oven to 325 degrees F. Grease a 1-quart casserole. Coarsely crush the macaroons. Line the bottom of the casserole with the macaroon crumbs. Spoon half of the wine over the macaroons. Now prepare the filling.

In a mixing bowl, mix the potato starch with ½ cup of sugar. In another bowl, with an electric mixer, beat the egg yolks until golden. Add to the sugar-starch mixture. Stir in the milk and remaining wine. Transfer the mixture to the top part of a double boiler and cook over hot water, stirring until the mixture thickens enough to coat the back of a spoon, like a custard. Pour the thickened mixture over the macaroons.

In a clean bowl, beat the egg whites until foamy, then gradually add the remaining 2 tablespoons of sugar. Continue beating until the whites are stiff but not dry. Spread the meringue over the pudding, making sure to bring the meringue to the edges of the casserole. Bake for about 18 to 20 minutes, until the meringue is golden brown. Chill before serving.

Variation:

Sprinkle grated coconut on the custard before putting the meringue on.

Saucy Surprise Pudding Cake

Serves 9

This wonderful dessert is a combination of cake and pudding. In baking, the cake (studded with raisins and fragrant with lemon peel) rises to the top, leaving a thick luscious toffee sauce beneath. To make pareve, use the margarine and substitute juice or pareve "milk" for the milk.

> Grease for the pan
> 1½ cups sifted all-purpose flour
> 2 teaspoons baking powder
> 1 teaspoon salt
> ½ cup unsalted butter or margarine,
> divided
> ⅔ cup sugar
> 1 cup milk
> ½ cup raisins
> Grated peel and juice of 1 lemon
> ½ cup light molasses
> 1¼ cups water

Grease an 8-inch-square baking pan and set aside. Preheat the oven to 350 degrees F.

Into a small bowl, sift together the flour, baking powder, and salt. In a medium-sized mixing bowl, cream ¼ cup of the butter or margarine. Gradually add the sugar. Cream until very light and fluffy. Add the milk alternately with the flour mixture, beating until smooth after each addition. Stir in the raisins and lemon peel. Spoon into the prepared pan.

In a small saucepan, combine the lemon juice with the remaining butter or margarine, molasses, and water. Bring to a boil. Remove from the heat; pour gently and evenly over the batter. Bake for 45 to 50 minutes, until the top springs back when lightly touched. Serve warm. Cut into squares and spoon sauce over each serving.

Pareve Ice Cream

Makes about ½ gallon

With the introduction of pareve whipping cream, making pareve ice cream is no longer a challenge. The challenge arises in creating exciting flavors. Use this basic ice cream recipe and let your imagination create some intriguing new flavors.

> 1 container (10 ounces) pareve whipping
> cream, cold
> 4 eggs (graded large), separated
> ¼ to ½ cup sugar, to taste
> 2 teaspoons vanilla extract

Three bowls are used. Clean beaters are used for whipping the cream and egg whites.

Bowl 1: Whip the cold pareve whipping cream until stiff. Refrigerate while beating the eggs.

Bowl 2: Beat the egg whites (room temperature) until soft peaks form. Gradually add the sugar, and continue beating until the egg whites are stiff. The amount of sugar to use depends upon personal preference as well as on the sweetness of the flavoring to be added.

Bowl 3: In a large bowl, using the egg white beaters, beat the egg yolks until light. Add the vanilla and beat together. Now add the flavoring of your choice (see below) and beat the mixture for 3 to 5 minutes.

Assembly: With a rubber spatula, fold the egg white meringue into the yolk mixture. Then gradually fold in the cold pareve whip. At this point add chopped nuts, chocolate chips, raisins, or any other goodies you desire.

When the ice cream mixture is completely prepared, transfer it to a half-gallon plastic freezer container. Close the lid tightly. Slipping the container into an air-tight plastic bag and sealing the end with a twister or rubber band will help keep the ice cream smooth and crystal-free. Freeze for several hours before serving.

Flavor suggestions:

Vanilla: Increase the vanilla extract to 1½ tablespoons.

Chocolate Chip: Fold in 1 cup of miniature chocolate chips.

Chocolate: Add 1 cup of pareve chocolate syrup.

Mocha: Stir in 2 tablespoons of unsweetened cocoa and 1 tablespoon of instant coffee mixed with enough water to form a paste. Or create a mocha flavor by dissolving a tablespoon of instant coffee granules dissolved in 2 tablespoons of hot water and adding this to the chocolate syrup flavoring.

Strawberry: Add a 10-ounce package of frozen strawberries, thawed. Add a few drops of red food coloring if desired.

Lemon: Add ½ cup frozen lemonade, thawed but not diluted.

Delightful Hash: Flavor the yolks with chocolate or mocha flavoring. After folding in the whip, fold in ½ to 1 cup chopped nuts and ½ to 1 cup miniature chocolate chips. When you transfer the ice cream to the freezer container, alternate layers of ice cream with a few spoonfuls of marshmallow fluff.

Peanut Fudge Ripple: Add ¾ cup chopped unsalted peanuts to the egg yolks. When you transfer the ice cream to the freezer container, alternate layers of ice cream with ¾ cup chocolate syrup. Swirl the layers with a spatula for a marbled effect.

Tropical: Add a can (20 ounces) of crushed pineapple, drained, and ½ to 1 cup toasted coconut.

Peanut Butter: Add ½ cup chunky peanut butter.

Spumoni: For each pint, stir in 1 tablespoon of rum and ¼ cup of chopped candied fruits.

Variations:

• Freeze in fluted aluminum foil party cups.

• To mold ice cream, line commercial ice cream molds with plastic wrap. Pack prepared ice cream that has been partially frozen into the molds. Freeze until very firm. Lift out the ice cream with plastic wrap. Unmold and serve immediately or freeze the molded ice cream, still covered with plastic wrap, until ready to serve.

• For Chanukah, use dreidel gel molds; for an anniversary or bridal shower, use heart molds; and so on. To prepare a quantity of ice cream molds, prepare the molds as instructed above, then reuse the molds until the number of servings needed have been accumulated in the freezer.

• To layer ice cream, partially pack one flavor before adding another. An attractive layered ice cream cake can be prepared in a 9- or 10-inch spring-form pan by using 2 or 3 different flavors. No need to line the pan. When frozen, remove the sides of the spring-form and the cake remains on the bottom. Decorate with pareve whipped cream if desired.

Quick Biscuit Tortoni

Serves 8 to 10

A refreshing dessert consisting of pareve ice cream and crunchy almonds garnished with minced macaroon crumbs and a maraschino cherry.

> 1 cup pareve whipping cream
> 3 tablespoons sugar
> ½ teaspoon almond extract
> ½ cup finely chopped blanched almonds
> Pareve vanilla cookie or macaroon crumbs

In a mixing bowl, with chilled beaters, whip the cream until stiff. Gradually add the sugar. Add the extract and blend gently. Fold in the almonds and spoon the mixture into fluted paper baking cups. Set the cups into muffin pans. Freeze until firm, 3 to 4 hours. Before serving, sprinkle cookie or macaroon crumbs on top of each. Garnish with a cherry or whole blanched almond.

Ice Cream Muffins

Makes 12 muffins

Just two ingredients and you have delicious muffins. The ice cream is baked in the muffins.

Grease for the pan
2 cups self-rising flour
2 cups softened vanilla ice cream

Grease well 12 muffin cups and set aside. Preheat the oven to 425 degrees F. Combine the flour and ice cream in the large bowl of an electric mixer. Beat until smooth. Fill the prepared muffin cups three-fourths full. Bake for 20 to 25 minutes, until golden brown.

Variation:

For a richer muffin, add 1 egg and 2 tablespoons of oil to the batter.

Fresh Cranberry Sherbet

Makes ½ gallon

This mildly tart dessert is a refreshing way to end a meal.

2 cups fresh cranberries
¾ to 1 cup sugar, to taste
2 egg whites (from eggs graded large)
1 tablespoon frozen orange juice
concentrate, thawed
1 teaspoon vanilla extract
⅛ teaspoon salt
1 cup pareve whipping cream

Grind the cranberries in a food processor (you will have about 1½ cups ground), and place in the large bowl of an electric mixer. Add the sugar and let stand for 5 minutes. Add the unbeaten egg whites, orange juice concentrate, vanilla, and salt. Beat the mixture at low speed until frothy, then at high speed for 6 to 8 minutes, until stiff peaks form.

In a clean medium-sized bowl with chilled beaters, beat the cream until soft peaks form. Fold the whipped cream into the cranberry mixture. Spoon into a half-gallon container and freeze.

Yolk-free Chocolate Mousse

Serves 6

Who can resist the tantalizing flavor of a chocolate mousse? *Voilà!* A chocolate mousse without yolks. Appreciated by cholesterol-conscious chocoholics.

> 6 ounces semisweet chocolate
> 1 tablespoon strong brewed coffee
> 1 tablespoon Sabra or another orange-
>   flavored liqueur or brandy (optional)
> 5 egg whites, at room temperature
> ¼ teaspoon cream of tartar
> Slivered orange peel

In the top of a double boiler, combine the chocolate with the coffee. Place over hot water and stir occasionally until the chocolate is melted. Remove from the heat. Beat in the liqueur or brandy until the mixture is smooth.

In the bowl of an electric mixer, beat the egg whites with the cream of tartar until the whites are stiff but not dry. To lighten the chocolate mixture, beat 2 or 3 tablespoons of the stiff egg whites into the chocolate. Then carefully fold in the remaining egg whites until no white is visible. Spoon into 6 individual champagne glasses. Refrigerate for at least 2 hours. Garnish with fine slivers of orange peel before serving.

Chocolate Banana Pops

Makes 12 pops

An ideal afternoon snack for children, but adults will enjoy them as well. They are quick to make and convenient to keep on hand.

6 bananas, fully ripened and unbruised
6 ounces semisweet chocolate
12 dowels or lollipop sticks

Peel the bananas. Cut each in half crosswise. Insert a dowel or lollipop stick into the center of the cut end of each banana. Wrap in wax paper and freeze. In the top part of a double boiler, melt the chocolate. Remove from the heat. Dip each frozen banana into melted chocolate. Arrange on aluminum foil. Refrigerate or wrap and store in the freezer.

Chocolate Rum Balls

Makes 54

These goodies are fantastically easy to prepare. One pan and no baking!

3 cups raisins
1 cup rum (dark or light, your choice)
12 ounces semisweet chocolate chips
1 tablespoon light corn syrup

Put the raisins in a plastic bag. Add the rum. Close the bag tightly so that it can be turned occasionally without leaking. Macerate the raisins in the rum for at least 3 hours, preferably overnight. Drain, but do not press. Save the liquor to use at a future time.

Melt the chocolate chips in the top of a double boiler over hot water. Add the corn syrup. Mix to blend. Remove the pan from the water. Stir in the drained raisins. Mix to coat all the raisins. Line a cookie sheet with wax paper. Drop the mixture by the teaspoonful onto the wax paper. Refrigerate to set the chocolate. To serve, place each in a petit four case. Freezes very well.

Note: The remaining rum makes an excellent addition to a cake, particularly a chocolate cake. Substitute the rum for part of the liquid in the recipe.

Chestnut Bon Bons

Makes about 40

In the Herald Square shopping area of New York City, the aroma of roasted chestnuts is a familiar one. Roasted chestnuts are delicious indeed, but there are ways to prepare chestnuts that are often overlooked.

In this recipe, the chestnuts are boiled, puréed, combined with sweeteners and flavorings, and then shaped into bon bons. Since chestnuts are lower in calories than most nuts, these confections should be a welcome addition to your sweet treat repertoire.

> ½ pound chestnuts
> Boiling water
> 1 tablespoon honey
> 1 tablespoon sugar
> ½ teaspoon cinnamon
> Dash of ginger
> ½ tablespoon brandy

Cut a slit into the flat side of the chestnut shell. Cook the chestnuts in boiling water to cover for 15 minutes, or longer if the chestnuts are large. Remove the nuts from the water and, while they are still warm and easy to peel, remove the outer shell and brown skin of each nut. Finely grate the chestnuts on a nut grinder, or purée in a food processor. Add the honey, sugar, cinnamon, ginger, and brandy. Mix well. Pack the mixture into 1-inch decorative molds. Unmold and set each into an individual petit-four case.

Fig Squares

Makes two 9-inch cakes,
36 portions in each

A baked confection akin to *tayglach* (see page 222). A honey dough filled with figs, nuts, and raisins dressed with a coating of honey and chopped nuts. A holiday favorite. No resemblance between these fig squares and fig newtons.

Dough:

Grease for the pan
1 pound honey, divided (1⅓ cups)
½ cup solid white vegetable shortening
½ cup sugar
2 eggs (graded large)
3¼ cups unsifted all-purpose flour
1 teaspoon baking powder
½ teaspoon cinnamon

Filling:

12 ounces figs, diced (about 1½ cups)
1 tablespoon sugar
1 cup raisins
½ cup chopped nuts
½ cup chopped dates (optional)
1 tablespoon solid white vegetable
  shortening for topping
Additional chopped nuts for garnish
  (optional)

Grease two 9-inch-square baking pans; set aside. Preheat the oven to 325 degrees F.

Place the honey (in its jar or in a heat-resistant measuring cup) in hot water in order to warm it. In a large mixing bowl, cream the vegetable shortening with the sugar. Add the eggs and beat until light. Gradually add 1 cup of the warmed honey, beating all the while. Sift together the dry ingredients and add to the egg mixture. Mix well to form a dough.

Combine all filling ingredients except for the shortening. Set aside.

Divide the dough in half. Transfer one piece of dough to a floured pastry cloth. Roll out the dough to ⅛-inch thickness. It should make an oblong about 14 x 18 inches. Measure off ¼ cup of warm honey and brush a portion of this generously over the dough. Sprinkle the dough with half of the filling mixture.

Roll up the dough (as for a jelly roll) by lifting the edges of the cloth nearest you. Make a roll 2 inches in diameter. Cut the roll off from the remainder of the dough. Cut into lengths to fit into the prepared pans. Arrange the rolls close together. Repeat this procedure until all the dough has been used. Continue with other piece of dough as for the first piece. When all the rolls of dough have been arranged in the pans, cut through the rolls, making 6 cuts across each. Bake for 20 to 35 minutes, until golden brown.

In a small saucepan, combine the tablespoon of shortening with ⅛ cup honey. Place over low heat until the shortening melts and is combined with the honey. Stir. Brush the tops of the fig squares with the honey mixture. If desired, garnish the top of the squares with additional chopped nuts.

Egg Noodle Snacks

Makes about 2½ quarts,
loosely packed

Cooked egg noodles are transformed into a sugary confection by deep-frying them until crisp and puffy. These are comparable to *cenci,* an old confection from Italy.

> 3 quarts water
> 1 tablespoon salt
> 8 ounces wide egg noodles or egg noodle
>   bows
> Oil for deep-frying
> Confectioners' sugar or a cinnamon-sugar
>   mixture

Bring the water to a rapid boil; add the noodles. Cook uncovered, stirring occasionally, until tender. Drain in a colander; rinse with cold water; drain again. Blot the noodles dry with paper towels.

In a deep-fryer or a skillet at least 2 inches deep, heat 1¼ inches of oil to 375 degrees F. Separate any noodles that may cling together, and drop a few at a time into the hot fat. Fry just enough at one time to cover the bottom of the fry basket or fryer. Cook for about 3 minutes, until evenly and lightly browned. If necessary, separate the noodles while frying. Spread on paper towels to drain. Sprinkle or shake in paper bag with confectioners' sugar. Or shake with a mixture of cinnamon and granulated sugar. Serve with coffee or tea, fruit or ice cream.

Note: If you do not use a commercially prepared cinnamon-sugar mixture, prepare one by blending a tablespoon of cinnamon with ½ cup of sugar.

13

Company Is Coming

Cakes

"*Abraham hastened into the tent to Sarah, and said, 'Quick, three seahs of choice flour! Knead and make cakes!'*" (Genesis 18:6).

New "Sponge" Cake

Serves 10 or more

A high-rise creation made without separating eggs! Hard to believe? The secret is the length of time that the batter is beaten. Your electric mixer plays the important role.

Because baking powder is added and because the baking pan is greased, this cannot be considered a truly authentic sponge cake. However, the taste and texture are virtually identical.

> **Grease for the pan**
> **6 eggs (graded large)**
> **1 tablespoon lemon juice**
> **1 teaspoon grated lemon rind**
> **1 cup sugar**
> **1½ cups sifted all-purpose flour**
> **½ teaspoon salt**
> **2 teaspoons baking powder**

Preheat the oven to 325 degrees F. Lightly grease and flour the bottom of a 10-inch spring-form pan; set aside.

Into the large bowl of an electric mixer, break the eggs. Add the lemon juice and lemon rind. Beat the eggs at highest speed until soft peaks form, about 12 to 16 minutes. After soft peaks form, keep beating at highest speed while you slowly pour in the cup of sugar in a fine stream, taking 2½ to 3 minutes to add all of the sugar.

Sift together the flour, salt, and baking powder. Carefully fold the dry ingredients into the egg batter. Bake for 45 to 50 minutes, until the cake is done, invert the pan onto a rack to cool. Cool to room temperature before removing the cake from the pan.

Golden Honey Sponge Cake

Serves 10 or more

This sponge cake keeps fresher longer than an ordinary sponge cake. Honey has the property of absorbing and retaining moisture and therefore retards the drying-out process.

> **1 cup sifted cake flour**
> **½ teaspoon salt**
> **5 eggs (graded large), separated**
> **1 cup honey**

Preheat the oven to 300 degrees F.

Sift together the cake flour and salt. Warm the honey by placing the jar of honey in hot water before measuring. In the large bowl of an electric mixer, beat the egg yolks until they are very thick and lemon-colored.

Very gradually, add the honey to the egg yolks, beating constantly. After all the honey has been added, continue beating the yolks for an additional 3 minutes. Add the flour gradually as you continue beating. After all the flour has been added, continue beating for an additional 5 minutes.

In a clean bowl with clean beaters, beat the egg whites until stiff but not dry. Fold the egg whites into the batter. Transfer the batter to an ungreased 9-inch tube pan. Bake for about 1 hour, until a toothpick inserted in the center comes out clean. Invert the pan and let the cake cool completely before removing.

Honey-Orange Chocolate Cake

Serves 12

A honey cake that chocolate-lovers will go for. The colored frosting and filling contrast nicely with the cake itself.

> **Grease for the pans**
> **½ cup solid white vegetable shortening**
> **½ cup sugar**
> **¾ cup honey, warmed**
> **2 egg yolks**
> **2 squares (2 ounces) unsweetened chocolate, melted**
> **3 cups unsifted cake flour**
> **1 teaspoon salt**
> **½ teaspoon baking soda**
> **2 teaspoons baking powder**
> **¾ cup pareve milk or water**
> **1 teaspoon vanilla extract**

Preheat the oven to 350 degrees F. Grease two 9-inch layer cake pans; set aside.

Sift together the flour, salt, baking soda, and baking powder; set aside. In the large bowl of an electric mixer, cream well the shortening, sugar, and warmed honey. Add the egg yolks and beat thoroughly. Stir in the melted chocolate. Add the sifted dry ingredients alternately with the liquid ingredients. Mix just until well combined. Pour the batter into the layer pans. Bake for 35 to 40 minutes, until tested done. Cool completely while preparing the Honey-Orange Frosting and Filling.

Honey-Orange Frosting and Filling:

> **½ cup honey**
> **½ cup sugar**
> **2 egg whites**
> **Dash of salt**
> **1 teaspoon grated orange rind**
> **Few drops orange vegetable coloring**
> **¾ cup white seedless raisins**
> **⅓ cup chopped walnuts**

Simmer the honey in the top of a double boiler over direct heat for 5 minutes; add the sugar and egg whites. Place the pot over boiling water and beat the mixture constantly with a rotary beater until it is stiff enough to hold its shape. Add the salt and orange rind. Tint the mixture with the orange coloring.

Transfer a third of the honey-orange mixture to a small bowl. Add the raisins and chopped nuts. When assembling the cake, spread this filling between the layers, then frost the entire cake with the balance of the mxiture.

Honey Fruit Cake

Serves 12 or more

A honey cake whose appealing flavor is enhanced by the orange juice. The baked cake comes out of the oven donned with an eye-appealing honey topping, a glaze crowned with slivered almonds.

> **Grease for the pan**
> **2 tablespoons solid white vegetable**
>   **shortening**
> **1¾ cups sugar**
> **4 eggs (graded large)**
> **½ cup orange juice**
> **4 cups unsifted all-purpose flour**
> **2 teaspoons baking powder**
> **2 teaspoons baking soda**
> **¾ cup warm brewed coffee**
> **1¼ cups honey**
> **¾ cup coarsely chopped nuts**
> **¾ cup chopped candied fruit**
> **⅓ cup honey for topping**
> **Blanched slivered almonds**

Grease a 10-inch tube pan and set aside. Preheat the oven to 325 degrees F.

In the large bowl of an electric mixer, cream the shortening with the sugar. Add the eggs one at a time, beating well after each addition. Blend in the orange juice.

Into a bowl, sift together the flour, baking powder, and baking soda. Combine the coffee and honey. To the beaten egg mixture, alternately add the dry ingredients and the coffee-honey mixture. Lastly, coat the chopped nuts and candied fruit with 2 teaspoons of flour. Fold into the batter. Pour the batter into the prepared pan. Bake for 30 minutes. Remove the cake and dribble the ⅓ cup of honey over the top. Arrange the blanched slivered almonds over the honey topping. Return the cake to the oven and continue baking for an additional 30 minutes or until a toothpick inserted into the center comes out dry. Cool before removing from the pan.

Picnic Gingerbread

Serves 6 to 8

When you think of gingerbread, do you invariably imagine an elaborate gingerbread house or cookies cut into fanciful shapes? Well, here is something a bit different: a spicy cake that is baked in a pan and served cut into squares. Easy to cart off in the pan for a picnic.

By the way, ginger has lately been touted as a remedy for motion sickness. So, on your next trip, why not take along some of these gingerbread squares? They might serve a double purpose.

Grease for the pan
1¾ cups unsifted all-purpose flour
1 teaspoon baking soda
1 teaspoon cinnamon
1 teaspoon ginger
½ teaspoon cloves
¼ teaspoon allspice
¼ teaspoon nutmeg
¼ teaspoon salt
1 stick (½ cup) unsalted margarine or
    butter
½ cup sugar
2 eggs (graded large)
½ cup dark molasses
½ cup water

Preheat the oven to 350 degrees F. Grease and flour an 8 x 8 x 2-inch pan; set aside.

Into a bowl, sift the flour with the baking soda, cinnamon, ginger, cloves, allspice, nutmeg, and salt. In the large bowl of an electric mixer, cream the butter or margarine with the sugar until light and fluffy. Add the eggs and beat well. Combine the molasses with the water. Alternately add the flour mixture and the liquid to the creamed mixture. Mix until smooth. Pour into the prepared pan. Bake for 45 to 50 minutes, until a toothpick inserted comes out dry.

Almond Carrot Cake

Serves 9

A past president of Sisterhood, Marilyn Gluck, shared with me countless recipes. This almond carrot cake was among her favorites. After baking the cake, which is studded with toasted almonds, the cake is glazed with honey and topped with additional almonds. Garnished with a dollop of whipped cream atop the glaze, the cake may be served to your most discriminating guests.

> **Grease for the pan**
> **1½ cups all-purpose flour**
> **1½ teaspoons baking powder**
> **1½ teaspoons cinnamon**
> **¾ teaspoon salt**
> **¾ cup oil**
> **1 cup plus 2 tablespoon sugar**
> **2 eggs (graded large)**
> **1½ teaspoons vanilla extract**
> **1½ cups grated carrot**
> **1 cup toasted slivered almonds, divided**
> **3 tablespoons honey**
> **½ cup heavy cream, whipped**

Grease a 9-inch-square baking pan and set aside. Preheat the oven to 300 degrees F.

Into a large mixing bowl, sift the flour, baking powder, cinnamon, and salt. Make a well in the center and add the oil, sugar, eggs, and vanilla. Beat until very smooth. Stir in the carrots and ¾ cup of the almonds. Pour the mixture into the prepared pan and bake for 50 minutes. Cool and cut into squares. Combine the honey with the remaining almonds. Serve the squares garnished with the honey topping and a dollop of whipped cream.

Fruit Cocktail Cake

Serves 10 or more

A large fruit cake made with canned fruits rather than dried ones. The colorful pieces of fruit add interest to each slice of the rum- or brandy-spiked cake.

> 3 cups sifted all-purpose flour
> 3 teaspoons baking soda
> 2 cups sugar
> 1 teaspoon salt
> 1 teaspoon cinnamon
> 1 can (17 ounces) fruit cocktail including juice
> 3 eggs (graded large)
> 2 tablespoons brandy or rum (extract may be substituted)
> 1½ cups chopped walnuts or pecans
> ¼ cup solid white vegetable shortening
> 2 tablespoons flour

Preheat the oven to 350 degrees F. Into a large bowl, sift together the dry ingredients. Add the fruit cocktail, eggs, brandy, and nuts. Stir until well blended.

Prepare a coating mix with the shortening and flour. Heavily coat an 8-inch tube pan with this mix. Pour the batter into prepared pan. Bake for 1½ to 2 hours, until a cake tester inserted into the cake comes out clean. Set on a rack to cool for 5 minutes. Run a knitting needle or small spatula around the tube and side of the pan. Turn out onto the rack to cool completely.

Apple Crumb Cake

Serves 12 to 15

A new French study reported in *Nutrition Research* has given credence to the old saying "An apple a day keeps the doctor away." The study reported that eating apples daily may help reduce cholesterol. So, on with the apple desserts. This crumb cake is a welcome substitute for apple pie and makes an instant hit with apple-lovers of all kinds.

Grease for the pan

Filling:

10 apples, peeled
1 cup sugar
½ cup water
Juice of 1 lemon
1 teaspoon cinnamon

Crumb Crust:

4 cups all-purpose flour
4 teaspoons baking powder
1½ cups sugar
1 teaspoon salt
1 cup solid vegetable shortening or
    unsalted margarine or butter
2 eggs (graded large)
2 teaspoons vanilla extract
¼ teaspoon cinnamon
1 tablespoon sugar

Grease a 9 x 13-inch baking pan and set aside. Preheat the oven to 350 degrees F.

Thinly slice the apples into a large saucepan. Add the sugar, water, lemon juice, and cinnamon. Cook over medium heat for 5 minutes, no longer. While the apples are cooking, prepare the crumb crust.

Into a large mixing bowl, sift the flour, baking powder, sugar, and salt. With a pastry blender, cut in the shortening or margarine or butter. Add the eggs and vanilla. Blend well. Pat half of the crumb crust into the greased pan. Spoon the apples with only half of the juice evenly over the layer in the pan. Cover the apples with the remaining dough. Sprinkle with cinnamon and sugar. Bake for 1 hour.

Eight-layer Torte

Serves 12

A magnificent eight-layer torte made from one jelly-roll-pan sheet cake. It is wonderful to look at and delicious to eat. A luscious rich chocolate filling spread between the layers and on the top makes it devilishly good. Chopped pistachio nuts make an attractive garnish.

Cake:

> ¾ cup sifted cake flour
> ¾ teaspoon baking powder
> ¼ teaspoon salt
> 4 eggs (graded large), unbeaten, at room
>   temperature
> ¾ cup sugar
> 1 teaspoon vanilla extract
> ½ teaspoon grated lemon rind
> Confectioners' sugar

Preheat the oven to 400 degrees F. Line with wax paper a 10 x 15 x 1-inch jelly-roll pan; set aside.

Set the sifted flour aside in a small bowl. In a medium-sized mixing bowl, combine the baking powder, salt, and eggs. Beat with a rotary beater, adding the sugar gradually, until the mixture is thick and very light in color. Gradually fold in the flour, vanilla extract, and grated lemon rind. Turn the batter into the prepared pan and bake for 13 minutes. Invert the cake out onto a cloth that has been sprinkled with confectioners' sugar.

Quickly peel off the paper and with a long knife cut off the crisp edges of the cake. Allow the cake to cool completely. When cool, cut the cake into 4 equal parts. Split each quarter through the middle, making 8 thin layers.

Frosting:

> 4½ squares (4½ ounces) unsweetened
>   chocolate
> 1 stick (½ cup) unsalted margarine or
>   butter (for dairy)
> 3 cups sifted confectioners' sugar
> ⅓ cup water or pareve "milk" or milk (for
>   dairy)
> 2 eggs whites, unbeaten
> 1 teaspoon vanilla extract

To make the frosting, place the chocolate and margarine or butter in a medium-sized saucepan over low heat. Stir occasionally. When the chocolate has melted and the mixture is smooth, remove the pan from the heat and add the sugar, water or milk, egg whites, and vanilla. Mix well.

Place the saucepan in an ice bath by placing the saucepan into a larger pan filled with ice cubes. Beat with a rotary beater until the mixture is of spreading consistency.

To assemble the cake, spread a thin layer of frosting, about ¼ cup, on a layer of cake. Place another layer of cake on top and repeat until all 8 layers of cake are used. Frost the sides and top of the torte with the remaining frosting. Chill before serving.

Chocolate Nut Cake

Serves 10 or more

Try this cake on any chocolate-lover. An intense chocolate flavor infuses the luscious cake, which is richly endowed with nuts.

> Grease for the pan
> 8 ounces bittersweet chocolate
> 9 eggs (graded large), separated
> 1 cup sugar
> ½ pound walnuts, ground
> 1 envelope (.43 ounces) vanilla sugar

Grease a 10-inch tube pan and set aside. Preheat the oven to 325 degrees F.

Place the chocolate in the top of a double boiler over moderate heat. Stir occasionally until completely melted and smooth.

In the large bowl of an electric mixer, beat the egg yolks until light. Gradually add the sugar and beat until light and lemon-colored. Add the ground nuts. Remove from the mixer and stir in the melted chocolate. Set aside the chocolate batter.

In a clean bowl with clean beaters, beat the egg whites at low speed for about 30 seconds. Increase the speed to high, and gradually add the vanilla sugar. Continue to beat until stiff peaks form. Gently fold the stiffly beaten egg whites into the chocolate batter.

Transfer the batter to the greased tube pan. Bake for 1 hour or until tested done. Place the pan on a wire rack and let the cake cool completely before removing from the pan. Do not invert the pan to cool.

Note: Vanilla sugar is sold commercially in .43-ounce packets. If you happen to buy it by the jar or make your own, the equivalent is 2½ teaspoons.

Chocolate Gâteau

Serves 8 or more

This is the ultimate—a wickedly delicious chocolate dessert. Intermingling with the melted chocolate and the finely ground almonds is either brandy or Scotch. This cake is a perfect party make-ahead, for it freezes very well and, in fact, improves with age.

> **Grease for the pan**
> **¼ cup raisins**
> **¼ cup brandy or Scotch**
> **7 ounces bittersweet chocolate**
> **3 tablespoons water**
> **1 stick (½ cup) unsalted margarine, cut into small pieces**
> **3 eggs (graded extra large), separated**
> **⅔ cup sugar**
> **4½ tablespoons cake flour**
> **⅔ cup finely ground almonds**
> **Pinch of salt**

Preheat the oven to 375 degrees F. Cut a round of wax paper to fit the bottom of a 9-inch cake pan. Grease the sides of the pan and the top part of the paper. Set aside.

Steep the raisins in the brandy or Scotch. Place the chocolate and the 3 tablespoons of water in the top of a double boiler over simmering water. Stir until the chocolate is melted and smooth. Remove from the heat and stir in the pieces of margarine. Stir until smooth.

In the large bowl of an electric mixer, beat the egg yolks with the sugar until the mixture is light and lemon-colored. Combine the melted chocolate with the beaten egg yolks. Stir the flour into the ground nuts and add to the batter. Stir in the raisins and the brandy or Scotch.

In a clean bowl with clean beaters, beat the egg whites with a pinch of salt until they are stiff but not dry. Stir a third of the whites into the chocolate to lighten the mixture, then fold the chocolate mixture back into the remaining whites. Pour the cake batter into the pan.

Bake the cake on the middle rack of the oven for 20 minutes. The outside of the cake will be firm, but the inside will be moist. Allow the cake to cool and set for 10 minutes. It will look rather flat. Unmold onto a wire rack, remove the wax paper, and invert back onto another rack. Allow to cool for a few hours, then decorate with the following icing.

Icing:

3 ounces bittersweet chocolate
3 tablespoons sifted confectioners' sugar
3 tablespoons unsalted margarine or butter

Place the chocolate in the top of a double boiler over moderate heat. When the chocolate is melted and smooth, stir in the sugar and then the margarine, a little at a time. Blend well. Immediately spread the icing over the top and sides of the cake.

Chocolate Nut Torte

Serves 8 to 10

A chocolate nut torte topped with raspberry jam subtly laced with rum. Ground walnuts may be substituted for the filberts. This flourless cake makes a wonderful Passover treat.

> Grease for pan
> 6 ounces semisweet chocolate
> 5 eggs (graded large), separated
> 1 cup sugar
> 1¾ sticks (14 tablespoons) unsalted
>   margarine or butter, at room
>   temperature
> 1 cup ground filberts (hazelnuts)
> 1 cup seedless raspberry jam
> Dark rum

Preheat the oven to 350 degrees F. Grease a 9-inch spring-form pan and set aside.

In the top of a small double boiler over low heat, melt the chocolate until smooth; set aside. In the large bowl of an electric mixer, beat the egg yolks with the sugar until light. Beat in the margarine or butter and the ground nuts. Blend in the melted chocolate. Remove a third of the chocolate batter and set aside.

In a clean bowl with clean beaters, beat the egg whites until stiff but not dry. Fold them into the remaining chocolate batter. Pour the batter into the prepared pan and bake for 30 to 35 minutes, until tested done. Cool the cake on a wire rack. Remove the sides of the spring-form.

In a small bowl, beat the raspberry jam, adding the rum a teaspoon at a time until the jam is of spreading consistency. Spread the jam in an even layer over the top of the cake, then spread the reserved chocolate batter over the raspberry jam.

Cheesecake

Serves 10 or more

The late Mrs. Abraham Ribicoff, wife of the former senator from Connecticut, shared with me and members of my Sisterhood this cheesecake recipe, which happened to be one of her husband's favorites. The slightly sweetened sour cream topping enhances the velvety rich cheesecake.

Crust:

> 1⅓ cups crumbs (graham cracker or
>   cornflake)

⅛ to ¼ cup sugar, to taste
1 stick (½ cup) unsalted butter or
   margarine, melted

Combine the ingredients and press the mixture onto the sides and bottom of a 9-inch spring-form pan, reserving some of the crumbs for the top of the cake. Set aside.

Filling:

2 pounds cream cheese
4 eggs (graded large), well beaten
1 cup sugar
1 tablespoon lemon juice
½ teaspoon salt

Topping:

2 cups sour cream
¼ cup sugar
1 teaspoon vanilla extract
½ teaspoon almond extract

Preheat the oven to 375 degrees F.

In the large bowl of an electric mixer, cream the cheese. In another bowl, with clean beaters, beat the eggs and the sugar until very thick and lemon-colored. Add the beaten eggs to the cheese along with the lemon juice and salt. Beat very well, at least 10 minutes at medium speed. Pour into the prepared spring-form pan and place in the oven.

While the cake is baking, prepare the topping. Blend the sour cream with the ¼ cup of sugar and the vanilla and almond extracts. After 20 minutes, remove the cake from the oven and spread the topping over the partially baked cake. Sprinkle the reserved graham cracker crumbs over all. Raise the oven heat to 475 degrees and bake for an additional 10 minutes. Remove from the oven and let cool. Refrigerate for several hours before serving.

Variation:

If desired, a fruit glaze may be added over the sour cream topping.

Noodle Cheesecake

Serves 6 to 8

Cream cheese and noodles partner in this different cheesecake. The haunting flavoring in the cake is the result of cooking the raisins together with the noodles. Sour cream and/or sliced strawberries make admirable toppings.

> **Grease for the pan**
> **8 ounces wide egg noodles**
> **¾ cup golden raisins**
> **1 pound cream cheese, softened**
> **2 eggs (graded large) beaten**
> **⅓ cup sugar, to taste**
> **½ teaspoon nutmeg**
> **½ teaspoon cinnamon**

Grease with butter or margarine an 8-inch baking pan; set aside. Preheat the oven to 375 degrees F.

Cook the noodles and raisins in boiling water until the noodles are tender. Meanwhile, combine the softened cream cheese with the eggs, sugar, nutmeg, and cinnamon. Stir until well blended. When the noodles are tender, drain well. Stir the noodles and raisins into the cheese-egg mixture. Pour the mixture into the prepared pan and bake for about 25 minutes, until set. Serve warm or at room temperature. Cut into wedges. This may be frozen.

Meringue Cheesecake

Serves 12

A delicious cheesecake with a cloudlike topping. The meringue contrasts nicely with the luscious cheesecake.

Dough:

> **1½ cups all-purpose flour**
> **1 teaspoon baking powder**
> **½ cup sugar**
> **2 sticks (½ pound) unsalted butter or**
> **margarine, at room temperature**
> **1 egg (graded large), beaten**

Filling:

>   2 pounds small-curd cottage cheese
>   1 whole egg plus 3 egg yolks (from eggs
>   graded large)
>   1 cup sugar
>   2 tablespoons cornstarch or potato starch
>   ½ teaspoon vanilla extract
>   Grated rind of 1 lemon
>   1 cup milk

Meringue:

>   3 eggs whites (from eggs graded large)
>   ¼ cup sugar

Preheat the oven to 375 degrees F.

To prepare the dough, into a mixing bowl sift together the dry ingredients. Blend in the butter or margarine and the beaten egg until well mixed. Roll the dough into a ball, wrap it in wax paper, and chill it in the refrigerator for 20 minutes. Roll out the dough between 2 sheets of wax paper, then line the bottom and sides of a 7 x 11-inch or 9 x 13-inch pan with the rolled-out dough.

In the large bowl of an electric mixer, beat the filling ingredients until well blended. Do not underbeat. Pour the mixture into the prepared pan and bake for 45 minutes to 1 hour, until the cake is well set. Remove from the oven.

To prepare the meringue, in the small bowl of an electric mixer beat the egg whites until soft peaks form. Gradually add the sugar and continue beating until the whites are stiff. Spoon the whites onto the baked cake and return to the oven for 10 to 15 minutes, until the meringue is nicely browned. Chill before serving.

Pareve Cheesecake

Serves 10 or more

Only relatively recently has tofu (bean curd) become popular in the West, although Asians have been using it for thousands of years. Tofu is an excellent protein food, low in calories and free from cholesterol.

Unadorned, tofu tastes very bland, but it readily absorbs the flavors of the ingredients with which it is partnered. Here, tofu serves as the basic ingredient for a cheesecake.

Crust:

2 cups graham cracker crumbs
¼ cup firmly packed brown sugar
1 stick (½ cup) unsalted margarine, melted

Blend the crumb ingredients thoroughly with a pastry blender or with the ultimate kitchen gadget—your hands! Spread the mixture over the bottom and sides of a 10-inch spring-form pan. Press firmly and evenly with the back of a spoon or with the palm of your hand. Refrigerate while preparing the filling.

Filling:

4 eggs (graded large), separated
¼ cup sugar
Juice of 1 lemon
¼ teaspoon lemon extract
2 tablespoons cornstarch
1 pound soft tofu
1 container (10 ounces) pareve cream

Adjust an oven rack one-third up from the bottom. Preheat the oven to 350 degrees F.

In a blender jar, place the egg yolks and sugar. Blend at high speed until the yolks are very light. Continue blending while adding the lemon juice and lemon extract. Add the tofu a little at a time so as not to overwork the blender motor. When all is liquefied, add the cornstarch and blend for about 30 seconds. Transfer the batter to a large mixing bowl. Stir in the container of pareve cream. Blend well.

In a large clean bowl, with clean beaters, beat the egg whites until stiff. Gently fold the beaten whites into the tofu batter. Pour the filling into the prepared pan and bake for 50 to 60 minutes, until the top is golden. Let cool thoroughly before serving. The cake has a tendency to fall slightly in the center.

Alternate Method:

In the bowl of a food processor, place the egg yolks and sugar.

Process until the yolks are very light. Continue processing while adding the lemon juice and lemon extract. Add the tofu a little at a time. When all is liquefied, add the cornstarch and process for about 30 seconds more.

Transfer the batter to a large mixing bowl. Stir in the container of pareve cream. Blend well. In a large clean bowl, with clean beaters, beat the egg whites until stiff. Gently fold the beaten egg whites into the tofu batter. Proceed as above.

Variations:

• To create an admirable stand-in for a cheese soufflé, bake in a greased pan without a crust.
• Top the cooled cake with a fruit filling of your choice.
• Substitute cornflake crumbs for the graham cracker crumbs.

Note: The same quantity of batter will also make two 9-inch "cheese" pies. A fruit topping of your choice can be added to the prepared pies.

Pareve Whipped Cream Cake

Serves 8 or more

This fine-textured cake is unusual in that pareve whipped cream is used in place of shortening. It is delicious served as is, or it can be served as an accompaniment to fruit or with a fruit sauce spooned over it. Or simply garnish it with additional whipped cream.

> **Grease for the pan**
> **1½ cups sifted all-purpose flour**
> **1 cup sugar**
> **2 teaspoons baking powder**
> **Pinch of salt**
> **1 cup pareve whipping cream**
> **2 eggs (graded large)**
> **1 teaspoon vanilla or almond extract**
> **½ cup finely chopped nuts (optional)**

Preheat the oven to 350 degrees F. Grease and flour the bottom and sides of an 8-inch spring-form pan. Set aside.

Sift together the flour, sugar, baking powder, and salt. Set aside.

In the large bowl of an electric mixer, whip the cream until it holds soft peaks. Add the eggs one at a time, beating well after each addition. Add the vanilla or almond extract. Fold the sifted dry ingredients and the nuts into the cream mixture, blending well.

Spoon the batter into the prepared pan. Bake for about 50 minutes, until the cake is lightly browned and a cake tester inserted comes out clean. Cool in the pan for about 15 minutes, then remove the cake from the pan and set it on a wire rack to cool completely. This cake freezes very well and may be served semifrozen.

Variations:

•Fold ¼ to ½ cup mini chocolate chips into the batter along with the nuts.

•One cup of golden raisins boiled for 5 minutes in water to cover and thoroughly drained and dried may be folded into the batter along with the nuts.

•For dairy, whipping cream may be substituted for the pareve cream.

14

From the Hearth

Pies, Pastries, Cookies & Bars

"The taste of it was like wafers made with honey" (Exodus 16:31).

Pie Crust

Makes two 9-inch pie shells
or the top and bottom for one pie

The addition of vinegar to the dough will not change the flavor significantly. It actually acts as a tenderizer, resulting in a flakier dough.

2 cups all-purpose flour
1 teaspoon salt
¾ cup solid white vegetable shortening
2 teaspoons vinegar
¼ cup cold water

Into a small mixing bowl, sift the flour and salt. With a pastry blender or 2 knives, cut in the shortening until the mixture resembles small peas. In a small glass, combine the vinegar with the cold water. Sprinkle the mixture, a tablespoon at a time, into the flour, tossing lightly with a fork after each addition, until the mixture is moist enough to come together. Shape the pastry into a ball, then divide it in half. On a lightly floured board with a floured rolling pin, roll out to the desired shape.

Basic Short Dough

Makes enough dough to line
one 9 x 2-inch cake layer pan

This basic dough is referred to as the 1-2-3 short dough because of the proportion of its basic ingredients. It is one part (pound) sugar to two parts (pounds) fat to three parts (pounds) flour. This very versatile dough makes an excellent crust for cheesecake.

> 1 cup sugar
> 2 cups unsalted butter or margarine
> Pinch of salt
> ⅛ teaspoon baking powder
> 1 teaspoon vanilla extract
> 1 egg (graded large)
> 3 cups unsifted all-purpose flour

In a large mixing bowl, cream together the sugar and fat. Add the salt, baking powder, vanilla, and egg. Beat until thick. Then, all at once, add about three-fourths of the flour. Knead in the remaining flour. At first the dough will be difficult to handle, but the secret is to work quickly so that the fat does not melt. Do not knead too much. Squeeze the dough together to form a smooth ball. Refrigerate for at least 1 hour before using. The dough, wrapped in wax paper, will keep in the refrigerator for several days.

Variation:

This dough may be used to make shortcake cookies. Roll out the dough and brush with a beaten egg. Liberally sprinkle with sugar and cinnamon. Or sprinkle on crushed nuts and roll them into the dough; then sprinkle with sugar and cinnamon. Cut the dough into the desired shapes—bars, squares, etc. Bake at 400 degrees F. for 7 to 10 minutes.

Dutch Apple Tart

Serves 6 to 8

It's hard to beat the taste of this spectacular-looking apple tart. A combination of apple pie filling topped with baked apple halves makes a good apple pie even better.

> **1 deep 9-inch pie shell, unbaked**
> **7 or 8 medium-sized tart apples**
> **½ to ¾ cup sugar, to taste**
> **2 tablespoons flour**
> **½ teaspoon cinnamon**
> **¼ cup light cream, pareve cream, apple**
>   **juice, or water**
> **2 tablespoons unsalted butter or margarine**

Preheat the oven to 400 degrees F.

Peel, halve, and core the apples. Reserve 10 apple halves. Slice the remaining halves into the pastry shell, making an even layer. Combine the sugar, flour, and cinnamon. Sprinkle half of the mixture over the sliced apples. Arrange the reserved apple halves, cut side down, in a single layer on top of the sliced apples. Sprinkle with the remaining sugar mixture. Slowly pour the cream, apple juice, or water near the center. Dot with butter or margarine.

Bake in the preheated oven for about 1 hour, until the apples are tender but still hold their shape.

When you take the tart out of the oven, gently press down the apple halves into the juices in the tart (the syrupy juices will thicken as the tart cools). Serve warm or cold.

Apple Custard Pie

Serves 8

Deep inside a spicy custard filling, crisp apple slices are baked until just tender and come to the table as an added surprise ingredient. Serve either warm or cold.

> **4 tablespoons flour, divided**
> **1 cup sugar, divided**

1 deep 9-inch pie shell, unbaked
3 medium-sized apples
1 egg (graded large), beaten
1½ cups dairy or pareve milk
¼ teaspoon nutmeg
½ teaspoon cinnamon

Preheat the oven to 450 degrees F.

Mix 2 tablespoons of the flour with ¼ cup of the sugar and sprinkle over the bottom of the pie shell. Peel and core the apples and slice into fairly thick slices, about ½ inch. Arrange the apples over the flour and sugar mixture in the pie shell.

Combine the beaten egg and milk and pour over the apples. Combine the remaining flour and sugar with the spices and sprinkle over the top. Bake at 450 degrees F. for 10 minutes, then reduce the heat to 325 degrees F. and bake 30 minutes longer, until the custard is firm.

Cranberry-Apple Meringue Pie

Serves 8

As an alternative to traditional apple pie, try this delicious cranberry-apple pie adorned with a golden brown meringue. A perfect pie for Thanksgiving.

⅔ cup sugar
3 tablespoons cornstarch
⅛ teaspoon salt
½ cup light corn syrup
¼ cup water
2 cups fresh cranberries
2 cups peeled, cored, and diced apples
½ teaspoon grated lemon rind
1 deep 9-inch pie shell, prebaked

Meringue:

3 egg whites (from eggs graded large)
¼ teaspoon cream of tartar
6 tablespoons sugar

In a medium-sized saucepan, combine the sugar, cornstarch, and salt. Add the corn syrup and water. Cook over medium heat until the mixture begins to boil, stirring constantly with a wire whisk. Add the cranberries and apples. Reduce the heat to low; cook covered, stirring occasionally, for 10 to 15 minutes, until the cranberry skins pop. Stir in the lemon rind. Remove from the heat. Set aside while preparing the meringue.

With the electric mixer at low speed, beat the egg white until foamy. Beat in the cream of tartar, then gradually increase the mixer speed to high. Beat until soft peaks begin to form. Gradually beat in the sugar, one tablespoon at a time. Beat until stiff peaks form. Preheat the oven to 350 degrees F.

Pour the filling into the pie shell. Cloak it with the meringue. Seal the filling in completely, making sure the meringue touches the pie crust at all points. Bake until golden brown, 10 to 12 minutes. Cool on a wire rack.

Note: To prevent a burned or overbrowned rim around a pie crust, cut the center out of an aluminum pie plate the same size as the pie, and invert it over the pie. Remove from the last 15 minutes of baking.

Lemon Sponge Pie

Serves 6 to 8

An old favorite goes modern. Frozen lemonade mix replaces the lemon juice.

> 1 deep 9-inch pie shell
> ¾ to 1 cup sugar, more or less depending on personal preference for tartness
> ¼ cup all-purpose flour
> 2 tablespoons oil or melted unsalted butter or margarine
> ⅛ teaspoon salt
> 2 eggs (graded large), separated
> ½ cup (from a 6-ounce can) frozen lemonade concentrate, defrosted
> 1 cup milk (for dairy) or water

Preheat the oven to 350 degrees F. Prebake the pie shell for 5 minutes; set aside to cool.

In the bowl of an electric mixer, place the sugar, flour, oil or butter or margarine, salt, and egg yolks. Beat until very light and fluffy, about 5 minutes. Beat in the lemonade concentrate. Add the milk or water, beating slowly.

In a clean bowl with clean beaters, beat the egg whites until stiff but not dry. Fold the whites into the lemonade mixture. Pour the filling into the prebaked pie shell. Return to the oven and bake for 40 minutes or until the top is firm and golden.

Variation:

Pour the batter into 8 lightly greased custard cups or into a greased 1½-quart casserole. Place the cups or casserole in a large pan and fill with hot water halfway up the sides. Bake for 40 to 45 minutes, until golden on top.

Amazing Coconut Custard Pie

Serves 8 to 10

This is so simple to prepare. Believe it or not, the pie makes its own crust as it bakes! To make pareve, use the margarine and substitute pareve "milk" for the dairy milk.

> **Grease and flour for the pan**
> **4 eggs (graded large)**
> **1 stick (½ cup) unsalted butter or pareve**
>   **margarine, at room temperature**
> **1 teaspoon vanilla extract**
> **2 cups milk**
> **¾ cup sugar**
> **½ cup unsifted all-purpose flour**
> **⅛ teaspoon salt**
> **¾ teaspoon baking powder**
> **1 cup flaked coconut, divided**

Preheat the oven to 350 degrees F.

Grease and flour a 10-inch pie pan (a 9-inch square pan can also be used). Put all the ingredients, reserving ½ cup of the coconut for topping, into a blender jar. Blend at high speed for 30 seconds. Pour the batter into the prepared pan. Sprinkle the reserved coconut over all. Bake for 40 to 45 minutes, until the coconut is golden brown.

Fresh Cranberry Crunch

Serves 6 to 9

Cranberries are traditionally served on Thanksgiving, but they need not be prepared only as a relish. Here, raisins and uncooked rolled oats team up with cranberries to make an energy-filled pastry.

Grease for the pan
1 cup sugar
1 tablespoon cornstarch
½ cup water
1 teaspoon vanilla extract
Pinch of salt
2 cups fresh cranberries
½ cup raisins
1 cup quick-cooking (not instant) rolled oats
1 cup firmly packed light brown sugar
½ cup unsifted all-purpose flour
⅓ cup unsalted margarine

Preheat the oven to 350 degrees F. Grease an 8-inch-square pan; set aside.

In a saucepan, combine the sugar, cornstarch, water, vanilla, and salt. Mix together. Stir in the cranberries and raisins. Bring to a boil over medium heat. Reduce the heat and simmer for 5 minutes. Cool slightly. Mix together the oats, brown sugar, and flour. Cut in the margarine until the mixture is crumbly. Sprinkle half of the mixture over the bottom of the prepared pan. Press the mixture to flatten. Spread with the cooled cranberry filling and top with the remaining oat mixture, patting lightly. Bake for 45 minutes. Serve warm or cold.

Yeast Strudel

Makes 6 rolls, 16 pieces per roll

The traditional Austrian and German stretched strudel is replaced here with an easy-to-prepare yeast dough. There is no stretching of dough and no waiting for the yeast dough to rise. The finished strudel freezes very well.

Dough:

1 envelope active dry yeast
1 cup warm water (110 to 115 degrees F.)
5 cups unsifted all-purpose flour
5 tablespoons sugar
Pinch of salt
2 cups solid white vegetable shortening
3 egg yolks (from eggs graded large)
1 stick (½ cup) unsalted margarine, melted

Filling:

¼ cup cinnamon sugar (scant ½ tablespoon
    cinnamon to ¼ cup sugar)
2 jars (12 ounces each) fruit preserves of
    your choice (strawberry, cherry, apricot)
1 cup chocolate minichips
1 cup raisins
1¼ cups shredded coconut
1 cup chopped nuts

In a small bowl, dissolve the yeast in the warm water. Sift the flour into a large mixing bowl. Blend in the sugar and salt. With a pastry blender or 2 knives, cut in the shortening until the mixture looks like small peas. Add the egg yolks and finally the dissolved yeast. Mix together and shape into a ball.

Preheat the oven to 350 degrees F. Divide the dough into 6 portions. Work with one part at a time, keeping the remainder in a covered bowl. Sprinkle a pastry cloth lightly but thoroughly with flour. Using a lightly floured rolling pin, roll out the dough very thin, about ⅛ inch, into a 12 x 16-inch rectangle.

Brush the dough with melted margarine, then sprinkle with some of the cinnamon sugar. Spread with some of the fruit preserves, followed by a sprinkling of chocolate bits, raisins, shredded coconut, and nuts. Increase or decrease any of the filling ingredients to taste. Now carefully roll up the dough jelly-roll-fashion. Brush the top with melted margarine and a sprinkling of cinnamon sugar. Transfer to a teflon or vegetable-sprayed 13 x 17-inch baking pan. Score the top of the roll 16 times. Repeat the process with the remainder of the dough. You will have 2 pans, with 3 rolls on each pan.

Bake for 20 to 25 minutes, until golden brown. Cut the strudel completely through at the score marks and remove the pieces to a rack to cool.

Variation:

This dough is very versatile. It is excellent to use for making knishes, as follows. Roll out the dough, fill with the savory filling of your choice, then roll up and brush with margarine. Slice the roll at 1½-inch intervals. Up-end each slice, placing it cut side down on the baking sheet. If you wish, flatten each slice slightly with your hand. Bake at 350 degrees F. for 20 to 25 minutes, until golden.

Rugelach

Makes about 30

Play it safe! Double the recipe because no one can eat just one rugel.

This cream cheese pastry can also be used to make cheese strudel. It has a wonderfully flaky texture.

Dough:

> 4 ounces cream cheese
> 1 stick (½ cup) unsalted butter
> 1 cup sifted all-purpose flour
> ¼ teaspoon salt (optional)

Filling:

> ½ cup fruit preserves of your choice
>   (cherry, raspberry)
> ½ cup chopped walnuts

1 teaspoon grated lemon rind
Cinnamon sugar
1 egg beaten with 1 teaspoon water

Have the cream cheese and butter at room temperature. In a mixing bowl, cream together the cheese and butter. Gradually add the flour, mixing until well blended. Form into a ball and refrigerate overnight, or place in the freezer for 1 to 2 hours.

Preheat the oven to 350 degrees F.

Cut the chilled dough into thirds. On a floured surface, roll out each third of dough into a 9-inch circle about ⅛-inch thick. Mix together the preserves, nuts, and lemon rind. Spread the circle with the filling and cut into 10 wedge-shaped sections. Lightly sprinkle with cinnamon sugar.

Starting at the wide end of a wedge, roll up the wedge, ending at its point. Shape into a crescent. Repeat with remaining wedges. Transfer the crescents to baking sheets, then brush each crescent with the egg wash. Bake for about 12 to 15 minutes, until lightly browned. Cool on wire racks.

Pareve Rugelach

Makes 64 or more

It is difficult to detect that these rugelach are not dairy. Their taste and texture is on a par with versions made with butter, cream cheese, or sour cream. Try them and determine for yourself. They are an excellent addition to the cookie larder. They freeze very well and need not be thawed before serving.

5 cups unsifted all-purpose flour,
approximately
4 sticks (1 pound) unsalted margarine
1 container (10 ounces) pareve whipping
cream
½ cup cinnamon sugar (½ tablespoon
cinnamon to ½ cup sugar)

Preheat the oven to 350 degrees F. Vegetable spray or lightly grease baking sheets; set aside.

Place the flour in a large bowl. Cut in the margarine and then the pareve whipping cream. Mix together until a smooth, rollable dough is formed, adding more flour if necessary.

Divide the dough into 8 portions. On a floured surface, roll out one portion at a time into a circle approximately 8 inches in diameter. Sprinkle with cinnamon sugar. Cut into 8 wedge-shaped sections (a pizza cutter is an ideal tool for this). Starting at the wide end and ending with the point, roll up each wedge. Curve to form crescent-shaped rolls. Place each roll, open end down, on the prepared baking sheets. Bake for about 20 minutes, until golden brown.

Variation:

Spread the rolling surface with cinnamon sugar. Roll out the dough on this mixture. Continue as above. Finely chopped nuts can be sprinkled on the circle.

Toasted Jelly Rolls

Makes 12

Sliced white bread is the base for these Toasted Jelly Rolls. They are a nonbaked pastry substitute.

> 12 slices white bread
> ¼ cup firmly packed light brown sugar
> ¼ cup soft margarine
> 1 cup flaked coconut
> Jelly of your choice

Preheat the oven to 425 degrees F.

Decrust each slice of bread. Roll each lightly with a rolling pin. In a mixing bowl, cream the sugar and margarine until fluffy. Spread each slice with the mixture. Sprinkle the coconut on a sheet of wax paper. Place the bread slices spread side down on the coconut. Press down so the coconut adheres to the bread. Spread jam on the top of the bread. Roll up to form jelly rolls. Place seam side down on a baking sheet. Bake for 4 to 5 minutes, until golden.

Variation (for peanut-butter lovers):
Spread the bread with peanut butter and/or jam.

Mandelbrot
(Almond Bread)

Makes about forty ½-inch slices

Mandelbrot is a German and Yiddish term literally meaning "almond bread." But actually it is more in the cookie than in the bread family. The dough is baked either as long rolls on a baking sheet or in a loaf pan. It is cut into diagonal slices after baking and returned to the oven to toast slightly.

> **3 cups unsifted all-purpose flour**
> **3 teaspoons baking powder**
> **½ teaspoon salt (optional)**
> **3 eggs (graded large)**
> **1 cup sugar**
> **½ cup oil**
> **1 teaspoon vanilla extract**
> **1 teaspoon almond extract**
> **1 tablespoon grated lemon rind (optional)**
> **½ to 1 cup chopped blanched almonds**
> **Grease for the foil sheet**

Preheat the oven to 350 degrees F.

Into a small bowl, sift the flour, baking powder, and salt. In the large bowl of an electric mixer, at medium speed, beat the eggs and sugar until fluffy and pale yellow in color. Add the oil and flavorings. Beat until well blended. Add the sifted dry ingredients. Stir in the chopped almonds.

Divide the dough into 4 parts. On individual pieces of greased aluminum foil, shape each portion into a roll about 2½ inches wide and 7½ inches long. After forming each roll on the greased foil, fold up the sides of the foil against the roll, then fold the corners together securely. This insures that the mandelbrot retains an even shape while baking. Transfer the loaves to a 10 x 15-inch baking sheet. Bake for about 25 minutes, until lightly browned. Open the foil.

With a serrated or sharp knife, slice each roll crosswise into half-inch slices. Lay the slices, one cut side down, on a clean ungreased baking sheet. Place the baking sheet in the oven and bake for about 7 minutes, then turn the cookies over and bake for another 7 or 8 minutes, until golden. With a metal spatula, carefully remove the cookies to wire racks to cool. Store in a tightly covered container.

Variations:

• Add coconut, tiny chocolate chips, or raisins to the batter.
• Dust the top of the rolls with a mixture of cinnamon and sugar before baking.

Note: Save crumbs for use in strudel, streusel, or kuchen.

Chinese Fortune Cookies

Makes about 18

Legend has it that fortune cookies did not originate in China but rather in San Francisco, where they were created by a Japanese chef. Whatever their origin, they are a deliciously crisp and fun ending to a Chinese meal.

The preparation of fortune cookies is similar to that of the French rolled lace cookies. Thin cookies are baked then quickly folded to enclose the fortune message. The cookies are not difficult to make, but they are time-consuming because they are baked almost individually. Nonetheless, they are well worth the effort.

> 1 egg white (from an egg graded large)
> ¼ cup sugar
> Pinch of salt
> 2 tablespoons plus 2 teaspoons melted
>   unsalted margarine
> Drop of vanilla extract
> ⅓ cup sifted all-purpose flour
> ¼ teaspoon unsweetened instant tea
>   powder (optional)
> 2 teaspoons water

Grease for the baking sheet
Freezer or white paper cut into 2 x ½-inch
strips with fortunes written or typed on
them

In a medium-sized bowl, combine the egg white, sugar, and salt. Stir. Continue stirring as you add first the margarine, then the vanilla, flour, instant tea, and water. Chill in the refrigerator for at least ½ hour. Preheat the oven to 350 degrees F. Bake only 2 cookies at a time. On a greased baking sheet, drop 1 slightly rounded teaspoon of dough for each cookie. Space them about 3 inches apart. It is important to spread the dough very thin— about 3 inches in diameter—with the back of a spoon. Bake for 3 to 5 minutes, until the edges turn light brown. Remove immediately. The cookies should be paper-thin.

Working very quickly, place a fortune in the center of each cookie. Fold the cookie in half, enclosing the fortune and forming a semicircle; then drape the folded cookie over the handle of a wooden spoon. Pinch the 2 points together so the cookie takes on the shape of a fortune cookie. Slide the cookie off the end of the spoon. Place each cookie in a small-size muffin tin, open edges up, until the cookie sets. Store in an airtight container.

Poppy Seed Cookies

Makes about 50

No need to wait for Purim to prepare these poppy seed cookies! They are appreciated all year long. Two active members of the Agudas Achim Sisterhood, Anita Kaplowitz and Irene Kronick, shared this favorite recipe with me.

1 cup solid white vegetable shortening
1 cup sugar
2 eggs (graded large)
3 tablespoons water
1 teaspoon vanilla extract
3½ cups unsifted all-purpose flour
¼ teaspoon salt
2 teaspoons baking powder
½ cup poppy seeds, scant

Preheat the oven to 350 degrees F. Grease 2 baking sheets; set aside.

In a mixing bowl, cream the shortening with the sugar until light. Beat in the eggs, water, and vanilla. Sift together the dry ingredients. Blend into the egg-shortening mixture. Knead by hand until all is well blended. Lastly, add the poppy seeds and knead again.

Pull off small pieces of dough and shape into 1-inch balls. Place 1½ inches apart on the prepared baking sheets. Flatten the balls with the bottom of a drinking glass. Bake for 12 to 15 minutes, until golden brown.

Shortbread Cookies

Makes 24 to 30

2 cups sifted all-purpose flour
¼ teaspoon baking powder
1 cup unsalted butter or margarine
½ cup sifted confectioners' sugar
½ cup finely chopped walnuts
Walnut halves

Into a small bowl, sift together the flour and the baking powder. In a mixing bowl, cream the butter or margarine with the sugar until light and fluffy. Gradually blend in the flour mixture. Stir in the finely chopped nuts. Cover and refrigerate until well chilled.

Preheat the oven to 300 degrees F. On a lightly floured surface, roll out the dough to ¼-inch thickness. Cut into desired shapes. Place on an ungreased cookie sheet. Press a walnut half in the center of each cookie. Bake for 20 minutes, until the edges are lightly browned. Cool on wire racks.

Yum Yum Squares

Makes twenty-four squares,
each approximately 2⅛ inches

Chocolate-lovers will delight over these raisin-rich Yum Yum Squares. Chopped nuts are an optional addition.

⅓ cup solid white vegetable shortening
1 cup sugar
1 cup raisins
2 ounces unsweetened chocolate
1 teaspoon cinnamon (optional)
1½ cups cold water
1 teaspoon vanilla extract
Pinch of salt
2 cups unsifted all-purpose flour
1 teaspoon baking soda

Preheat the oven to 350 degrees F. Grease and flour a 9 x 13 x 2-inch pan; set aside.

In a saucepan, combine the shortening, sugar, raisins, chocolate, cinnamon, and water. Place over medium heat and bring to a boil. Stir occasionally until the chocolate is melted. Boil for 4 minutes. Set aside to cool. Add the vanilla and salt. In a mixing bowl, combine the flour and baking soda. Add the cooled chocolate mixture and beat. Pour the batter into the prepared pan. Bake for 30 to 40 minutes. Cut into squares, approximately 2⅛ inches.

Note: Unsweetened cocoa can be substituted for the unsweetened chocolate. One ounce of chocolate equals 3 tablespoons cocoa powder plus 1 tablespoon shortening.

Coconut-Lemon Bars

Makes fifty-four bars, each
approximately 1 x 2⅛ inches

The combination of dates and nuts flavored with tangy lemon juice and topped with coconut makes these bars great for dessert or for just plain snacking.

½ cup firmly packed brown sugar
½ cup soft vegetable shortening or
   margarine
1 cup sifted all-purpose flour
2 eggs (graded large)
1 cup firmly packed brown sugar
2 to 3 tablespoons lemon juice, to taste
1 teaspoon grated lemon rind
½ teaspoon salt
1 cup chopped pitted dates
1 cup chopped nuts
1 cup shredded coconut

Preheat the oven to 350 degrees F.

In a large bowl, cream the ½ cup brown sugar with the shortening until light and fluffy. Stir in the flour. Press the mixture onto the bottom of an ungreased 9 x 13 x 2-inch pan. Bake for 10 minutes.

Meanwhile, beat the eggs very well with the cup of brown sugar. Add the lemon juice, grated rind, and salt. Stir in the dates, nuts, and coconut. Spread the batter over the partially baked crust. Return to the oven for an additional 20 minutes, until light brown on top. Cool in the pan on a wire rack. Cut into bars, each approximately 1 x 2⅛ inches.

Nutty Noodle Bars

*Makes thirty-six bars, each
approximately 1½ x 2⅛ inches*

The chow mein noodles in this recipe do not give the cookies a Chinese character, but they do provide a definite crunch.

First Layer:

Grease for the pan
1¼ cups sifted all-purpose flour
½ cup firmly packed light brown sugar
⅓ cup solid white vegetable shortening or
   unsalted margarine

Second Layer:

> 2 eggs (graded large), beaten
> 1 cup firmly packed light brown sugar
> 1 teaspoon vanilla extract
> 3 tablespoons all-purpose flour
> ¼ teaspoon salt (optional)
> 1 teaspoon baking powder
> 1½ cups crushed chow mein noodles
> ⅔ cup moist flaked coconut
> ⅔ cup chopped walnuts
> Confectioners' sugar

Preheat the oven to 350 degrees F. Grease a 9 x 13 x 2-inch baking pan; set aside.

For the first layer, in a small bowl combine the flour and brown sugar. Cut in the shortening until the mixture resembles coarse meal. Pat onto the bottom of the prepared pan. Bake for 5 minutes. Cool on a wire rack.

For the second layer, with an electric mixer beat together the eggs and brown sugar. Add the vanilla and beat. Sift together the flour, salt, and baking powder. Add the sifted dry ingredients to the egg-sugar mixture. Beat until blended. Stir in the noodles, coconut, and walnuts. Spread the mixture evenly over the cooled first layer. Return to the oven and bake for 25 minutes at 350 degrees F. While still warm, cut into bars, each approximately 1½ x 2⅛ inches. Dust with confectioners' sugar when cool.

Easy Date Bars

Makes twelve bars, each
approximately 1¾ x 3⅔ inches

An easy date bar to prepare, especially if you use precut pitted dates. The flavors of dates and nuts naturally go together, and this recipe is no exception.

> Grease for the pan
> 2 eggs (graded large)
> 1 teaspoon vanilla extract

⟶

      ½ cup sugar
      ¼ cup all-purpose flour
      ½ teaspoon baking powder
      ¼ teaspoon salt
      1½ cups (8 ounces) cut-up pitted dates
      ½ cup coarsely chopped walnuts

Preheat the oven to 350 degrees F. Grease a 7 x 11 x 1½-inch baking pan; set aside.

In the bowl of an electric mixer, beat the eggs until very light. Add the vanilla. Gradually beat in the sugar. Into a bowl, sift together flour, baking powder, and salt. Toss the cut-up dates and chopped nuts with the flour mixture. Fold this mixture into the beaten egg mixture. Spread the batter in the prepared pan. Bake for 20 to 22 minutes, until nicely browned. Cool thoroughly. Cut into bars, each approximately 1¾ x 3⅔ inches.

Oat Date Bars

*Makes thirty-six bars, each
approximately 1½ x 2⅛ inches*

    Date bars requiring a little more time to prepare. The dates have to be cooked before the bars can be baked.

    Rolled oats are combined with flour to make a crumbly dough. It's a luscious combination: a date filling baked between a crumbly oatmeal crust.

      Grease for the pan

Filling:

      1 package (8 ounces) pitted dates
      ½ cup sugar
      1 tablespoon flour
      1 cup boiling water
      1 teaspoon vanilla extract

Dough:

      ¾ cup solid white vegetable shortening
      1 cup firmly packed brown sugar
      1½ cups unsifted all-purpose flour

½ teaspoon baking soda
⅓ teaspoon salt
1½ cups quick-cooking (not instant) rolled
    oats

Preheat the oven to 350 degrees F. Grease a 9 x 13 x 2-inch pan; set aside.

To prepare the filling, cut up the dates and place in a saucepan. Add the sugar, flour, boiling water, and vanilla. Cook over low heat, stirring constantly until thickened, about 8 to 10 minutes.

Set aside to cool while preparing the dough.

In a mixing bowl, cream the shortening with the sugar. Sift together the flour, baking soda, and salt. Mix in the rolled oats. Blend the dry ingredients with the creamed mixture. Press half of this crumb mixture onto the bottom of the greased pan. Spread with the cooled filling. Top with the remaining crumb mixture, patting gently. Bake for 30 to 45 minutes, until lightly browned. While still warm, cut into bars, each approximately 1½ x 2⅛ inches.

Variations:

• Prepare a pineapple filling by combining one 8½-ounce can of undrained crushed pineapple with 1 cup of sugar (or less), 2½ tablespoons of cornstarch, 1 tablespoon of unsalted margarine and 1 cup of water. Cook as above, until thickened.
• Use one can of your favorite prepared pie filling.

Holiday Fruit Bars

Makes thirty-six bars, each
approximately 1½ x 2⅛ inches

Fruit bars rich with candied fruit and nuts. You get all the goodness of a fruitcake in these bar cookies baked in a pan.

Grease for the pan
1¼ cups unsifted all-purpose flour
½ cup sugar
½ teaspoon baking powder
½ teaspoon salt

→

> ½ cup unsalted margarine, melted
> 3 eggs (graded large)
> 1 cup mixed candied fruit
> 1 cup chopped nuts
> ½ cup raisins
> ½ cup diced pitted dates

Glaze:

> 1 cup sifted confectioners' sugar
> 3 to 4 tablespoons orange juice

Preheat the oven to 350 degrees F. Grease a 9 x 13 x 2-inch baking pan; set aside.

Into the large bowl of an electric mixer, sift together the dry ingredients. Add the melted margarine and the eggs. Mix at low speed until thoroughly blended. Stir in the candied fruit, nuts, raisins, and diced dates. Pour the batter into the prepared pan and bake for 25 to 30 minutes, until golden.

In a small bowl, make a glaze by combining the confectioners' sugar with 3 tablespoons of the orange juice. Add more orange juice if the glaze is too thick. Spread the glaze over the warm cake. Cool and cut into bars, each approximately 1½ x 2⅛ inches.

Coconut Bars

Makes thirty-nine 1 x 3-inch bars

These are two-layer cookie bars. Rich and sweet, they freeze very well and need not be completely thawed to be enjoyed.

Dough:

> ½ cup solid white shortening or unsalted
> margarine
> ½ cup firmly packed dark brown sugar
> 1 cup all-purpose flour

Topping:

> 2 eggs (graded large)
> 1 cup firmly packed dark brown sugar
> 1 teaspoon vanilla extract

2 tablespoons flour
½ teaspoon baking powder
1 cup moist shredded coconut
½ cup chopped nuts

Preheat the oven to 350 degrees F.

To prepare the dough, cream the shortening and sugar thoroughly. Stir in the flour. Blend well. Press and flatten with the back of a spoon or palm of the hand to cover the bottom of an ungreased 9 x 13 x 2-inch pan. Bake for 10 minutes.

To prepare the topping, beat the eggs with the dark brown sugar and vanilla until well blended. Sift together the flour and baking powder. Beat into the egg-sugar mixture. Stir in the coconut and chopped nuts.

Spread the topping on the baked crust. Return to the oven and bake for an additional 25 minutes or until golden brown. Cool slightly, then cut into 1 x 3-inch bars.

Raspberry Bars

Makes sixteen bars, each
approximately 1¾ x 2¾ inches

These bars are reminiscent of the Linzer torte, the famous Austrian pastry.

Crust:

⅓ cup solid white vegetable shortening
3 tablespoons confectioners' sugar
Dash of salt (optional)
1⅓ cups sifted all-purpose flour
1 egg (graded large)

Preheat the oven to 375 degrees F.

Cream the shortening. Add the sugar and salt; beat well. Stir in the flour and egg. Mix well. Press the dough into an 7 x 11 x 1½-inch baking pan. Bake for 12 minutes. Remove from the oven and cool.

Topping:

> ¾ cup raspberry jam
> ¼ cup chopped blanched almonds
> 2 eggs (graded large)
> ¾ cup granulated sugar
> 1 teaspoon almond extract
> 2 tablespoons flour
> ½ teaspoon baking powder
> ¼ teaspoon salt
> Confectioners' sugar

Spread the raspberry jam over the baked crust. Sprinkle the chopped nuts over the jam. In a small bowl, beat the eggs. Add the sugar and beat until light. Add the almond extract. Sift together the flour, baking powder, and salt; stir the sifted ingredients into the egg mixture. Spread this mixture over the jam and nuts. Bake for about 30 minutes, until set. While still warm, cut into bars, each approximately 1¾ x 2¾ inches. When cool, sprinkle with confectioners' sugar.

Cherry Bars

Makes sixteen bars, each
approximately 1¾ x 2¾ inches

A coconut filling baked on a shortbread-cookie-type crust is topped by a scattering of cherries. About as good as a sweet can be.

Crust:

> 1 cup unsifted all-purpose flour
> 2 tablespoons confectioners' sugar
> 2 sticks (½ pound) unsalted margarine

Filling:

> 1 cup sugar
> ¼ cup unsifted all-purpose flour
> ½ teaspoon baking powder
> ½ cup chopped nuts
> ½ cup shredded coconut

1 teaspoon vanilla extract
2 eggs (graded large), well beaten
1 can (17 ounces) sour cherries, drained

Preheat the oven to 350 degrees F.

Into a medium-sized bowl, sift the flour and sugar. With a pastry blender or 2 knives, cut in the margarine. Pat the mixture into a 7 x 11 x 1½-inch baking pan. Bake for 15 minutes.

Into a medium-sized bowl, sift the sugar, flour, and baking powder. Stir in the chopped nuts and coconut. Add the vanilla to the well-beaten eggs, then blend with the dry mixture. Pour this mixture onto the baked crust. Spoon the drained cherries over the top. Return to the oven and bake for 30 minutes. Cut into rectangles, each approximately 1¾ x 2¾ inches.

15

The Staff of Life

Breads, Coffeecakes & Related Items

"*Man doth not live by bread alone*" (Deuteronomy 8:3).

Easy Blender Challah

Makes 1 large or 2 small loaves

Nothing quite introduces the Sabbath spirit like a loaf of home-baked *challah*. In fact, one of my fondest childhood memories is the aroma that came from my mother's kitchen when she was baking challah on Friday mornings.

Discover the joy of baking bread. Start with this easy blender challah, which requires no kneading.

> **3 cups unsifted all-purpose flour**
> **1 cup warm water (110 to 115 degrees F.)**
> **1 envelope active dry yeast**
> **¼ cup vegetable oil**
> **⅓ cup sugar**
> **1 egg (graded large)**
> **½ teaspoon salt**
> **1 egg (graded small)**
> **1 tablespoon water**
> **Sesame or poppy seeds (optional)**

Into a large bowl, measure 2 cups of the flour. Set aside. Into a blender jar, pour the water, yeast, and remaining cup of flour. Cover and blend at low speed (whip). Uncover and continue blending while adding the oil, sugar, large egg, and salt. Blend until the mixture is smooth.

Pour the batter over the reserved flour. Mix thoroughly with a spoon until a ball of dough forms. Place in a lightly greased bowl, turning to grease all sides. Cover and let rise in a warm draft-free place for 1½ hours or until doubled in bulk. Stir down.

Preheat the oven to 375 degrees F.

Shape the dough into challahs, braided or unbraided. To shape into 2 small braided challahs, divide the dough in half. Divide each part into 3 equal parts. Roll each part into a long coil of even thickness. Pinch together the tops of all 3 pieces. Start to braid by taking the outer right strip and crossing it over the center strip, bringing it to the center. Then take the outer left strip and cross it over the middle strip, bringing it to the center. Repeat the procedure by alternately bringing the right strip to the center and the left to the center until all are braided. Pinch the ends together. Tuck the ends in carefully. Transfer the bread to a greased loaf pan, 9⅝ x 5½ x 2¾ inches. Repeat with the remaining dough. If you choose to make one large braided challah, use a 9 x 13 x 2-inch baking pan.

For a round challah, shape the dough round with your cupped hands. Place in a greased 9-inch round baking pan. For a round spiral challah, roll the dough into a long coil. Form into a spiral by twisting the dough 'round and 'round into a spiral that thins toward the top.

Cover and let rise in a warm place until doubled in bulk, about 1 hour. Beat the remaining egg with the tablespoon of water just to blend. Brush the top of the breads with the egg wash. Sprinkle with sesame or poppy seeds if desired. Bake for about 40 minutes, until the breads are well browned and sound hollow when tapped with a knife handle or spoon. Remove to racks to cool.

Alternate method:

Into the large bowl of an electric mixer, measure 2 cups of the flour. Prepare the other mixture as above and pour this over the flour in the mixer bowl. Using a dough hook, beat on low speed until the dough clings to the hook and cleans the sides of the bowl, about 3 minutes. Continue to knead for an additional 3 minutes. Cover the bowl and set in a warm draft-free place until doubled in bulk. Continue as above.

Note: When baking challah, grease the pan with solid vegetable shortening rather than oil. Oil has a tendency to be absorbed into the bread dough whereas a solid vegetable shortening does not. Also, the pans will be easier to clean.

Fast-and-Easy Onion Rolls

Makes 6 rolls

These onion rolls are a gustatory delight when served with cream cheese and lox. For onion-lovers, the recipe offers the opportunity to be as extravagant as one wishes with the onion filling. You may increase or decrease the amount of onions that you reconstitute. You may also increase or decrease the amount of poppy seeds.

> **¼ cup dried onion flakes**
> **Water**
> **2 tablespoons unsalted margarine, melted**
>   **(or butter for dairy)**
> **½ teaspoon salt (optional)**
> **½ tablespoon poppy seeds**
> **6 frozen egg-twist rolls (frozen dough, not**
>   **prebaked rolls)**
> **Grease for the baking sheet**
> **1 egg, beaten**

Reconstitute the dried onions in water, then squeeze dry and place in a small bowl. Stir the melted margarine into the reconstituted onion flakes. Season with salt, then stir in the poppy seeds.

Thaw the frozen egg roll dough. On lightly floured surface, roll out each roll into a 5½-inch circle. Spoon a portion of the onion filling on three-fourths of each circle, reserving some of the filling for the top of the rolls. Fold a third of the dough over the onion filling; fold a third over from the other side. Place the rolls seam side down on a lightly greased cookie sheet. Brush the rolls with the egg wash and top with the remaining onion mixture. Let rise in a warm draft-free place until doubled in bulk. Preheat the oven to 375 degrees F. Bake for 15 to 20 minutes, until nicely browned.

Tzibileh Kichel

(Onion Biscuits)

Makes about 50

Old-time onion biscuits, not to be confused with onion *pletzlach*, which are made with a yeast dough.

Grease for the baking sheets
2 large onions
2 eggs (graded large)
½ cup oil
2¾ cups sifted all-purpose flour
2 teaspoons baking powder
1½ teaspoons sugar
½ teaspoon salt
¾ teaspoon black pepper
½ cup poppy seeds
2 tablespoons water

Preheat the oven to 425 degrees F. Grease baking sheets and set aside.

Grate the onions into a medium-sized bowl. Beat in the eggs and oil. Sift together the flour, baking powder, sugar, salt, and pepper; add to the onion mixture. Mix well. Add the poppy seeds and water. Drop the mixture by the tablespoonful onto the greased baking sheets. Bake for 10 to 15 minutes, until nicely colored.

Variations:

• More flour may be added so that the dough can be rolled out and cut with a cookie cutter or cut with a knife into triangles and rectangles. Bake in a moderate oven, 350 degrees F., until golden brown.

• More salt and pepper adds additional zest to the biscuits, which are good stand-ins on the hors d'oeuvre table.

Balubishkis

Makes about 20

Balubishkis, an Old World recipe I inherited, are baked yeast dumplings that are traditionally served with a stew. My late mother-in-law would serve them with a *jakaya* (Russian for meat stew). She would cloak the balubishkis with a dressing made from the stew gravy and two or three cloves of garlic chopped fine or crushed into it. Her contention was that a jakaya tastes infinitely better when served with balubishkis rather than with mashed potatoes, noodles, or rice.

Balubishkis are luscious enough to stand on their own merit without being enhanced with a gravy. They can be substituted for petit pain rolls.

> 2 tablespoons sugar
> ½ teaspoon salt
> ½ cup hot water
> 1 envelope active dry yeast
> 2 tablespoons warm water (110 to 115 degrees F.)
> 2 cups sifted all-purpose flour
> 2 tablespoons oil
> 1 egg (graded large), lightly beaten
> ¼ cup oil

In a large bowl, combine the sugar, salt, and hot water. Cool to lukewarm. Pour the warm water into a small bowl. Stir in the yeast and let stand for 5 minutes. Stir the yeast into the water mixture. Add ¾ cup of the flour. Beat well. Cover and let rise for about 1 hour, until foamy.

Stir in the 2 tablespoons of oil and the egg. Work in the remaining flour to make a light dough. Turn out onto a lightly floured board. Knead lightly. Cover and place in a warm draft-free place to rise until doubled in bulk, about 1 hour.

Preheat the oven to 400 degrees F.

Punch down the dough. Knead once or twice. Pull off pieces of dough and shape into 1 to 1¼-inch balls. Roll the balls in the ¼ cup of oil and arrange in a 9-inch cake layer or pie pan. Cover and let rise until doubled, about 30 minutes. Bake for 20 minutes or until browned. To serve, break off individual balub-ishkis and set on a serving dish alongside stewed meat. Spoon a garlicky gravy over them and serve.

Variation:

Before baking, sprinkle ¼ teaspoon garlic powder or garlic salt over them. Or garnish the formed balls with a tablespoon of finely chopped parsley.

Babka

Makes 2 loaves

Babka is a rich cakelike bread. Here is a pareve version, one that is tastefully united with a chocolate filling. The rich choco-late ribbons running through the bread are created simply and quickly by blending chocolate pudding mix with a little milk and spreading it on the yeast dough.

> **2 envelopes active dry yeast**
> **¼ cup warm water (110 to 115 degrees F.)**
> **½ cup sugar**
> **1 stick (½ cup) soft unsalted margarine**
> **1 teaspoon salt**
> **1 cup pareve milk, scalded**
> **5 cups sifted all-purpose flour,**
> **approximately**
> **2 eggs (graded large)**
> **½ cup chocolate pudding mix**
> **½ cup chopped nuts, your choice**
> **3 tablespoons pareve milk**
> **2 tablespoons unsalted margarine, melted**

In a small bowl, proof the yeast in the warm water. Measure the sugar, margarine, and salt into a large bowl. Pour in the pareve milk and stir until the sugar dissolves. Cool to lukewarm. Stir in about 1½ cups of the flour and mix until smooth. Beat in the yeast and the eggs. Stir in enough additional flour to make a soft dough.

Turn out the dough onto lightly floured surface and knead until smooth and satiny, 8 to 10 minutes. Shape into a ball. Place in a lightly greased bowl, turning to coat all sides. Cover and let rise in warm draft-free place until doubled, about 1½ hours. Punch down. Divide the dough in half and shape into smooth balls. Cover and let rise for 10 minutes.

In a bowl, blend the pudding mix and nuts with 3 tablespoons of pareve milk.

Preheat the oven to 350 degrees F. Roll out half of the dough into a 9 x 24-inch rectangle. Lightly brush with melted margarine. Spread the dough with half of the chocolate mixture. Roll up from the narrow end. Place seam side down in a greased 5½ x 9½-inch loaf pan. Repeat with the remaining dough. Brush with water or melted margarine. Let rise until doubled, about 45 minutes. Bake for 35 to 40 minutes, until golden brown. Immediately invert and remove the cakes from the pans. Place upright on the racks and cool thoroughly.

Variations:

• After spreading the filling on the dough, roll up the dough from each end, jelly-roll-fashion, toward the center. Turn the dough over and place it in the prepared pan, seam side down. Lightly brush with melted margarine.

• *Chocolate Rolls:* Roll out each piece of dough into a 10 x 12-inch oblong. Brush with the melted margarine, then spread filling on the dough. Fold the dough into thirds at the 12-inch side. The dough should now be 4 inches wide. Place each roll on a greased cookie sheet with overlap down (bottom up). Brush top with margarine or egg wash (1 egg well beaten with 1 teaspoon of water) and bake for 30 to 35 minutes.

• *Cinnamon Babka:* Mix 2 teaspoons cinnamon with ½ cup sugar, ½ cup chopped nuts of your choice, and ½ cup golden raisins. After lightly brushing the dough with margarine, spread the dough with half of the cinnamon-sugar mixture. Sprinkle with half of the chopped nuts and raisins and proceed as above.

Coffeecake Swirls

Makes 12 swirls

A basic dough that is sweet but not too sweet. This recipe calls for rolling out the dough then filling it, rolling it up, and slicing it into individual rounds. Alternatively, this may be filled and baked as a loaf, or it may be plaited.

This is a pareve recipe. For dairy, substitute hot milk for the water and butter for the margarine.

Dough:

> ¼ cup hot water
> ¼ cup sugar
> ½ teaspoon salt
> 3 tablespoon unsalted margarine
> ¼ cup warm water
> 1 envelope active dry yeast
> 1 egg (graded large), beaten
> 2¼ cups sifted all-purpose flour
> Grease for the pan

Filling:

> 4 tablespoons (¼ cup) unsalted margarine,
>   divided
> ¼ cup firmly packed brown sugar
> ¾ teaspoons cinnamon, divided
> ¼ cup chopped pecans or walnuts (optional)
> 2 tablespoons granulated sugar

In a mixing bowl, combine the hot water with the sugar, salt, and margarine. Stir until the margarine is melted. Cool to luke-warm. In a separate bowl, sprinkle the yeast over the ¼ cup warm water. Stir until thoroughly dissolved. Blend in the sugar mixture. Add the beaten egg and 1½ cups of the flour. Beat until smooth. Stir in an additional ½ cup of flour. Turn out the dough onto a floured board and knead in approximately ¼ cup of the remaining flour. Continue kneading until the dough is satiny and smooth, about 5 minutes.

Place the ball of dough in a greased bowl; turn it so that all sides are lightly greased. Cover and set in warm draft-free place until doubled in bulk, about 1 hour. Punch down the dough, then turn it out onto a floured board and knead it slightly, 10 or more times.

Grease twelve 2-inch muffin cups and set aside. Preheat the oven to 350 degrees F.

Roll out the dough into a rectangle 8 x 12 inches. Melt the margarine and brush the dough with 2 tablespoons' worth. Combine the brown sugar, ½ teaspoon of the cinnamon, and the nuts. Sprinkle the mixture evenly over the margarine. Roll up the 12-inch side of the dough tightly, sealing the edges well. Cut into 12 one-inch slices, and place each slice into a greased muffin cup. Brush the top of each swirl with a little of the remaining melted margarine (about a teaspoon's worth in all). With a fork, gently pull up the center of each roll to form a peak. Cover, set in warm draft-free place, and let rise until doubled in bulk.

Bake the swirls for about 20 minutes, until browned. While they are baking, combine the remaining cinnamon with the granulated sugar. Brush the hot rolls with the remaining melted margarine and sprinkle with the cinnamon-sugar mixture.

Strawberry Bread

Makes 2 loaves,
each serving 8 to 10

You will find this bread particularly delicious when served with the strawberry-cheese spread.

> 3 cups unsifted all-purpose flour
> 1 teaspoon baking soda
> 1 teaspoon cinnamon
> 2 cups sugar
> 1 teaspoon salt
> 1¼ cups oil
> 4 eggs (graded large), well beaten
> 2 packages (10 ounces each) frozen strawberries, well drained (reserve the juice)
> 1 package (8 ounces) cream cheese, at room temperature

Preheat the oven to 350 degrees F.

In a large bowl, combine the flour, baking soda, cinnamon, sugar, and salt. Make a well in the center of the dry ingredients. Pour in the oil, eggs, and strawberries. With a large wooden spoon, stir until the ingredients are thoroughly combined. Pour the batter into 2 greased and floured 9 x 5 x 2½-inch loaf pans. Bake for 1 hour. Cool thoroughly.

For the spread, measure ½ cup of the reserved strawberry juice. In a blender jar, combine the cream cheese with the strawberry juice. Blend until the mixture is of spreading consistency.

Note: Blueberries, bananas, or any other fruit may be substituted for the strawberries.

Popovers

Makes 6

Popovers are a phenomenon. They are high, crisp on the outside and almost hollow on the inside. Serve them as the bread at breakfast, lunch, or dinner; or fill them to make a nice entrée. This recipe is for pareve popovers. For dairy, use one cup of milk in place of the pareve milk-and-water combination.

A popover can be thought of as the American equivalent of an individual Yorkshire Pudding. In England, it is traditional to serve Yorkshire Pudding with roast beef. The pudding is baked in the pan with the beef.

> **Grease for the cups**
> **½ cup pareve milk**
> **½ cup water**
> **1 cup sifted all-purpose flour**
> **½ teaspoon salt**
> **2 eggs (graded large)**

Generously grease six 6-ounce custard cups or the cups of a cast-iron popover pan. Preheat the oven to 450 degrees F.

Combine the pareve milk with the water. Sift together the flour and salt. With a rotary beater or with an electric mixer at low speed, beat the eggs slightly. Beat in the milk until the mixture is very smooth.

Divide the batter among the greased cups. (A ladle is useful in transferring the batter into the cups.) If using custard cups, arrange them on a cookie sheet. Bake the popovers in the preheated oven for 15 minutes. Reduce the oven temperature to 350 degrees F. and continue baking for an additional 20 to 25 minutes, until the popovers are golden brown. Remove from the oven.

To serve, split the popovers and serve plain; or fill with chicken à la king, chicken salad, creamed fish, or the filling of your choice. Or spread generously with butter, margarine, or jelly.

Variations:

For variety, add to the batter either a dash of paprika; a pinch of a favorite herb; ¼ cup ground blanched almonds; or 2 teaspoons sugar sifted with ½ teaspoon ground cinnamon. The choice is yours.

Edible Salad Bowl

Makes one 9-inch bowl

Using *pâté à choux* (cream puff paste), bake a salad bowl. Filled with a colorful salad, it makes a spectacular dish. The guests eat the salad and the bowl!

> ½ stick (¼ cup) unsalted margarine or oil
> ½ cup boiling water
> ½ cup all-purpose flour
> ⅛ teaspoon salt
> ⅛ teaspoon onion powder (optional)
> 1 teaspoon sesame seeds (optional)
> 2 eggs (graded large)
> Grease for the pan

Preheat the oven to 400 degrees F.

In a 1-quart saucepan, combine the margarine or oil with the boiling water. Place over medium-high heat. Combine the flour, salt, onion powder, and sesame seeds. When the margarine-water mixture comes to a bubbling boil, remove the pan from heat. Immediately pour in the flour mixture and mix vigorously to blend thoroughly. Return to low heat and continue mixing vigorously until the mixture forms a ball and leaves the sides of the pan clean. Remove from the heat.

Let cool for about 3 minutes so that the eggs will not cook when they are added to the mixture. Add the eggs one at a time, beating well after each addition, until the eggs are well absorbed and the mixture is smooth and velvety. Spread the batter evenly in the bottom of a lightly-greased 9-inch pie pan. Be sure batter touches the sides of the pan. Bake for 40 to 50 minutes. The batter will form a bowl, high on the sides and flat in the center. Cool slowly, away from drafts. The bowl may be frozen for later use.

Just before serving, fill the bowl with tuna, salmon, egg, or chicken salad. Garnish as desired. Cut wedges of the bowl with the filling, serving them together. Or, first line the bowl with dry shredded lettuce, then top with prepared salad.

Variation:

This dough is tremendously versatile. You can prepare many delicacies with it. To make cream puffs, éclair shells, doughnuts, etc., omit the onion powder and sesame seeds. Double the basic recipe for 10 to 12 cream puff shells or 36 miniature puff shells for hors d'oeuvres.

French Toast Dolls

Serves 3

What could be more appealing to a child than French toast served as a doll? Would the child prefer a facsimile of a pet? Cut animal shapes out of the bread with animal cookie cutters.

> 6 slices bread
> 2 eggs (graded large)
> ½ cup milk
> ¼ teaspoon salt (optional)
> 2 tablespoons unsalted butter or margarine
> Confectioners' sugar, cinnamon sugar, or
> the jelly of your choice

With a cookie cutter, cut the bread into dolls or other shapes. In a medium-sized bowl, beat the eggs with the milk and salt just until well combined. Dip the bread figures into the egg batter, coating each side. Melt the butter or margarine in a large skillet. When hot, sauté the cutouts on each side until crisp and golden. Drain the toast on paper towels. Sprinkle lightly with confectioners' sugar or cinnamon sugar, or serve with jelly.

Variations:

• Dip each cutout into thawed frozen orange juice concentrate. Shake to remove excess. Place on a cookie sheet and bake in a preheated 250-degree F. oven until lightly toasted, about 15 to 20 minutes. Sprinkle with cinnamon if desired.

• Brush each cutout very lightly on both sides with melted butter or margarine, then sprinkle with cinnamon sugar. Place on a cookie sheet and toast in a 400-degree F. oven for about 8 minutes, until crisp and golden brown.

• Bread that has been cut with aspic cutters and then toasted makes very attractive soup garnishes. Make hearts for an anniversary party dinner. Or, using numeral cookie cutters, cut out numerals, toast them, and float them on soup as a garnish. Of course, numerals can be used for bithdays as well.

• A large dreidel crouton makes an outstanding garnish for vegetable, green pea, or tomato soup served on Chanukah. Smaller dreidel croutons make an attractive base for Chanukah canapés.

Bread Boat

Creamed seafood, stews, vegetables, or salads look very appealing when served in this Bread Boat.

Sliced white bread
Margarine

Preheat the oven to 350 degrees F.

Decrust slices of fresh white bread. Arrange the slices overlapping around the inside and bottom of a greased loaf pan. Brush each slice with melted margarine. Press a smaller loaf pan part way into the larger pan to hold the slices in place. Toast in the oven for 15 minutes, then remove the inner pan and continue to toast till golden brown. Lift from the pan and set on a serving dish. Fill as desired.

Note: Trimmed-off crust can be cubed, toasted, and be sprinkled on the filling as a garnish.

Croustades

(Toast Cups)

Crisp toasted bread cups make impressive containers for chopped liver, liver sauté, or fricassee. Prepare one Toast Cup for each portion.

Sliced fresh white bread (¼ inch thick)
Margarine or butter, melted

Preheat the oven to 350 degrees F. Decrust the slices of white bread. Brush or spread melted margarine or butter on each side. Press each slice into a custard cup, muffin pan, or small pie pan so that the bread forms a cup. Bake for 10 to 15 minutes until crisp and golden brown.

Variation:

To make Sandwich Cones, decrust sliced white bread. With a rolling pin, roll each slice thin. Spread with soft margarine or butter. Roll each into a cone and secure with a toothpick. Place on an ungreased baking sheet. Bake for 10 to 15 minutes, until lightly browned. Remove the picks. Carefully spoon the desired filling—egg, tuna, or salmon salad or perhaps chopped liver—into the cones. To serve attractively, arrange on a serving dish spoke-fashion, with the point of each cone toward the center of the dish. Garnish and serve.

Baked French Toast

Serves 4

This is a creative way to serve toast. Add zip to breakfast by serving Baked French Toast in place of plain toast.

¾ **cup cornflake crumbs**
2 **eggs (graded large)**
¾ **cup milk**
½ **teaspoon vanilla extract**
6 **slices day-old bread, cut into halves diagonally**
½ **stick (¼ cup) unsalted butter or margarine, melted**
Grease for the baking dish

Preheat the oven to 450 degrees F.

Into a shallow dish, measure the cornflake crumbs. In a second shallow dish or pan, beat the eggs until foamy. Stir in the milk and the vanilla. Dip the bread into the egg mixture, turning once. Allow time for the bread to absorb the liquid. Then dip the bread into the crumbs, coating evenly.

Arrange the slices on a well-greased baking sheet. Dribble with melted butter or margarine. Bake for about 10 minutes, until lightly browned. Serve with warm maple syrup, jelly, honey, cinnamon, or the topping of your choice.

Sucherkis

(Biscuits)

This was my mother-in-law's Russian version of melba toast. Thick slices of one or two-day old challah or white bread are toasted in the oven until thoroughly dried and nicely browned. A stick-to-the ribs borsht or soup served accompanied by slices of *sucherkis* makes an exceptionally satisfying dish.

One- or two-day old white bread, sliced thick

To prepare, arrange the thick slices of bread on an ungreased baking sheet. Toast in a preheated 350-degrees F. oven for 10 minutes or until dried through and nicely browned. Prepare at least 1 slice per person.

16

For Good Cheer

Beverage & Spirits

"What that maketh glad the heart of man" (Psalms 104:15).

Tea

Tea is a comparatively inexpensive beverage to serve, and its popularity is ever increasing. The virtues of tea are many. William Ewart Gladstone, nineteenth-century prime minister of Great Britain, put it succinctly when he wrote:

If thou art cold, tea will warm thee.
If thou art hot, tea will cool thee.
If thou art sad, tea will cheer thee.
If thou art cross, tea will calm thee.

The tea you serve need not be ordinary. Create an exciting flavor with the subtle use of spice. The aroma will be tantalizing to your most discerning guests. Simply add the selected spice to the teapot when brewing the tea. Use the aromatic addition sparingly. Do not let the added flavor overpower the real tea flavor.

Tea leaves or tea bags

To brew tea, scald a teapot with boiling water and drain. Measure the tea leaves into the pot. Vary the proportion of tea leaves or tea bags to water to suit personal taste. As a rule, use 1 teaspoon of tea leaves or 1 tea bag for each cup desired, plus 1 extra teaspoon or tea bag "for the pot" for good measure.

Into a kettle measure freshly drawn cold water for each cup of tea; bring to a bubbling boil. Pour the briskly boiling water over the tea leaves or tea bags in the teapot. Cover and let steep for 3 to 4 minutes to develop full flavor. The longer the brewing time, the stronger the essence becomes. Stir the tea just before serving. If using tea leaves, strain the infusion. Dilute, if necessary, to desired strength with clear boiling water.

Serve the tea with sugar, honey, fruit preserves, lemon or orange slices. A whole clove stuck into the center of a slice of orange or a lemon circle makes a flavorful garnish for a cup of tea.

At a dairy meal, milk or cream may be served as a substitute for the lemon or orange slices.

Variations:

• For an Orange-spice Blend, add whole cloves and a piece of dried orange peel.

• For a Cinnamon-spice Blend, add a piece of cinnamon bark and a piece of lemon peel.

• The addition of allspice berries or a piece of fresh ginger root makes for an interesting beverage as well.

Tea With Spiced Juice

Serves 6

Spiced juices team up with hot tea to make a refreshment with a difference. Serve the beverage plain or dress it up with a slice of orange or lemon or a few swirls of lemon rind.

> ½ cup water
> ¾ cup sugar
> ¼ cup orange juice
> ¼ cup lemon juice
> 6 whole cloves
> 1 stick cinnamon
> 5 cups water
> 3 to 4 tea bags

In a 1-quart saucepan, bring the ½ cup of water and the sugar to a boil. Remove from the heat and add the fresh juices, the cloves, and the stick of cinnamon.

In a small covered saucepan, bring the 5 cups of water to a boil. Remove from the heat and immerse the tea bags in the boiled water; let steep for 3 to 4 minutes. Combine the steeped tea with the spice mixture and serve immediately.

Coffee and . . . .

Coffee connoisseurs believe that nothing should be added to coffee that would detract from its natural flavor. And, of course, many dieters prefer to drink their coffee black. In the absence of milk or cream, enhance the taste of coffee as follows:

- Add a little honey for sweetening.
- Add a twist of orange or lemon peel and a pinch of cinnamon. The result is an orange- or lemon-spiced coffee.
- Add a whole cinnamon stick, using it as a stirrer to create an elegantly cinnamony coffee.
- Add a spoonful of cocoa to create a mocha flavor.

Jewish Coffee

This is a delicious takeoff on Irish coffee! Here, Sabra, the Israeli chocolate-orange liqueur, substitutes for Irish whiskey.

3 tablespoons (1 jigger) Sabra liqueur
Strong black coffee
Sugar (optional)
Whipped cream

For each serving, pour 3 tablespoons of Sabra into a 7 or 8-ounce mug or goblet. Add strong black coffee, filling to 1 inch from the rim. Add sugar and stir. Top with lightly-whipped well-chilled nondairy cream or whipped cream for a dairy meal.

Note: Insert a teaspoon into a glass goblet before pouring in the hot water. This will prevent the goblet from cracking.

Coffee Cordial

Serves 8

Coffee and brandy or vodka are hand-in-hand partners in this delightful cordial. For a caffein-free drink, substitute decaffeinated instant coffee for the regular instant coffee.

> ¼ cup instant coffee powder or coffee
>   crystals
> ¼ cup sugar
> 3 cups boiling water
> ¼ cup brandy
> 8 strips orange peel

In a coffeepot, mix together the coffee powder or crystals and the sugar. Add the boiling water, then the brandy. Pour into 8 demitasse cups. Twist the orange peel strips and add a strip to each cup.

Coffee-Apricot Cooler

Serves 2

Iced coffee with a difference. A refreshing beverage on a hot summer day.

> ¾ cup chilled brewed coffee
> ½ cup chilled apricot nectar (juice)
> ⅓ cup cold milk
> ½ pint coffee ice cream, softened

Combine the liquids in a blender jar. Add the ice cream; blend until smooth. Serve in chilled glasses.

Foreign Toasts
"Here's to You!"

British	*Cheers!*
French	*A vôtre santé!*
Hebrew	*L'chayim!*
Italian	*Alla salute!*
Russian	*Za vashe zdarovya!*
Spanish	*Salud!*
Yiddish	*Tzu gezunt!*

Orange Nog

Serves 4 or 5

A nutritious breakfast beverage. In the summer, add crushed ice to the blender if you want a refreshingly cold thirst-quencher.

> 4 eggs
> 1 teaspoon vanilla extract
> 1 tablespoon sugar or honey
> 3¼ cups cold orange juice

Combine all the ingredients in a blender jar. Blend at high speed. Chill.

Raisin Wine Drink

Serves 6 to 8

Do not confuse this with raisin wine. Raisin wine is fermented. Raisin wine drink can be served in twenty-four hours or less. The color of the raisins will determine the color of the drink. Use white raisins for a light-colored drink and dark raisins for a deeper-colored drink.

> 1½ cups raisins
> ½ cup sugar

4 cups boiling water
2 thin lemon slices (optional)

Place the raisins in a decanter. Thoroughly dissolve the sugar in the boiling water and pour over the raisins. Add the lemon slices if desired. Chill overnight or longer. Strain before serving.

Gogel Mogel

Serves 2

This European recipe is reputed to be a good remedy for throat hoarseness or soreness. A fine way to use leftover egg yolks.

4 egg yolks
6 tablespoons firmly packed brown sugar
¼ teaspoon vanilla extract

In the small bowl of an electric mixer, beat the yolks until very smooth. Gradually add the brown sugar and vanilla extract. Beat until thick. Serve in a small coupe glass and eat with a spoon.

Sangria

Makes about 1½ quarts

Sangria is a Spanish punch made from fruit juices, wine, and usually fresh fruit. This recipe may be prepared in advance, but add the club soda, apple and orange slices, and the ice cubes immediately before serving.

½ cup sugar
½ cup lemon juice
½ cup orange juice
1 bottle (⅘ quart) dry red wine
¼ cup brandy
1 bottle (7 ounces) club soda, chilled
Unpeeled apple slices
Unpeeled orange slices
1 tray ice cubes

In a large pitcher, completely dissolve the sugar in the fruit juices. Add the wine, brandy, and club soda. Blend together. Garnish with unpeeled apple slices and orange slices. Add a tray of ice cubes. Mix together and serve.

Note: Oranges or lemons will yield more juice if immersed in warm water for a short time before squeezing.

Mock Sangria I

Makes 3 quarts

This nonalcoholic version of Sangria is ideal for entertaining. Each guest pours his or her own drink.

> **2 bottles (25 ounces each) purple grape
>   juice, well chilled
> 1 bottle (28 ounces) club soda, chilled
> 1 orange, sliced
> 1 lemon, sliced
> 1 apple, cored and sliced but unpeeled
> Half of a small pineapple, peeled and cut
>   into small chunks**

In a large pitcher or punch bowl, combine the chilled grape juice and the chilled club soda. Add the orange, lemon, and apple slices, then add the pineapple chunks. Add a tray of ice cubes. Mix all the ingredients and serve.

Note: The ice cubes to be used in this punch may be enhanced by freezing a slice of orange or lemon or a piece of pineapple in each cube.

Mock Champagne

Makes about 1½ pints

The chilled ginger ale gives this beverage a champagne sparkle. A nice Passover beverage.

> **½ cup water
> ½ cup sugar**

½ cup grape juice or wine
¼ cup orange juice
1 pint ginger ale, chilled

In a small saucepan over low heat, boil the water and sugar until the sugar dissolves. Let cool, then add the grape juice or wine and the orange juice. Chill until ready to serve. Pour into a pitcher and add the chilled ginger ale before serving. Stir briefly.

Note: A connoisseur once commented that the best way to revive a glass of "authentic" champagne that has become flat is to drop one or two raisins into the champagne and watch it come to life.

Champagne Punch

Serves 16

Perhaps the greatest advantage of serving punch is convenience. Mixing time is minimal, so you are free to socialize.

¼ cup sugar
Juice of 2 lemons
1 lemon, very thinly sliced
½ orange, very thinly sliced
2 slices pineapple, cut into small pieces
Ice cubes
2 bottles champagne, chilled

In a small bowl, dissolve the sugar in the lemon juice. Add the fruit and pour the mixture over a block of ice or ice cubes in a punch bowl. Just before serving, add the champagne; stir.

Borsht Punch

Serves 10 to 12

A borsht punch garnished with borsht ice cubes is very nice for a dairy buffet. To make borsht ice cubes, pour a mixture of half borsht and half water into an ice cube tray. Add a curl of lemon peel to each cube. Freeze until hard.

> 1 jar (32 ounces) borsht, strained
> 1 cup orange juice
> ¾ cup sugar
> 2 cups ginger ale
> 1 quart lemon ice
> Borsht ice cubes

In a large saucepan, combine the borsht, orange juice, and sugar. Cook over medium heat for 8 to 10 minutes. Cool. When ready to serve, add the ginger ale. Place the lemon ice in a punch bowl; pour the punch over it. Garnish with borsht ice cubes.

Crème de Framboises

(Raspberry Liqueur)

Makes 1¼ pints

If you want to embark on an exciting adventure, make your own liqueurs. Their preparation is economically feasible, and when you serve them, you will experience a grand feeling of pride. It is imperative to start preparation early so the liqueurs will have sufficient time to age.

> 1⅓ cups vodka
> ¾ cup Basic Sugar Syrup (see below)
> ½ cup bottled red raspberry syrup (available
>   in 25.4-ounce bottles)
> 2 teaspoons vanilla extract

Combine the vodka, sugar syrup, raspberry syrup, and the vanilla extract in a one-quart screw-top jar. Close the bottle and store in a cool, dark place for at least a week.

Basic Sugar Syrup

(For Fruit Liqueurs)

Makes 3¾ cups

> **1 lemon**
> **3 cups granulated sugar**
> **2 cups water**

Peel very thinly the bright-colored rind from the lemon; do not remove any of the pith (inner white portion). Blot the rind on paper towels to remove any excess oil.

In a large saucepan, combine the sugar, water, and rind; heat to boiling, stirring often. Lower the heat; simmer for 5 minutes. Strain the syrup into a glass container and cool to room temperature before using to prepare liqueurs.

Easy Raspberry Liqueur

The three basic ingredients needed for making liqueurs at home are alcohol, sugar (either as a syrup or in granular form), and a flavoring agent. Here is a raspberry liqueur that eliminates the need to prepare a sugar syrup.

> **Bottled red raspberry syrup**
> **Vodka, brandy, or Slivovitz**

In a screw-top jar, dilute raspberry syrup with the amount of vodka, brandy, or Slivovitz necessary to obtain the strength of liqueur desired. Let age for a few days before using.

Prune Liqueur and Shikker Prunes

Makes 3 cups

A combination of liqueur and a dessert of spiked prunes.

> **1 cup firmly packed dark brown sugar**
> **3 cups vodka**
> **½ vanilla bean**
> **1 pound unpitted prunes**

Combine the brown sugar and vodka in a 1½-quart jar. Stir together. Cut the vanilla bean into quarters and add it to the jar along with the prunes. Cover and store in a dark place at room temperature. Periodically shake the jar. Let the prunes steep in the vodka for at least 6 weeks. Pour off the liqueur, strain, and transfer to a serving decanter. Place the prunes in a separate bowl. Discard the vanilla bean. Serve the prunes as a dessert, garnished with chopped nuts.

Appendix

Table of Equivalent Amounts

dash	⅛ teaspoon	2 to 3 drops
1 teaspoon	⅓ tablespoon	⅙ ounce
3 teaspoons	1 tablespoon	½ ounce
1 tablespoon	3 teaspoons	½ ounce
2 tablespoons	⅛ cup	1 ounce
4 tablespoons	¼ cup	2 ounces
5⅓ tablespoons	⅓ cup	2⅔ ounces
6 tablespoons	⅜ cup	3 ounces
8 tablespoons	½ cup	4 ounces
10 tablespoons	⅝ cup	5 ounces
10⅔ tablespoons	⅔ cup	5⅓ ounces
12 tablespoons	¾ cup	6 ounces
14 tablespoons	⅞ cup	7 ounces
16 tablespoons	1 cup	8 ounces
⅛ cup	2 tablespoons	1 ounce
¼ cup	4 tablespoons	2 ounces
⅜ cup	¼ cup plus 2 tablespoons	3 ounces
⅝ cup	½ cup plus 2 tablespoons	5 ounces
⅞ cup	¾ cup plus 2 tablespoons	7 ounces
1 cup	16 tablespoons	8 ounces
1 cup	½ pint	8 ounces
2 cups	1 pint	16 ounces
4 cups	1 quart	32 ounces
16 cups	1 gallon	128 ounces

Approximate Metric Size Equivalents

1 inch = 2.50 centimeters
2 inches = 5 centimeters
3 inches = 8 centimeters
5 inches = 13 centimeters

8 inches = 20 centimeters
9 inches = 23 centimeters
10 inches = 25 centimeters
13 inches = 33 centimeters

Metric Equivalents for Cooking

- Gram (gr.) is the basic unit of weight (mass). There are about 28 grams to the ounce.
- A kilogram equals 1,000 grams.
- A kilogram is just under 2¼ pounds.
- ½ kilogram equals 500 grams, slightly more than 1 pound.
- ¼ kilogram equals 250 grams, marginally more than ½ pound.
- ⅛ kilogram equals 125 grams, slightly more than ¼ pound.
- 1 ounce equals 28 grams.
- ½ ounce equals 14 grams.
- A kilogram is frequently referred to as a kilo.

- Milliliters (ml.) and liter (l.) are the basic units used for measuring liquid volume. There are about 28 milliliters in a fluid ounce.
- 5 milliliters equal 1 teaspoon.
- 15 milliliters equal 1 tablespoon.
- A liter is a little more than 1 quart. Used for milk, wines, or cooking oil.

To Convert a Recipe to Metric Measure

Approximate conversion for weight

When you know	Multiply by	To find
ounces	28	grams (gr.)
pounds	.45	kilograms (kg.)

Approximate conversion for volume

teaspoons	5	milliliters (ml.)
tablespoons	15	milliliters
fluid ounces	30	milliliters
cups	.24	liters (l.)
pints	.47	liters
quarts	.95	liters
gallons	3.8	liters

Approximate conversion for length

inches	2.5	centimeters (cm.)

To Convert a Recipe From Metric Measure

Approximate conversion for weight

When you know	Multiply by	To find
grams	.035	ounces
kilograms	2.2	pounds

Approximate conversion for volume

milliliters	.03	fluid ounces
liters	2.1	pints
liters	1.06	quarts
liters	.26	gallons

Approximate conversion for length

centimeters	0.4	inches

Temperature Conversion

Fahrenheit	subtract 32 and multiply by 5/9 to find Celsius temperature
Celsius	multiply by 9/5, then add 32 to find Fahrenheit temperature

Oven Temperatures

Degrees Fahrenheit		Degrees Celsius
200	extremely low	100
225	very low	110
250	very low	120
275	low	135
300	low	150
325	moderately low	165
350	moderate	175
375	moderately hot	190
400	hot	205
425	hot	220
450	very hot	230
475	very hot	245
500	extremely hot	260
525	extremely hot	275

Boiling Point: 212 degrees Fahrenheit
100 degrees Celsius

Cake Pan Conversions

If cake calls for:	It will also bake in:
1 8-inch layer	1 11 × 4½ × 2¾-inch rectangle
	9 to 12 2½-inch cupcake pans
2 8-inch layers	2 thin 8 × 8 × 2-inch squares
	18 to 24 2½-inch cupcake pans
	1 13 × 9 × 2-inch rectangle
3 8-inch layers	2 9 × 9 × 2-inch squares
1 9-inch layer	1 8-inch square
	15 2½-inch cupcake pans
2 9-inch layers	2 8 × 8 × 2-inch squares
	3 thin 8-inch layers
	1 15 × 10 × 1-inch rectangle
	30 2½-inch cupcake pans
1 8-inch square	1 9-inch layer
2 8-inch squares	2 9-inch layers
	1 13 × 9 × 2-inch rectangle (with leftover batter)
1 9-inch square	2 thin 8-inch layers
2 9-inch squares	3 8-inch layers (with leftover batter)
	1 15 × 10½ × 1-inch rectangle
1 12 × 8 × 2-inch rectangle	2 8-inch layers
1 13 × 9 × 2-inch rectangle	2 thin 9-inch layers
	2 8 × 8 × 2-inch squares
	2 8-inch rounds
1 8 × 4 × 3-inch loaf	1 8 × 8 × 2-inch square
1 9 × 5 × 3-inch loaf	1 8-inch round
	1 9 × 9 × 2-inch square
	1 11 × 4½ × 2¾-inch rectangle
	24 to 30 2½-inch cupcake pans
1 9 × 3 ½-inch tube pan	2 9-inch layers
	24 to 30 2½-inch cupcake pans
1 10 × 4-inch tube pan	2 9 × 5 × 3-inch loaves
	1 13 × 9 × 2-inch rectangle
	2 15 × 10 × 1-inch rectangles

What Makes What

When your recipe calls for: **You will need:**

Crumbs

When your recipe calls for:	You will need:
1 cup soft breadcrumbs	2 slices bread
1 cup dry breadcrumbs	3 slices dry bread
1 cup crushed cereal flakes (corn or wheat)	3 cups cereal
1 cup potato chip crumbs	2 cups firmly packed potato chips
1 cup pretzel crumbs	24 thin pretzels
1 cup fine graham cracker crumbs	12 crackers
1 cup fine gingersnap crumbs	18 2-inch crackers
1 cup fine vanilla wafer crumbs	28 to 30 2-inch crackers
1 cup fine zweiback crumbs	9 zweiback
1½ cups matzo farfel	2½ matzos, finely broken

Macaroni and rice products

When your recipe calls for:	You will need:
2 cups cooked cornmeal	½ cup uncooked
2 cups cooked elbow macaroni	1 cup uncooked or half an 8-ounce package
4 cups cooked small shells	2 cups uncooked
3½ cups cooked noodles	5 cups uncooked or one 8-ounce package
4 cups cooked spaghetti	8-ounce package
4 cups cooked rice	1 cup uncooked rice or 2 cups uncooked instant rice

Dairy

When your recipe calls for:	You will need:
8 tablespoons butter or margarine	¼ pound or 1 stick or ½ cup
2 cups butter or margarine	1 pound
1 cup freshly grated cheese	¼ pound
1 cup cottage cheese	8 ounces or ½ pound
1 cup whipped cream	½ cup cream for whipping
1 cup sour cream	8 ounces or ½ pint
⅔ cup evaporated milk	1 small can

Eggs

1 cup whole eggs	4 to 6 eggs
1 cup egg whites	8 to 10 whites
1 cup egg yolks	12 to 14 yolks

Meats

2 cups ground raw meat	1 pound raw meat
2 cups ground cooked meat	1 pound cooked meat
3 cups diced cooked meat	1 pound cooked meat
4 cups diced cooked chicken	a 5-pound cooked chicken

Fruits, juices, and peels

1 cup candied fruits	8 ounce jar
1 cup cut-up dates	8 ounces or ½ pound
2 cups cooked prunes	½ pound prunes
4 cups sliced apples	4 medium-sized apples
2 cups sliced strawberries	1 pint strawberries
2 cups pitted cherries	4 cups unpitted cherries
4 cups sliced fresh peaches	2 pounds or 8 medium-sized peaches
4 cups cranberries	1 pound cranberries
1 teaspoon grated orange rind	½ orange
1 cup orange juice	3 medium-sized oranges
1½ teaspoons grated lemon rind	1 lemon
3 tablespoons lemon juice	1 lemon
1 cup lemon juice	4 to 6 lemons
1 cup mashed bananas	3 medium-sized bananas
3 cups seedless raisins	1 pound raisins

Nuts

1 cup blanched whole almonds	5 ounces shelled almonds
1 cup toasted slivered almonds	5 ounces shelled almonds
1 cup chopped walnuts	¼ pound or 4 ounces shelled walnuts
1 cup pecans	3 ounces shelled pecans
1½ cups whole peanuts	7 ounces
1½ cups chopped peanuts	7 ounces

1 cup cashew nuts	¼ pound or 4 ounces shelled cashew nuts
1 cup grated coconut	¼ pound or 3½ ounces fresh coconut
2 cups chestnut meats	1 pound in shell

Vegetables

4 cups sliced raw potatoes	4 medium-sized potatoes
4 cups diced raw potatoes	4 medium-sized potatoes
3 cups mashed potatoes	1½ pounds raw unpeeled potatoes or 2 cups instant potato buds
3 cups sliced sweet potatoes	3 medium-sized potatoes
4 cups cooked cut green beans	1 pound
1 cup shelled peas	1 pound
1 cup chopped onion	1 large onion
4 cups shredded cabbage	1 pound head of cabbage
2½ cups cooked fresh tomatoes	4 medium-sized or 1 pound
2 cups canned tomatoes	1 pound can
5 medium carrots	½ pound
1 cup grated raw carrots	1 large carrot
2 cups diced carrots	3-4 medium-sized carrots
2 cups diced beets	4 medium-sized carrots

Recipe Conversion

To convert a recipe from one category—*milchig* (dairly), *fleshig* (meat), or *pareve* (neutral) to another category, substitute ingredients as follows:

For	Adapted for	Substitute
Butter	Fleishig	Pareve margarine
		Solid white shortening
		Chicken fat
		Oil or a combination of oil plus one of the above

Butter	Pareve	Pareve margarine Solid white shortening Oil Combination of oil plus margarine or shortening Mock chicken fat (see recipe)
Cheese	Fleishig or pareve	Pareve cheese or tofu
1 cup milk	Fleishig or pareve	½ cup pareve milk plus ½ cup water 1 cup water plus 2 tablespoons pareve shortening for pareve baking Potato water in baking Water Fruit juice Black coffee Water from cooked vegetables
1 cup skim milk	Fleishig or pareve	¼ cup pareve milk plus ¾ cup water
1 cup condensed milk	Fleishig or pareve	1 cup pareve milk
1 cup buttermilk	Fleishig or pareve	1 tablespoon vinegar plus pareve milk to make 1 cup
1 cup cream	Fleishig or pareve	Prepare "cream" sauce (cornstarch or potato starch, pareve fat, and liquid to the desired consistency) before adding to the mixture. 1 cup pareve milk can be liquid used.
1 cup Half-and-Half	Fleishig or pareve	1 cup pareve milk
Chicken or meat stock	Pareve	For each cup of stock, one pareve boullion cube dissoved in 8 ounces of hot water; or an equal quantity of water flavored with a pareve soup mix powder.

| Ground meat | Milchig | Textured soy granules |
| Chunks of meat | Milchig | Soy chunks |

One may want to convert a nonkosher recipe to kosher. I recommend the following substitutions for some nonkosher foods.

When the recipe calls for:	Use:
Bacon	Kosher beef fry or bacon-flavored soy chips (Bacos)
Smoked meats	Pastrami, salami, or smoked veal shoulder

Some fish recipes utilizing nonkosher fish may be adapted for year-round use by substituting kosher fish. The substitute fish is cut into bite-size pieces, either chunks or strips of varying lengths, and prepared to simulate the appearance of the fish being substituted. Note that semifrozen or chilled fish can be cut into cubes more easily.

When the recipe calls for:	Use:
Shrimp	Flounder fillets
Scallops	Halibut, haddock, or cod chunks
Crab meat salad	Halibut or sole
Lobster	Haddock or halibut

Temporarily Out?

For the best results, we recommend that you use the ingredients called for in the recipe, but in an emergency, chances are that you might have a suitable substitute right on hand. There may be a slight variation in the texture or taste, but the overall results are very difficult to discern.

Instead of:	**You may use:**
1 cup skim milk	⅓ cup instant non fat dry milk plus ¾ cup water
	4 tablespoons powdered whole milk plus ⅞ cup water
	4 tablespoons powdered nonfat dry milk, 2 tablespoons melted fat (butter or margarine) plus 1 cup water
	½ cup pareve milk plus ½ cup water
	1 cup fruit juice or 1 cup potato water (for baking)
	⅞ cup liquid skim milk plus 3 tablespoons melted buter (for cooking only)
1 cup whole milk	¼ cup pareve milk plus ¾ cup water
	½ cup evaporated milk plus ½ cup water
1 cup light cream	1 cup undiluted evaporated milk
1 cup heavy cream	¾ cup milk plus ⅓ cup melted butter (for cooking only, not whipping)
1 cup sour milk or buttermilk (for baking)	1 tablespoon lemon juice or 1 tablespoon vinegar plus enough milk to measure 1 cup (allow to stand 5 minutes)
1 cup buttermilk	1 cup yogurt
Sweet milk and baking powder (for baking)	Equal amount of sour milk plus ½ teaspoon soda
1 teaspoon baking powder	¼ teaspoon baking soda plus ½ teaspoon cream of tartar
1 teaspoon double-acting baking powder	1½ teaspoons phosphate baking powder, ¼ teaspoon baking soda, plus ½ teaspoon cream of tartar
1 tablespoon flour for thickening	½ tablespoon cornstarch or potato starch
	1 tablespoon quick-cooking tapioca

1 tablespoon cornstarch for thickening	2 tablespoons flour (as thickener)
	1 tablespoon potato starch
	4 teaspoons tapioca
1 tablespoon tapioca	1½ tablespooons all-purpose flour
1 whole egg for thickening	2 egg yolks
1 whole egg for baking	2 egg yolks plus 1 tablespoon water
1 cup butter	⅞ cup vegetable oil
	1 cup margarine
1 ounce (square) unsweetened chocolate	3 tablespoons cocoa plus 1 tablespoon shortenng or fat
	3 tablespoons carob powder, sifted, plus 2 tablespoons water
1 cup cake flour	1 cup all-purpose flour minus 2 tablespoons
1 cup all-purpose flour	1 cup cake flour plus 2 tablespoons
1 cup self-rising flour	1 cup all-purpose flour plus 1 teaspoon baking powder plus ⅛ teaspoon salt
1 cup biscuit mix	1 cup flour plus 1½ teaspoons baking powder plus ½ teaspoon salt plus 2 tablespoons shortening
1 cup honey	1¼ cups sugar plus ¼ cup liquid
1¼ cups sugar	1 cup honey less ¼ cup liquid called for in recipe
1 cup corn syrup	1 cup sugar plus ¼ cup liquid (plus liquid called for in recipe)
1 cake compressed yeast	1 package active dry yeast
1 cup breadcrumbs	¾ cup cracker crumbs
1 teaspoon dry mustard	1 tablespoon prepared mustard
1 cup tomato juice	½ cup tomato sauce plus ½ cup water
1 cup canned tomatoes	1⅓ cups chopped fresh tomatoes simmered for 10 minutes

1 cup ketchup or chili sauce	1 cup tomato sauce plus ¼ cup sugar plus 2 tablespoons vinegar plus 2/8 teaspoon ground cloves (for cooking)
1 teaspoon Italian seasoning	¼ teaspoon each of basil, oregano, thyme, rosemary, sage, and a dash of cayenne
½ pound mushrooms	1½ ounces dried mushrooms, reconstituted
10-ounce package frozen strawberries	1 cup sliced fresh strawberries plus ⅓ cup sugar
½ cup seedless raisins	½ cup cut pitted dried prunes or dates
1 teaspoon pumpkin pie spice	½ teaspoon cinnamon plus ¼ teaspoon ginger plus ⅛ teaspoon each ground nutmeg and cloves
1 teaspoon allspice	½ teaspoon cinnamon plus ⅛ teaspoon ground cloves
1 average-size lemon, juice	2 tablespoons bottled lemon juice
1 small onion, chopped	1 tablespoon instant minced onion, rehydrated, or ¼ cup frozen chopped onion
1 clove garlic	¼ teaspoon garlic powder, or to taste
1 tablespoon chopped fresh herbs	1 teaspoon crushed dried herbs
¼ cup soy sauce	3 tablespoons Worcestershire sauce plus 1 tablespoon water
½ cup tartar sauce	⅜ cup mayonnaise or salad dressing plus ⅛ cup chopped pickle relish

Portion Converter

When you want to alter the yield of a recipe, here are some helpful hints to help you save time.

Amount	One-half recipe	One-third recipe
¼ teaspoon	⅛ teaspoon	pinch
½ teaspoon	¼ teaspoon	pinch
1 tablespoon	1½ teaspoons	1 teaspoon
2 tablespoons	1 tablespoon	2 teaspoons
3 tablespoons	1 tablespoon plus 1½ teaspoons	1 tablespoon
4 tablespoons	2 tablespoons	1 tablespoon plus 1 teaspoon
5 tablespoons	2 tablespoons plus 1½ teaspoons	1 tablespoon plus 2 teaspoons
6 tablespoons	3 tablespoons	2 tablespoons
7 tablespoons	3 tablespoons plus 1½ teaspoons	2 tablespoons plus 1 teaspoon
8 tablespoons	4 tablespoons or ¼ cup	2 tablespoons plus 2 teaspoons
⅛ cup	1 tablespoon	2 teaspoons
¼ cup	2 tablespoons	1 tablespoon plus 1 teaspoon
⅓ cup	2 tablespoons plus 2 teaspoons	1 tablespoon plus 2⅓ teaspoons
⅜ cup	3 tablespoons	2 tablespoons
½ cup	¼ cup or 4 tablespoons	2 tablespoons plus 2 teaspoons
⅝ cup	¼ cup plus 1 tablespoon or 5 tablespoons	3 tablespoons plus 1 teaspoon
⅔ cup	⅓ cup or 5 tablespoons plus 1 teaspoon	3 tablespoon plus 1⅔ teaspoons

¾ cup	¼ cup plus 2 table-spoons or 6 tablespoons	¼ cup or 4 tablespoons
⅞ cup	¼ cup plus 3 table-spoons or 7 tablespoons	4 tablespoons plus 2 teaspoons
1 cup	½ cup or 8 table-spoons	⅓ cup or 5 table-spoons plus 1 teaspoon

Index

About the Author

Born in New York City, Frances R. AvRutick received her secular education at the City College of New York and pursued her Jewish studies at the Seminary College of the Jewish Theological Seminary of America. In 1946, Mrs. AvRutick and her husband, Rabbi Abraham N. AvRutick, moved to West Hartford, Connecticut (from Newburgh, New York), where Rabbi AvRutick served as spiritual leader of Congregation Agudas Achim until his death in 1982.

Mrs. AvRutick has long been active in Jewish community affairs. She currently serves on the board of directors of the Hartford Jewish Historical Society. A former member of the National Commission on Adult Education of the Women's Branch of the Union of Orthodox Jewish Congregations of America, she has conducted holiday cooking workshops at state and national conventions.

For UOJC she has also written several holiday publications, including the acclaimed "A Passover Sampler: From Appetizer to Afikomon." Her *Complete Passover Cookbook*, published in 1981 (Jonathan David), has enjoyed enormous success. Subsequent to its publication, Mrs. AvRutick served for three years as Passover foods stylist for Hoods, a large New England dairy.

Frances AvRutick has three married daughters; eight grandchildren, two of whom are married; and a great-grandson, her latest pride and joy.